Identity, Culture and Memory in Japanese Foreign Policy

This book is part of the Peter Lang Regional Studies list.
Every volume is peer reviewed and meets
the highest quality standards for content and production.

PETER LANG
New York • Bern • Berlin
Brussels • Vienna • Oxford • Warsaw

Identity, Culture and Memory in Japanese Foreign Policy

Edited by
Michal Kolmaš and Yoichiro Sato

PETER LANG
New York • Bern • Berlin
Brussels • Vienna • Oxford • Warsaw

Library of Congress Cataloging-in-Publication Data

Names: Kolmaš, Michal, editor. | Sato, Yoichiro, editor.
Title: Identity, culture and memory in Japanese foreign policy / Edited by
Michal Kolmaš and Yoichiro Sato.
Description: New York: Peter Lang, 2021.
Includes bibliographical references and index.
Identifiers: LCCN 2020033435 (print) | LCCN 2020033436 (ebook)
ISBN 978-1-4331-7202-1 (hardback) | ISBN 978-1-4331-7327-1 (ebook pdf)
ISBN 978-1-4331-7328-8 (epub) | ISBN 978-1-4331-7329-5 (mobi)
Subjects: LCSH: Japan—Foreign relations. | Cultural identity—Japan. |
Collective memory—Japan. | Japan—Politics and government.
Classification: LCC DS845 .I34 2021 (print) | LCC DS845 (ebook) |
DDC 327.52—dc23
LC record available at https://lccn.loc.gov/2020033435
LC ebook record available at https://lccn.loc.gov/2020033436
DOI 10.3726/b16049

Bibliographic information published by **Die Deutsche Nationalbibliothek**.
Die Deutsche Nationalbibliothek lists this publication in the "Deutsche
Nationalbibliografie"; detailed bibliographic data are available
on the Internet at http://dnb.d-nb.de/.

The paper in this book meets the guidelines for permanence and durability
of the Committee on Production Guidelines for Book Longevity
of the Council of Library Resources.

Table of Contents

Preface

Yoichiro Sato
Ritsumeikan Asia Pacific University

The return of the Liberal Democratic Party (LDP) to power in late 2012 under the leadership of Abe Shinzo left an important mark in Japanese politics. Who would have expected Abe would renew the Japanese record of the longest serving prime minister, previously held by Katsura Taro who led the nation through the challenging war against Russia and for two more terms afterward? Abe's resignation in September 2007 at less than a year of serving as a prime minister in his first term cited a health issue. The LDP lost power in September 2009 as its two prime ministers after the first Abe Cabinet failed to recapture popular support for the scandal-tainted ruling party amid the stubborn economic deflation and the deteriorating regional security environment.

The typical characteristics of prolonged leaderships in Japan—do nothing controversial to avoid making enemies—is probably not the way most observers would describe Abe. While making compromises is required of him just as his predecessors have gone through, Abe has from time to time pushed through considerable policy changes, such as endorsing the country's participation in collective defense (Sato 2017b). The conservative vision he presented has guided the policy recourse during the past seven and a half years.

When we held our workshop to critique the initial chapter drafts of this book in November 2018, Japan was booming with international visitors under the government's drive to promote inbound tourism as a new source of economic revenue. With the upcoming Tokyo Olympic then scheduled in summer 2020, both "whole-of-government" and "public-private" cooperation was at work under the central government's slogan, "Yokoso [welcome to] Japan." The reflationist economic policy Abe promoted by placing like-minded Kuroda Haruhiko in the governorship of the Central Bank of Japan brought back a period of economic growth, which albeit limitedly resembled the bubble economy boom era from the late 1980s to the early 1990s. All came to a sudden halt in the spring of 2020 when the coronavirus pandemic reached the country.

Japan's responses to the pandemic under Abe have revealed some of its core values. Japan did not have a law that would give its executive leader a power to declare and enforce a mandatory lockdown of any part of its territory for a reason of epidemic. Abe had to propose an amendment to the existing law against influenza epidemic, which was put in place several years earlier to deal with a new more toxic strain of influenza virus, to expand its scope to cover the new coronavirus (SARS COV-2). The law, however, merely authorized the prime minister to declare an emergency to specific municipalities and the relevant governors to request a voluntary curfew and business closures. Success of Japan's attempt to curb the rise of infections depended on compliance of its citizens. The country's relatively small number of available intensive care units per population invited a major concern, but in the end Japan wiggled through the tense months of April and May 2020 with one of the lowest rates of deaths per population. Hotel rooms and public halls the municipal governments earmarked for transferring the patients in less serious conditions in order to free up hospital capacities for those in serious conditions were barely utilized. The contrast between Tokyo's calm restraint and similarly gigantic cities like Wuhan and New York where the infected overloaded the medical systems despite the more forceful lockdown orders was stark.

Japan's soft approach was not only inevitable because of the lack of a powerful constitutional authority of the executive, but also was realistic given the strong public reservation against giving the executive such power even during a crisis. It is not too difficult to imagine a root of such attitude is found in the country's painful total defeat in World War II. Abe's Finance Minister Aso Taro, whose outspokenness earned him a pro-Nazi labeling by some liberal Western journalists, caused yet another controversy when he cynically bragged Japan's success owed to its "[higher] level of civility" [*mindo ga chigau*].[1] Liberal Japanese media and leftist opposition parties were quick to question Aso's remark, but the silence of the large segment of the public indicated that the pride is a shared feeling. The Japanese displayed the same sense of pride in their own self-discipline and public mindedness during the Great Eastern Japan Earthquake of March 2011.

Outside Japan, the pandemic has sharpened the ideological conflict between the United States and China. The propaganda war over the origin of and responsibility over the pandemic added fuel to the trade war. United States President Donald Trump's cease-fire after the first stage agreement with China to improve the US trade balance is now at the risk of being abandoned. China continues to build up military infrastructure and presence throughout the South China Sea region, and the United States counters the Chinese move by increasing the frequency of its naval transit operations to challenge China's claims. But, Japan's previously growing activism in the South China Sea (Sato 2017a) appears to have peaked in the 2017–2018 period. The upgraded bilateral alliance between the United States and Japan as a result of the latter's reinterpretation of the constitution and the national security legislation in 2015 (Sato 2017b) brings Japan closer to a hypothetical conflict, but a simple neorealist bandwagoning logic does not seem to explain the ways Japan is coping with divergence from its prime ally. Alliance dilemma is present and has grown (Atanassova-Cornelis and Sato 2019), and its material manifestations are inseparable from less tangible ideas, values, beliefs, and cultures. In the ongoing competition for a new order, Japan too utilizes old and new ideas which are consistent with its material interests (Rothman, Vyas, and Sato 2017).

The collection of chapters that follows will illustrate nuanced applications of constructivism and poststructuralism to study of Japanese foreign policy that is more conducive to dialoging with the more traditional materialist-utilitarian theories (Sato and Hirata eds. 2008) as well. We believe that material factors cannot (by any means) give a holistic picture of Japan's foreign policy behavior, interests, and perceptions; and only through dialogue with these immaterial concepts we can try to grasp hints of Japanese uniqueness and policy conduct. Our collection of chapters brings together scholars of international relations, security studies and policy studies, and offers a compelling food for thought that adds to contemporary debates on Japanese foreign policy and also on Japanese self-perception and understanding of its past.

Note

1 Asahi Shimbun Digital, June 4, 2020. https://www.asahi.com/articles/ASN6455CGN64UTFK008.html.

References

Atanassova-Cornelis, E., & Sato, Y. (2019). The US-Japan alliance dilemma in the Asia-Pacific: Changing rationales and scope. *The International Spectator: Italian Journal of International Affairs*, 54(4), 78–93.

Rothman, S., Vyas, U., & Sato, Y. (2017). Introduction. In *Regional institutions, geopolitics and economics in the Asia-Pacific* (pp. 1–10). London: Routledge.

Sato, Y. (2017a). Japan's maritime security: Continuity and post-Cold War evolution. In N. Tarling & X. Chen (Eds.), *Maritime security in East and Southeast Asia: Political challenges in Asian waters* (pp. 125–144). London: Routledge.
Sato, Y. (2017b). Conclusion: Abe's Japan—Manifestation of a Quiet Transformation in Power and Values. In H. Sato & Y. Sakai (Eds.), *Rerising Japan: Its strategic power in international relations* (pp. 243–252). New York: Peter Lang.

Acknowledgments

We would like to express our thanks to the Czech Science Foundation for its financial support under standard research grant no. 18-05339S. We would also like to thank the Ritsumeikan Center for Asia Pacific Studies (RCAPS) at Ritsumeikan Asia-Pacific University for organizing a workshop in 2018, which helped us to meet and discuss the initial drafts of the chapters. And our thanks also go to our family members and friends for support and advice.

Introduction: National Identity and the Study of Japan

MICHAL KOLMAŠ
Metropolitan University Prague

Introduction

Has pacifism retreated from Japan? Is the country returning to its prewar militarist identity, or is it just reacting to the security developments in Asia and in the world? Or are ongoing political changes in Japan merely small steps on a long trajectory of incremental "normalization"? These questions have been in the forefront of Japan research for at least three decades now. The reasons are perhaps straightforward: There is indeed something happening with Japan. Japanese politicians have become less concerned with the promotion of pacifism into the world. They have visited the Yasukuni shrine, where souls of dead soldiers are enshrined, and called for the rejuvenation of Japanese role in the world. They have become critical of the postwar Constitution and its war-renouncing Article 9, which they no longer consider as an asset to Japan's foreign policy, but rather a hindrance to it. They have changed security legislature in order to allow the Japanese military more freedom in participating in foreign missions.

Indeed, the extent and scope of changes is breathtaking. Japan has become much more active in the world. It has created a first overseas military base in Djibouti and has sent troops in a variety of peacekeeping missions around the world. It has transformed its institutional structure to allow for a better cooperation among ministries of defense and foreign affairs. Under the Prime Minister Shinzo Abe, it has enacted a series of laws that allow for easier intelligence coordination with its allies, predominantly the United States. But what does that tell us about Japan? Do all these developments signal that the revisionist political leadership has succeeded in transforming Japanese pacifist identity? Or is it too soon or even wrong to suggest such a thing? And what would that mean for Japan, Asia, and the world?

There is no consensus on the answers. Some of the commentators (i.e., Dobson 2017; Hagstrom and Hanssen 2015; Hughes, 2015; Schulze 2016) have argued that Japan has indeed transformed into a different country—one that possesses a strong military no matter of the peaceful constitution, that has succeeded in detaching itself from its postwar torpor in foreign and security policy, and whose society no longer feels united under the antimilitarist banner. They have illustrated the ways of how the leading elite—and Abe in particular—have transformed the narrative of Japanese pacifism into Japanese proactive pacifism, which no longer stresses the necessity of following the Yoshida doctrine, but instead calls for a more active and playmaker role for Japanese foreign policy. There are others, however, who are not so inclined to the notion of Japanese change. These scholars (i.e., Oros 2010, 2015; Liff 2015; Lande 2017; Easly, 2017, for a broader discussion on this topic, see Kolmaš 2018, 2019) believe that the change under Abe is much more limited, if happening at all. They speak of Japanese incrementalism and show that the recent security changes are just minor advances on a long journey that started right after the war. Some of them have argued that the Constitution and the institutional brakes that it possesses have—although under attack—remained more-or-less intact in countering revisionist pressures (for in-depth discussion of the continuity/change spectrum see Kolmaš 2019).

Notwithstanding the fact that there is no consensus on the Japanese political trajectory, it is apparent that there is significant interest in the ideational side of Japanese change. The prescription of changing/non-changing Japan simply boils down to the question of Japanese national identity. Since the identity is so closely linked to the postwar constitution and the role of Japanese military, any attempt to transform these is directly linked to the very idea of Japanese self. Aware of this, Japanese politicians aim not only to change Japanese legislature, but also the underlying understanding of Japan as a nation—only by persuading the society that pacifism is no longer necessary—or indispensable—for Japan can they broaden the options for revisionist policy making. We thus believe that it is of utmost importance to engage in the debate of Japanese national identity and its effect on policy making.

We intend to do it by eclectically building on the prevailing scholarship on the role of ideas, identity, and culture in Japanese political change. Our main interest will be in the ideational background of Japanese policy making, but—differently to the abovementioned studies—we aim to broadly analyze these ideas within not merely Japanese postwar pacifism, but also education, popular culture, and economic model. We present a collection of chapters connected by the belief that rationality and calculated interests cannot simply explain changing Japanese trajectory. The chapters in our book show that identities and ideas matter, and that they constitute basis from which Japanese state operates. Instead of other identity-based studies, we do not merely focus on the state level of identity, but we illustrate the role of ideas on all levels of Japanese society.

Identity, Culture, and the Study of Japan[1]

Identity will serve as the main conceptual tool for our understanding of contemporary Japan. For most parts of the twentieth century, however, identity has been overlooked as a concept of interest for international relations scholars. Dominated by rationalist theories, International Relations (IR) scholars were interested in power, cooperation, institutions, and anarchy, rather than identity. If studied at all, state identity was understood in terms of power (superpowers, middle powers, small states, etc.). The surge of interest in identity and its relationship to foreign policy has resulted from the fourth great debate in IR theory during the 1980s and 1990s. The debate emancipated rationalists' post-positivist enemies; and theories such as social constructivism, post-structuralism, environmentalism, and gender theory became more-or-less widely applied in international relations. Identity has been one of the key concepts these "new" theories worked with. Social constructivists, in particular, have been widely interested in the way how identity works and how it influences individual and state behavior. Building on sociology and psychology, constructivists focused on the context in which meanings are created and believed that this context (cultural, historical, and discursive) is essential for our understanding of the world—and IR.

Although sharing the conviction that identity is—and should be—a fundamental concept in IR, constructivists were far from consensual on the meaning of this term. Paul Kowert (1998: 4) wrote that identity is a "notoriously slippery concept on a par with the much maligned political culture." Berenskoetter (2010: 3598) noted that even after "a decade of using it, the concept remained vague and its analytical role difficult to grasp, prompting some disillusionment among IR scholars." Nicholas Onuf (2003: 26), one of the pioneers of constructivism, went as far as to say that identity is "one of the most fashionable," but also "one of the murkiest concepts"—"so difficult to fathom" that he has been "reluctant to use it." Similarly, Abdelal, Herrera, Johnston, and McDermott (2006) argued that the insufficient analytical grasp reminds of a "definition anarchy," which hampers further attempts at conceptual clarity. One of the reasons for this inconsistency might lie in the fact that identity is very difficult to identify. Not only we have problems recognizing identity (What constitutes it? How do we define it? How do we see it?), we have further problems in defining what it leads to and what it does. Is identity a basis of national interest? Can identity be understood as a causal link to state's foreign policy? Is identity produced through history, culture, and socialization of a certain community, or is identity a simple "practice" defined on various policy and social levels? Does identity exist outside of our interactions with others or does it exist only within it? Is there only one identity or are there infinite identities that materialize in various settings? (Kolmaš 2018, 2019).

The questions connected to our study of identity are simply numerous. As Paul Kowert (1998: 4) notes then, it is no surprise that "even those otherwise prepared to make distinctions among national identities might well balk at the sheer implausibility of devising acceptable definitions." It should thus be of no surprise that there is a plethora of various understandings of national identity and its role, almost as many as there are authors focusing on it. Some of them try to answer the questions of what states are through connection to power (as abovementioned Waltz 1979; Mearsheimer 2001). Others (Kowert-Legro 1998; Onuf 1989; Wendt 1999; Guzzini 2000) connect identity to social rules, orders, and norms. There are researchers who try to understand identity in its historical and cultural context (Katzenstein and Okawara 1993) and others who aim at the same but do it through discursive interpretations (Herrmann, Isernia and Segatti 2009; Wodak, de Cillia, Reisigl and Liebhart 2009). Some go as far as to shed any grounding of national identity and believe that identity resides exclusively in its practice (Campbell 1998; Hansen 2006; Suzuki 2015, Kolmaš 2019).

Japan, in particular, has emerged as a widely used case study for national identity theorizing. This is perhaps not too perplexing given the radical transformation of Japanese self pre- and postwar and the fluidity and evolution of Japanese state (in terms of both economy and policy) in the last couple of decades. Initial interest in Japanese national identity came when realist prescriptions of Japan did not pan out. Realists believed that rising Japan would eventually shed the constraints placed on its foreign and security policy and reemerge as a powerful actor in world politics. Once their prescription did not materialize, they began to speak of Japan in the terms of abnormal or an anomaly (i.e., Green 2001; Kennedy 1994; Waltz 1993). Social constructivists tried to rescue realism from this situation. By departing from the concept of identity, constructivists believed that the sluggish change in Japanese politics can be explained by the existence of pacifist norms they called the "culture of antimilitarism" (Berger 1993, 1998; Katzenstein 1996; Katzenstein and

Okawara 1993). These norms were, according to them, grounded in Japanese domestic politics, or transferred from abroad and sedimented within the domestic politics. Most notably, these authors were interested in the norms sedimented in Japan's war-renouncing constitution. Although written by American lawyers, constructivists traced how these norms eventually became intersubjectively shared within Japanese policy-making institutions. In doing so, they approached the norms as a form of independent variable, which helps to explain the limited nature of Japanese change (dependent variable).

There is much to be grateful to social constructivists for their study of Japan. They have emancipated the study of culture and identity as key concepts for IR and thus tried to bridge the gap between IR and area studies. Their interpretation of Japanese change was a huge improvement on the preceding realist interpretation. And yet, their take on identity had several shortcomings that became apparent a bit later on. Namely, constructivists overstate the importance of the state and its domestic structure and underplay the constitutive relationship with Others. Since constructivists approach identity in terms of singular entities (states), they are prone to simplification stemming from labeling these entities in binary terms. Constructivists' idea that the Japanese Self was created in the wake of World War II dwells on a distinction between militarist prewar Japan and antimilitarist postwar Japan. But it would be misleading to say that postwar Japanese society was simply antimilitaristic and prewar simply militaristic. Many studies (i.e., Miyashita 2006) have illustrated that postwar Japanese society was far from antimilitaristic. There was a significant popular support for the Self-Defense Forces, and the peaceful war-renouncing Constitution was heavily disputed in the first years after the occupation for speaking in a foreign language and stripping Japan of its autonomy, identity, and foreign policy. It took more than two decades for Japanese pacifism to root into the society. Political institutions were supporting this process, with the Yoshida Doctrine (*Yoshida Rosen*), Eisaku Sato's three nonnuclear principles or Miki Takeo's one percent cap on defense spending aiding the promotion of Japanese pacifism.

Second point of criticism to constructivist interpretation points to its preoccupation with domestic institutions. Katzenstein and Berger define the cultural norms of antimilitarism as a product of the postwar peaceful Constitution, and the resulting foreign policy as a product of these intersubjective norms. Here it is fair to say that neither Katzenstein nor Berger believe that the Constitution is a purely domestic normative source. Quite to the opposite, constructivists believe that norms are fluid and constituted through connection to other (outside). But once the norm becomes sedimented, they prescribe only a limited possibility for change, which can happen only gradually (through cultural change) or via systemic shock such as a war. But contemporary Japan and its perception of pacifism surely seems different from that of fifty years ago: The narratives have changed, values associated with pacifism have too, and political actions once thought unthinkable (such as sending troops abroad to collective security operations) now seem normal. Post-structural interpretation is perhaps better in accounting for this change.

This approach builds on dynamic, relational approach to studying identity and accounting for its influence (Kolmaš 2019). Post-structural authors (see, i.e., Campbell 1998; Hansen 2006; Neumann, 1996, 1998; Rumelili 2004; Suzuki 2007, 2015; Tamaki 2015; Waever 2002) believe that identity is constantly produced and reproduced within a performative practice. It is, in fact, ritualized—the Self is being constantly contested and negotiated through interactions with broadly defined Others. The interactions are formulated within discourse and only there the identity exists. There is no objective component of identity, and there is no distinction between identity, interests, and ideational and material factors (discourse defines interests—the very notion as security might mean something completely different for different identities). Everything is a mere product of othering—a practice in which identity is created through distinguishing. Post-structural authors have identified a variety of others to which the Japanese self differentiates. Some were spatial (The West, the United States, China, and Russia); others were temporal (Japan's past such as Showa or Meiji Japan); or ethnical/societal (the Ainu, Korean, or Okinawan minority in Japan, etc.). They have shown that the definition of Japanese self is created (and constantly contested) through the discourse on these others. In this vein, even antimilitarism/pacifism is a product of the discursive practice and exists only within it. Since the narratives seem to have changed (Japan no longer sees pacifism as an asset to foreign policy), the very notion of pacifism, according to them, has either disappeared or has become severely limited.

Post-structuralism has succeeded in defining Japanese identity (identities as there are various discourses through which various identities are formed) in fluid and dynamic terms. They have discarded constructivist preoccupation with culture, history, and the postwar Constitution and have shown that Japanese antimilitarism/pacifism is actually a very contested concept that has been under constant pressure throughout the second part of the twentieth century. But they have overstated the defining factors of the narratives. Although it is true that the discussions about pacifism have changed very much over the past decades, the policy—and society—changes have been much slower. A vast majority of Japanese still oppose the change to the constitutional Article 9, Japanese soldiers are dispatched only with limited mandates and are under heavy popular scrutiny, and every revisionist law that Japanese administration proposes is met with significant popular protests. Thus it seems far-fetched to speak of Japanese pacifism as nonexistent.

In short, both theories have greatly helped us to understand contemporary Japan and its identity. There are still challenges, however, that contemporary identity research tries to overcome. These can be broadly summed up in three discussions: (1) the role of identity entrepreneurs (agents) in identity change, (2) hierarchization of identities, and (3) the role of popular emotions. Our chapters, as will be illustrated later, touch upon these broad discussions.

Japanese Identity and Agency

First, the use of agency in the identity discussion is based on the claim that agents are aware of how identity entrepreneurship can help them achieve their goals. These goals and strategies on how to achieve them take place in the least sedimented level and take on the form of contestation politics of identity (Campbell 1998: 218; Neumann 1996: 165; Guillaume 2011). Agents realize that much is at stake in the battle for the narrative of the state Self, and act accordingly. The form of the narrative can be more or less instrumental depending on the qualities and interests of particular agents. Their aim may be to describe, interpret, or straightforwardly formulate political issues. They use discursive practices such as naming, dramatization, comparison, exaggeration, or downplaying in order to inscribe their visions of state's Self into the state identity. This is what post-structuralists call the practice/performativity of identity in which the Self of the state resides (Campbell 1998: 218). Agents of this performativity do not necessarily have to take form of the elite representatives of the state such as the president, government, or the parliament. Media, epistemic communities, businesses, etc., might possess and entrepreneur their own visions of identity. Bukh (2015), for instance, showed the process in which local politicians of the Japanese Shimane prefecture incorporated the disputed Takeshima (Dokdo in Korean, officially known as Liancourt rocks, i.e., Kim, 2016) islands into Japanese national identity (vis-a-vis Korean Other) by the adoption of the so-called Takeshima Day in 2005. Subsequently, the prefecture pressured on the national government in Tokyo to accept this narrative in order to strengthen Japan's claim over the contested islands and question the Korean claim (Kolmaš 2019).

Here, however, lies the question to what extent is it possible to distinguish agents and a specific kind of narrative/system in which they operate. Some authors (ie. Kowert and Legro, 1996) argue that agents are independent on the structure and thus capable of consciously manipulating identity to reach their own goals. Others (Hagstrom and Gustafsson 2015: 8–9; Wodak, de Cilia, Reisigl and Liebhart 2009) believe that there is a limit to the identity agency. According to them, agents operate in a specific discursive field/narrative, which agents transform, but also accept and thus his actions can be traced to a particular underlying identity. Ruth Wodak (et al. 2009) illustrates this issue on the example of postwar American foreign policy, in which agents pursuing changes to security identity constructed the image of the American Self vis-a-vis the Soviet Other; yet only in compliance to the broader practice of American identity as constructed against the Other defined as a lack of order. Referencing to the National Security Council (NSC-68) documents, Wodak argues that the Soviet Union might have played the role of a significant Other, in distinction to which American foreign policy narrative was constituted; however, American politicians themselves admitted that the absence of order, possibility of anarchy, fear of totalitarianism, and other negative elements were more sedimented fears for them than the fear of Soviets. Even if the Soviet Union would not exist then (and American identity could not have been constructed vis-a-vis the Soviet Other), United States would still pursue similar foreign policy focused on eliminating the absence of order (Kolmaš 2019; Wodak, de Cilia, Reisigl and Liebhart 2009: 31–32).

The agency discussion helps us in two ways: First, contrary to much of postmodern thinking, it allows us to focus on individuals and not be utterly preoccupied with structure. Second, it differentiates between the actors we understand as key in identity formation and reformation. Both of these ways allow us to be ontologically clear.

Japanese Identity and Hierarchy

Understanding national identity in its discursive formulation always resides on the interplay between various others and various selves. Constructivists (i.e., Hopf 1998) believe that this struggle is in a relational form, but that does not necessarily have to be a hierarchical positioning for an identity to emerge. In case of Japan, however, hierarchization has played a key role in the formation and recreation of national identity. The deepest sedimented identities, such as modern state, have been produced hierarchically, by distinguishing from both Asia and the West. This struggle for meaning started with the Meiji restoration, but even before the restoration, Japan found itself in constantly contested hierarchical position within the Chinese tributary system. Understood as a "border case," Japanese elites often made an explicit distinction between Chinese civilization, which they revered, and the Chinese state, which they often held in contempt (Kang 2010: 593–594).

For most parts of Japan's modern history, the narratives compared Japan to a broadly defined superior and inferior states. These categories changed over time, but ultimately, Japanese identity has been produced within these hierarchical contestations. The West (superior) and Asia (inferior) have served for much of Japan's post-Meiji identity production and have contributed greatly to Japan's colonial ventures. Tokyo legitimized its World War II offensive by arguing it is "liberating" Asia from Western "predators," and argued that the struggles between Japan and China are no more than a rivalry between older and younger brother in one household (*Ajia no ikka*, see Tamaki 2015). After the war, Japan found itself in a hierarchical position toward the United States, and much of the postwar discussions on Japan's role in the world revolved around the key issue of whether Japan had been robbed of its identity and autonomy. The postwar Constitution and its war-renouncing Article 9 were—and still are—key to these discussions. Many leading LDP members including Kishi and Yoshida protested against the Constitution and argued that "It is not the policy of an independent nation to have troops of a foreign country based on its soil" (Samuel 2007: 30). What is often missed in these discussions is the fact that they originate in the fear of losing "autonomous" identity. As Suzuki (2015: 100) wrote: "Whatever one's political colors were, debates surrounding Article 9 were intimately linked to a persistent fear that Japan had a 'weak' or 'subservient' identity that allowed it to be dominated by foreign powers" (for a broader discussion, see Kolmaš 2018, 2019).

The Yoshida doctrine and the 1960 defense treaty in many ways codified this status and the debates became muted. But with the collapse of the Soviet Union at the beginning of 1990s, discussions about Japanese autonomy and independence returned. Advocated of autonomy (including Ozawa Ichiro, Shinzo Abe, Shintaro Ishihara, and others) criticized the US-imposed Constitution and postwar masochistic (*jigyakuteki*) regime that has robbed Japan of its place in the world. They argued that this "robbery" has placed Japan in a victim position to the dominant United States, and thus the country needs to detach itself from the postwar torpor on foreign and security policy, stand up again and become a self-confident and "normal" nation. Security reconstruction was framed as a "normalization" of Japanese identity, which, in itself, was produced through hierarchical position of Japan vis-a-vis its various others. Although the United States served as the most significant other for Japan for much of the second part of the twentieth century, since the end of 1990s, China has gradually emerged as the key other for Japanese hierarchical positioning (see Suzuki 2015).

This Japanese case reflects a broader theoretical discussion regarding identity production and change. Traditional constructivists generally believe that identities are not necessarily always hierarchical; and in some cases, identities of individuals can exist without others to confirm them. When describing individual identity, Alexander Wendt (1999: 226) wrote that "The characteristics that underlie type identities are at base intrinsic to actors. The qualities that make Max a teenager exist whether or not Others are present to recognize them as meaningful, and to that extent he can be a teenager all by himself." Post-structuralists reject this claim and instead believe that there are hidden hierarchies in every aspect of human life, including identity formation. Chapters in this book, albeit loosely tied to either constructivism or post-structuralism, highlight these hierarchical discourses, as will be illustrated later.

Japanese Identity and Emotions

Analyzing emotions has become increasingly popular in contemporary international relations literature (see, i.e., Coicaud 2014; Herrmann, Isernia and Segatti 2009; Mercer 2005). For most parts of the modern IR history, however, we have tended to disregard emotions as a constitutive part of national identity and/or foreign policy. The big IR theories such as realism and liberalism were preoccupied with the notion that states are unitary actors that behave rationally, and neither the emotions of the population nor the discursive interpretation of the emotions of the state played any role in foreign policy practice. Since the end of the 1990s, new approaches emerged which transcended/criticized the rationality of states and began to advocate for a range of emotions stemming from shame, anger, sympathy, or friendship. Ted Hopf (2010), for instance, came up with the concept of habit as a possible motivation for state behavior. Hopf believed that in some instances, neither logic of consequentialism nor the logic of appropriateness can provide a plausible explanation of the construction of political decision. He described cases of long-term cooperation or conflict, in which rationality presupposed by other logics of behavior does not exist and states behave instinctively. He used the term "habit," which—according to him—manifests as amity or enmity toward other states based in emotion, rather than instrumental rationality (Hopf 2010: 541). The habitual affect against particular Other presupposes the existence of particular identity—depending on the context, it can define states as friends, enemies, but can also influence/define behavior among identities such as Christian, Asian, modern, democratic, etc.

The relevance of Hopf's study does not only discard the preoccupation with rationality, but also shows how the very rationality/irrationality nexus is constituted by identity (and thus there is no objective rationality). This is ever more apparent in defining collective identity. In the formation of international organizations, or building up classical alliances among states, identity can form the emotional feeling of belonging similarly as within the groups of individuals. According to Jan Assmann (cited in Wodak et al. 2008: 7–8), "collective identity is a matter of identification on the part of the participating individuals. It does not exist 'in itself', but only ever to the extent that specific individuals subscribe to it. It is as strong or as weak as it is alive in the thoughts and actions of the group members, and able to motivate their thoughts and actions." When one identifies with a particular notion, one feels part of a certain collective. It follows that without emotional attachment, identities are difficult to construct. In such a situation, identity entrepreneurs appear more seldom and are much less likely to succeed (Hagstrom and Gustafsson 2015: 10). This, however, works both ways—in the cases of a highly passionate situation (emotional debates), there is the highest possibility of agents trying to instrumentalize these for their visions of identity (clearly visible in discussions of migration and identity). In the case of Japan, there is growing distress regarding the rise of China and its perceived undemocratic, irrational, bullying, or unlawful behavior, which constructs Japan as a democratic, rational, and lawful country (for this discussion in detail, see Kolmaš 2019, Suzuki 2015).

But emotional interpretation of states or a collective of states is not the only place in which emotions influence/form identities. Emotions can very well be found on intrastate levels as well. Emotions are connected to ways how individuals, groups, or social classes perceive facts or even construct meanings of social events and/or history. Several chapters of this collective monograph make use of emotions in their identification of historical memory, understanding, and reconciliation with Japan's past mistakes.

Outline of the Book and Chapter Summary

This book is rather a collection of chapters dealing with different aspects of Japanese identity, ideas, and emotions. It does so on a variety of levels described above. Some (such as Hosoda, Yoshimatsu and Kaseda's) focus on the state level of identity production and deconstruct discursive interpretations of Self and Other and social norms constituting these distinctions. Others (Heo, Kozisek and Sykora's) are more interested in substate narratives of belonging and forgetting and the ways these interact with official discourses. Many of these studies apply the identity framework for specific parts of foreign policy in order to better understand changing Japanese trajectory.

An example of this approach is Yoshimatsu Hidetaka's chapter titled "National Identity and Asian Diplomacy under Abe." Yoshimatsu examines key characteristics of Japan's national identity pursued under the Prime Minister Abe in its Asian diplomacy. He shows the complicated nexus between Japan's autonomous identity, its Asian belonging, and the alliance with the United States. Yoshimatsu shows how Abe's identity was represented within his value-oriented diplomacy, which later transformed to the currently much-mentioned concept of Indo-Pacific. Yoshimatsu shows how Abe has projected his vision of identity into Japan's foreign policy, namely the relationship with India and the proposed Free and Open Indo-Pacific (FOIP).

Similarly to Yoshimatsu, Utpal Vyas presents a chapter that builds on constructivist identity framework in order to interpret contemporary Japanese foreign policy. Vyas's chapter is titled "Japan-UK Relations before and after the Brexit Referendum" and tries to understand the sudden change in Japanese perception of the relation with the UK after the Brexit referendum. Although Japan-UK relations were amicable before the referendum, Japanese reaction has been rather cautious and incredulous. The referendum created a confusion and surprise in a country that craves stability and reliable partners outside of its own tense region. Vyas shows how Abe's vision of identity helps us to understand this confusion and argues that Japan's identity drives for diversification of its international partners and lesser reliance on the United States.

The chapter of Yoshinori Kaseda looks more closely on the change that has been ongoing in Japan's security policy. But instead of focusing solely on security evolution, Kaseda investigates the role of ideas in the constitution of these changes, that is, how has Abe's nationalism created Japan's security renaissance. Kaseda does a holistic and thorough evaluation based on a variety of primary sources of all the components of this ideational change and argues indeed there is a strong ideational background, rather than a simple strategic interest, in the ongoing policy change.

The chapter by Yoichiro Sato investigates the change within the realm of economy. Japan has been praised for its "East Asian miracle" of intense economic growth in the postwar years. This "high growth" helped Japan to recover pride in its achievements, and was more or less successfully emulated by many other Asian countries. In the chapter, Sato analyzes how this economic model reflects Japanese identity and how it has been transformed because of its interaction with Chinese mercantilist, and American liberal economic models.

The chapter of David Kozisek looks at Japanese identity through its discursive interpretation. Differently to the two abovementioned chapters,

David adopts a post-structural othering framework in order to illustrate how Japanese perception of China changes, and how this leads to changes in Japanese perception of self. This is by no means involuntary, but rather a product of a revisionist state policies and narratives spearheaded by the Prime Minister Abe. Methodologically, David Kozisek dissects media discourse and shows the ways in which media contribute, or hamper, positive/negative images of the country and ruling elites.

The chapters of Jan Sýkora and Emilia S. Heo engage with the discussion on historical memory and identity change. They investigate how much have shared understandings and feelings influenced the ways in which we perceive the past. Jan Sýkora's chapter focuses on the shared understanding and perceptions of Japanese surrender in 1945. The event has been dramatized by several movies both in Japan and abroad, which significantly contributed to the stereotypical myth in which the historical figures were labeled as heroes or villains. Sýkora's chapter analyzes the different images of the two controversial historical figures involved in the tragic endgame of the war in Japan, namely Emperor Showa and the Minister of Army General Korechika Anami, as portrayed in two film adaptations (1967 and 2015) of the Kazutoshi Hando's book "Japan's Longest Day." The different approaches to the historical facts reflect the changing content of war narrative and explore the process of the recreation of the national identity through the myth making in the contemporary Japanese society.

Emilia S. Heo's chapter titled "Through the Eyes of Others: Postwar Reconciliation Narrative in Contemporary Japan" explores to what extent Japanese youth's understanding about the country's past affects the way they perceive their relations with neighboring countries today. Working with data through an online survey and multiple class observations, Emilia elucidates that Japanese university students, especially those exposed to a global educational environment, display critical engagement with conflict knowledge acquired at school and the way it is taught. The research outcome also shows how they connect themselves with the country's past influences their perspective on what role youth can play in promoting peace with former enemy states. Learning history with and through others is crucial for younger generation to become an active agent of reconciliation.

Note

1 This section is a shortened and revised version of my earlier book *National Identity and Japanese Revisionism*, which was published by Routledge in 2019.

References

Abdelal, R., Herrera, Y., Johnston, A.I., & McDermott, R. (2006). Identity as a variable. *Perspectives on Politics*, *4*, 695–713.

Berenskoetter, F. (2010). Identity in international relations. In R A. Denemark (Ed.), *The International studies encyclopedia* (pp. 3595–3611). Chichester: Wiley-Blackwell.

Berger, T.U. (1993). From sword to chrysanthemum: Japan's culture of anti-militarism. *International Security*, *17*(4), 119–150.

Berger, T.U. (1998). *Cultures of antimilitarism*. Baltimore: John Hopkins Press.

Bukh, A. (2010). *Japan's national identity and foreign policy*. London: Routledge.

Bukh, A. (2015). Shimane Prefecture, Tokyo and the territorial dispute over Dokdo/Takeshima: regional and national identities in Japan. *The Pacific Review*, *28*(1), 47–70.

Campbell, D. (1998). *Writing security. United States foreign policy and the politics of identity*. Minneapolis: University of Minnesota Press.

Coicaud, J.-M. (2014). Emotions and passions in the discipline of international relations. *Japanese Journal of Political Science*, *15*(3), 485–513.

Dobson, H. (2017). Is Japan really back? The "Abe Doctrine" and global governance. *Journal of Contemporary Asia*, *47*(2), 199–224.

Drulak, P. (2009). *Metafory studene valky* [Metaphors of the Cold War]. Prague: Portal.

Easley, L.-E. (2017). How proactive? How pacifist? Charting Japan's evolving defense posture. *Australian Journal of International Affairs*, *71*(1), 63–87.

Guzzini, S. (2000). A reconstruction of constructivism in international relations. *European Journal of International Relations*, 6(2), 147–182.

Hagström, L., & Gustafsson, K. (2015). Japan and identity change: Why it matters in international relations. *The Pacific Review*, *28*(1), 1–22.

Hagström, L., & Hanssen, U. (2015). The North Korean abduction issue: Emotions, securitization and the reconstruction of Japanese identity from 'aggressor' to 'victim' and from 'pacifist' to 'normal'. *The Pacific Review*, *28*(1), 71–93.

Hansen, L. (2006). *Security as practice. Discourse analysis and the Bosnian War*. London: Routledge.

Herrmann, R.K., Isernia, P., & Segatti, P. (2009). Attachment to the nation and International Relations: Dimensions of identity and their relationship to war and peace. *Political Psychology*, *30*(5), 721–754.

Hopf, T. (2010). The logic of habit in international relations. *European Journal of International Relations*, *16*(4), 539–561.

Hughes, C.W. (2015). *Japan's foreign and security policy under the 'Abe Doctrine'*. New York: Palgrave Macmillan.

Kang, D.C. (2010). Hierarchy and legitimacy in international systems: The tribute system in early modern East Asia. *Security Studies*, *19*(4), 591–622.

Katzenstein, P.J. (1996). *Cultural norms and national security: Police and military in postwar Japan*. Ithaca, NY: Cornell University Press.

Katzenstein, P.J., & Okawara, N. (1993). Japan's national security. Structures, norms and policies. *International Security, 17*(4), 84–118.
Kennedy, P. (1994). Japan: A twenty-first-century power? In C.C. Garby & M. Brown Bullock, (Eds.), *Japan: A new kind of superpower?* (pp. 193–199). Baltimore, MD: John Hopkins University Press.
Kolmaš, M. (2018). Identity change and societal pressures in Japan: The constraints on Abe Shinzo's educational and constitutional reform. *The Pacific Review, 33*(2), 185–215.
Kolmaš, M. (2019). *National identity and Japanese revisionism.* London: Routledge.
Kowert, P. (1998). National identity: Inside and out. *Security Studies, 8*(2–3), 1–34.
Kowert, P., & Legro, J. (1998). Norms, identities and their limits: A theoretical reprise. In P. Katzenstein (Ed.), *The culture of national security* (pp. 451–497). New York: Columbia University Press.
Lande, E. (2017). Between offensive and defensive realism—The Japanese Abe government's security policy toward China. *Asian Security, 14*(2), 172–192.
Liff, A.P. (2015). Japan's defense policy: Abe the evolutionary. *The Washington Quarterly, 38*(2), 79–99.
Mearsheimer, J.J. (2001). *The tragedy of great power politics.* New York: W.W. Norton.
Medhurst, M., Ivie, R., Wander, P., & Scott, R. (1997). *Cold War rhetoric: Strategy, metaphor and ideology.* East Lansing: Michigan State University Press.
Mercer, J. (2010). Emotional beliefs. *International Organization, 64*(1), 1–31.
Mercer, J. (2005). Rationality and psychology in international relations. *International Organization, 59*(1), 77–106.
Neumann, I.B. (1996). Self and other in international relations. *European Journal of International Relations, 2*(2), 139–174.
Neumann, I.B. (1998). *Uses of the Other. The "East" in European identity formation.* Minneapolis: University of Minnesota Press.
Oguma E. (2002). *Genealogy of 'Japanese' self-images.* Melbourne: Trans Pacific Press.
Onuf, N. (1989). *World of our making.* Columbia, University of South Carolina Press.
Onuf, N. (2003). Parsing personal identity: Self, other, agent. In F. Debrix (Ed.), *Language, agency and politics in constructed world* (pp. 26–49). Armonk: M.E. Sharpe.
Oros, A.L. (2008). *Normalizing Japan: Politics, identity and the evolution of security practice.* Stanford: Stanford University Press.
Oros, A.L. (2015). International and domestic challenges to Japan's postwar security identity: 'Norm constructivism' and Japan's new 'proactive pacifism'. *The Pacific Review, 28*(1), 139–160.
Rumelili, B. (2004). Constructing identity and relating to difference: Understanding the EU's mode of differentiation. *Review of International Studies, 30*(1), 27–47.
Samuels, R.J. (2007). *Securing Japan: Tokyo's grand strategy and the future of East Asia.* Ithaca, NY and London: Cornell University Press.

Schulze, K. (2016). Japan's new assertiveness: Institutional change and Japan's securitization of China. *International Relations of the Asia Pacific*, *18*(2), 221–247.

Suzuki, S. (2007). The importance of "othering" in China's national identity: Sino-Japanese relations as a stage of identity conflicts. *The Pacific Review*, *2*(1), 23–47.

Suzuki, S. (2015). The rise of the Chinese 'Other' in Japan's construction of identity: Is China a focal point of Japanese nationalism? *The Pacific Review*, *28*(1), 95–116.

Tamaki, T. (2015). The persistence of reified Asia as reality in Japanese foreign policy narratives. *The Pacific Review*, *28*(1), 23–45.

Urrestarazu, U.S. (2015). Identity in international relations and foreign policy theory. In H. Gunter & K.E. Jorgensen (Eds.), *Theorizing foreign policy in globalized world* (pp. 126–149). London: Palgrave Macmillan.

Wæver, O. (2002). Identity, communities and foreign policy: Discourse analysis as foreign policy theory. In L. Hansen & O. Waever (Eds.), *European integration and national identity: The challenge of the Nordic states* (pp. 20–49). London: Routledge.

Waltz, K. (1979). *Theory of international politics*. New York: McGraw Hill.

Waltz, K.N. (1993). The emerging structure of international politics. *International Security*, *18*(2), 44–79.

Wendt, A. (1999). *Social theory of international politics*. New York: Cambridge University Press.

Wodak, R., de Cilia, R., Reisigl, M., & Liebhart, K. (2009*). The discursive construction of national identity*. Edinburg: Edinburgh University Press.

1. National Identity and Asian Diplomacy under Abe

HIDETAKA YOSHIMATSU
Ritsumeikan Asia Pacific University

Introduction

In the 2010s, Japan's diplomatic policies and relations have collected keen interests in the world in general and in Asia in particular. This is largely because the Abe administration has implemented distinctive diplomatic policies that have had significant impacts on regional politics and the global political economy. Shinzo Abe has assumed a prime ministerial post for more than eight years including one year of the first administration in 2006–2007. The Abe administration has presented distinctive diplomatic ideals towards Asia such as value-oriented diplomacy and the Free and Open Indo-Pacific.

Prime Minister Abe is known as a conservative nationalist who puts stress on Japan's traditional values and national pride. Abe's particular personal identity should have had meaningful impacts on Japan's national identity shown in its diplomacy towards Asia. Moreover, the external policies and relations of Japan, like other middle powers, have been constrained by great power politics. Under such constraints, Japan's national identity has swung in relation to two great powers, the US and China. While the US has been a sole ally with close political and economic ties, China's growing power and presence have significant influences on Japan's diplomatic stance and external relations.

This study seeks to examine the key characteristics of Japan's national identity pursued by the Abe administration in its Asian diplomacy. In so doing, this chapter takes into account two analytical angles. The first is relevant to the "layered identity" of state and state leader. The national identity is a state's identity that is developed in historical sequences and social and cultural contexts as well as social interactions with other states. The national identity is formed as the structure with stable and fixed character at the more institutionalised layer. The heads of state and government, agents of the state, are, in a normal condition, unable to establish or transform state identity. However, the production and reproduction of state identity might become possible under a strict condition when the state holds a distinctive political leader who has a strong aspiration for remodelling the state, high capabilities to employ languages for discourses to mobilise resources in the public space, and a long-term reign enough to realise political goals. Such identity entrepreneurs who operate at the less institutionalised layer can construct, reproduce, and alter state identity at the more institutionalised layer (Hagström and Gustafsson 2015: 8).

Abe has a distinctive character as prime minister. He is a "thoroughbred" politician with prime minister Nobusuke Kishi as a grandfather, another prime minister Eisaku Sato as an uncle, and Shintaro Abe, foreign minister and a faction leader of the Liberal Democratic Party (LDP), as the father. In September 2006, Abe became the youngest prime minister in Japan's postwar period. Since coming back to power in December 2012, Abe has enjoyed a solid political position. Within the Diet, the fragmented opposition parties have never challenged the dominance of the LDP. Within the LDP, the *Seiwa-kai*, a faction to which Abe belongs, has maintained the dominant position. Abe as a determined political leader has specific ideals and identity, and his identity is reflected in his administration's foreign policy. Abe as an agent seeks to reflect his own identity on Japan's status in the international arena through the advocacy of specific ideals. The diffusion and acceptance of the ideals and the embeddedness of such ideals into regional institutions are effective means to influence the international system in which Japan is located.

The second aspect is relevant to "relational" national identity. The national identity is formed intersubjectively through interactions with other actors in the social sphere (Suzuki 2007: 25). Accordingly, the national identity requires both a state's self-perception and the understanding and acceptance of such perception by other states. This implies that the national identity is produced and developed in relation to a state's surrounding fellow members through social interactions and social contestation. Given a state's imperative to maintain national interests under constraints from uneven distribution of power, it has to pay due attention to relations with great powers, which involve not only linkages in material terms but also an ideational perception. Under such conditions, the state tends to regard one great power as a senior fellow that shares the sameness and/or another great power as one with the otherness.

In the post-Second World War period, the political and security partnership with the US has been the primary pillar of Japan's foreign and security policy. The conservative LDP regime has put stress on the stable alliance with the US, and Japan's foreign and security policy has been tuned with the political and security partnership with the US. Japan has maintained an identity as a Western ally and a junior partner of Washington in the hierarchical international system. At the same time, several Japanese leaders have pursued Japan's autonomous status by emphasising its identity as an Asian nation. This was typical for Yukio Hatoyama who asserted a shift to the self-reliance diplomacy from America-obedient one, and pursued a closer affiliation with Asian nations through an East Asian community (EAC). As will be explained in the following section, Abe is a conservative nationalist, who has been eager to preserve Japan's traditional social and cultural values, and enhance Japan's national pride and self-confidence. Abe has accepted the value of the alliance with the US particularly as the great power to counter the China risk. But, Abe is likely to pursue the enhancement of Japan's autonomous identity when he considers that the partnership with Washington undermines Japan's national prestige. It is necessary to examine whether this is a case when Abe pursues a more autonomous identity in relation to the US.

Before investigating the Abe administration's concrete external policies towards Asia, the following section explores Abe's personal identity.

Abe's Identity as a Conservative Nationalist

Abe is regarded as a conservative nationalist. Abe's nationalist belief is strongly influenced by his grandfather, Nobusuke Kishi, who assumed prime ministership from February 1957 until July 1960. Abe recalls that growing up amid critical comments that his grandfather was "the embodiment of reactionary conservatism" or "a class-A war crime suspect" might bring about "the opposite effect of making me embrace 'conservatism' " (Abe 2006: 18–19). Abe's advocacy of "departure from the postwar regime" is consonant with Kishi's thirst to break the San-Francisco regime, and Kishi and Abe share a strong aspiration to revise the US-imposed post-war Japanese Constitution.

Abe as a conservative nationalist sought to re-establish Japan's national identity, seeking "to transform Japanese society and state into a more confident, autonomous, but also traditional and unique entity" (Kolmaš 2020: 187). Abe's such desire was revealed in the slogan of departure from the post-war regime, the revision of the Basic Education Act, and an attempt to revise the Japanese Constitution (Kolmaš 2020; McNeill and Lebowitz 2007; Ryu 2018). The concepts such as respect for history and culture, the spirit of the public, and the importance of nature were stressed in the revised education act (Togo 2015: 6). These elements are also emphasised in the LDP's draft of the revision of the Japanese Constitution (LDP 2012). Abe's conservative identity has been also embedded in his affiliation with various conservative political groups. Abe is the founder of an arch-conservative political association, *Sosei Nippon* (Reborn Japan), as well as a key member of the Diet's cross-party Alliance for Promoting the Assessment of a New Constitution (Hughes 2015). The concrete policy directions and affiliation with conservative political groups surely indicate Abe's identity as a conservative nationalist.

In external relations, Abe has maintained the LDP's long-honoured tenet to maintain close political and security ties with the US. However, Abe has maintained a historical revisionist posture, which was demonstrated, for instance, during his formal visit to India in 2007. Abe made a visit to the bereaved family of Chandra Bose who fought against the British army in collaboration with the Japanese army during the Pacific War. Abe also visited the son of Radhabinod Pal, an Indian Justice of the International Military Tribunal for the Far East who asserted innocent of class-A war criminals of the Pacific War. These visits could be interpreted as linking to Abe's affiliation with Kishi and revisionist historical views. Bose died in Taiwan due to an airplane accident in August 1945, and his remains were buried in a temple in Tokyo because India was under the control of Britain. Kishi and Indian Prime Minister Jawaharlal Nehru undertook a ceremonial service at the temple during Nehru's visit to Tokyo in October 1957 (Kusaka 2014: 67).

In addition to the character of a conservative nationalist, Abe is also regarded as a pragmatist who seeks to protect Japan's interest in evolving political and security environments in Asia (Mochizuki and Porter 2013; Nilsson-Wright and Fujiwara 2015; Pyle 2018). Even during the first administration in 2006–2007, Abe exhibited this pragmatism by respecting the 1993 Kono statement and the 1995 Murayama statement, which enabled him to make an "ice-breaking" visit to Beijing in September 2006 (Mochizuki and Porter 2013: 35–36). After forming the second administration, Abe's pragmatism became more salient. His pragmatism and learning were shown in the composition of the second Abe cabinet. While the cabinet included vocal conservatives such as Tomomi Inada (Regulatory Reform) and Hakubun Shimomura (Education), it also contained moderates such as Fumio Kishida (Foreign Affairs) and Sadakazu Tanigaki (Justice) (Nilsson-Wright and Fujiwara 2015: 4).

Abe's pragmatism had much to do with learning. Abe, who learned from his failure to manage the government skilfully during the first administration, has been very careful in governing policy formation and political interactions after returning to power. Abe recalled later that the setback and experiences at the time of the first administration that lasted for one year became an important fertiliser for six years after the start of the second administration (Sankei Shimbun 2018). As for the formation of the cabinet, Abe also learned from the failure of Kishi who was forced to step down as prime minister in July 1960 because of a broad spectrum of conservative politicians within his cabinet that later invited an internal party rebellion (Nilsson-Wright and Fujiwara 2015: 5).

In summary, Abe has a distinctive identity as a conservative nationalist who puts stress on the preservation of a strong and prestigious Japan. At the same time, he is a pragmatist who adjusts policy stances flexibly aiming to gain practical outcomes by observing the reality of complicated political conditions. The following sections analyse how Abe's identity has been reflected in the development of Japan's diplomacy towards Asia.

National Identity and Value-Oriented Diplomacy

In the 2000s, the Japanese government began to show new diplomatic postures to take advantage of Japan's specific identity. A representative is value-oriented diplomacy during the first Abe administration in 2006–2007. The administration stressed value-oriented diplomacy, a particular type of diplomacy that puts emphasis on universal values such as democracy, freedom, human rights, and rule of law. As a strategy to promote the liberal values of democracy, human rights, and rule of law, Foreign Minister Taro Aso stressed the necessity of building an "arc of freedom and prosperity" around the outer rim of the Eurasian continent through diplomacy that would emphasise these universal values. The arc of freedom and prosperity was a marked diplomatic ideal in Japanese diplomacy in the sense that it combined the geopolitical perspective and ideational values.

The stress on universal values is based on Japan's national identity as a law-abiding democratic nation that shared similarities with Western democracies and political commonalities underpinning international cooperation and the rule of law. This identity is expected to develop close partnerships with democratic nations such as the US, Australia, India, and the European Union (EU) members. In fact, strength in diplomatic ties with Australia and India—in addition to the US—became crucial diplomatic goals during the first Abe administration (Yoshimatsu 2012).

The value-oriented diplomacy had two distinctive characteristics. The first is that it was a means to preserve Japan's self-image as a great nation.

Japan had maintained an identity as an economic great power with the world's second-largest economy since 1968. However, it is projected that this status would be superseded by China soon, and India would follow. Moreover, its long-term economic recession and growing financial deficits led to the reduction of official development assistance (ODA), Japan's key diplomatic tool. Japan's ranking in terms of ODA provision declined from the first in 1989 to fifth in 2005. Under such environments, the Japanese government needed a new diplomatic vision to articulate Japan's presence in the world and inspire the Japanese people. Second, the value-oriented diplomacy implied a departure from Japan's past diplomatic posture. Japanese diplomacy was called "leadership from behind" or "quiet diplomacy", which indicated invisible and passive posture in the surface (Hook et al. 2011; Rix 1993). However, the advocacy of value-oriented diplomacy meant an assertive diplomatic posture, helping other countries proactively to pursue specific ideals that were linked to Japan's identity and its past experiences of nation-building.

The value-oriented diplomacy represented Abe's long-term perception of Japan's national identity. Abe ascribes, in a book published just before becoming prime minister, distinctive features of the Japanese society that pays respect to freedom, democracy, and fundamental human rights on the basis of rule of law (Abe 2006: 157–161). Abe also expressed a strong desire to convene a summit or ministerial meeting among Japan, Australia, the US, and India with an eye to holding talks on how to contribute to and cooperate on the sharing of these universal values with Asian countries. Abe's perception of value-oriented diplomacy, which was linked to Japan's national identity, was so strong that he located it as a key diplomatic pillar even in the second administration that began in December 2012. At the Diet speech in February 2013, Abe stated that "my diplomacy is based on 'strategic diplomacy'", "diplomacy that emphasises universal values", and "insisting diplomacy" to "protect national interests. I will rebuild the injured Japanese diplomacy and clarify Japan's firm position standing in the world" (Abe 2013a).

The value-oriented diplomacy represented a common national identity between Japan and the US. The realisation of values of democracy and human rights could be regarded as Tokyo's effort to underpin the military alliance with Washington "in terms of democratic principles and shared political values" (Mochizuki and O'Hanlon 1998: 128). Moreover, the value-oriented diplomacy had strategic implications. The arc of freedom and prosperity accorded with the geographic areas of an unstable belt that the US government showed in the 2001 Quadrennial Defence Review (QDR), and was resonant with an idea with "a growing community of democracies" in the

2006 US National Security Strategy (Hoshiyama 2007: 10). Japan's explicit support for universal values was particularly important in the trend that the Bush administration was losing its international credibility under the strong criticism of the Iraq War. Besides, the value-oriented diplomacy was expected to strengthen the "bilateral-plus" approach in that the new security links outside the US-Japan alliance could be developed as drives to strengthen the alliance's bilateral efforts (Suzuki 2010: 506–507).

The value-oriented diplomacy incorporated nuanced identity relations with China. The first diplomatic task for the Abe administration was to reconstruct damaged diplomatic relations with Beijing during the previous Koizumi administration. Abe selected China as the first destination of foreign visit and established a "mutually beneficial relationship based on the strategic interest". Afterwards, he carefully avoided obvious anti-Chinese rhetoric, even making it ambiguous whether he would visit the Yasukuni Shrine (Park and Vogel 2007: 29). However, Abe perceived Japan's specific identity in relation to China. In his 2006 book, Abe allocated one chapter to "Japan and Asia/ China". In discussing Japan's relations with China, Abe stressed that "for the past 60 years, Japan humbled itself for nation-building and international contribution under freedom, democracy, fundamental human rights, and the rule of law. Meanwhile, Japan has never shown a militant attitude, such as once" (2006: 150). This passage indicates his hope to articulate Japan's national identity as a pacifist democratic nation in contrast with China, an authoritarian state.

While stress on universal values through the value-oriented diplomacy surely served to highlight China's "other" nature as a dissenter from common values represented by Japan and its allies, Abe's first term in office was too short to articulate components of China's otherness (Hemmings and Kuroki 2013: 61). Such an articulation was done just after the beginning of the second administration. During a visit to Southeast Asia in January 2013, Abe prepared for a planned speech entitled "The Bounty of the Open Seas: Five New Principles for Japanese Diplomacy".[1] In this speech, Abe presented five principles for Japanese diplomacy to build the future. The first three principles were "protecting freedom of thought, expression, and speech", "ensuring that the seas, which are the most vital commons to us all, are governed by laws and rules, not by might", and "pursuing free, open, interconnected economies as part of Japan's diplomacy" (Abe 2013b). The stress on free, open, interconnected economies and freedom of thought, expression, and speech as well as the governance of seas by laws and rules, not by might, aimed to delineate China as the other. This approach sought to highlight the contrast between Japan and its regional and global partners, on the one hand, and an authoritarian China, on the other (Nilssen-Wright and Fujiwara 2015: 9).

National Identity and the Free and Open Indo-Pacific

In 2016, Prime Minister Abe advocated a new ideal that has significant implications for the international relations of Asia. In August, Abe presented the Free and Open Indo-Pacific (FOIP) strategy at the 6th Tokyo International Conference on African Development (TICAD VI) held in Kenya. The FOIP strategy is based on an assumption that the peace and prosperity of the international society are reliant on the free and open maritime order, and thereby such a maritime order should be fostered from the Pacific to the Indian Ocean. In this strategy, Japan intended to promote concrete policies such as: the promotion of basic values of the rule of law; democracy and freedom of navigation; the fostering of economic prosperity through the strength of infrastructure in ports, railways, and others, and enhanced economic partnerships; and strength in cooperation in the field of maritime safety such as maritime law-enforcement capabilities, piracy combating, and counter-terrorism.

The FOIP derived from Abe's long-term perceptions of two terms, "Indo-Pacific" and "free and open". Abe's use of the Indo-Pacific has a relatively long history (Yoshimatsu 2019). During the first administration, Abe made a formal visit to India in August 2007, exactly half a century after Kishi's visit to the country. An epoch-making event during this visit was a 25-minute speech at the Indian Parliament entitled the "Confluence of the Two Seas". The Confluence of the Two Seas was a new policy idea to comprehend the Pacific and Indian Oceans as a united geographical zone. After forming the second administration, Abe gradually developed the Confluence of the Two Seas into a new geographical concept. In a speech at the Centre for Strategic and International Studies in February 2013, Abe spelled out Japan's task to remain a leading promoter of rules "when the Asia-Pacific, or the Indo-Pacific region gets more and more prosperous" (2013c). Abe used the term, Indo-Pacific, for the first time in a speech as prime minister. The FOIP is an extension of the Confluence of the Two Seas from the Pacific and Indian Oceans to Africa. Abe stressed the FOIP's key role in creating regional stability and prosperity through confluences between the "two continents" of Asia and Africa and the "two oceans" of the Pacific and Indian.

The free and open is a normative belief that is applied to the management of maritime affairs. The "free and open" implies freedom of navigation and rule of law, specific norms that Abe advocated to maintain the stable maritime order. Abe had stressed the importance of such norms before the launching of the FOIP idea. At the Shangri-La dialogue in May 2014, Abe presented the Three Principles on the Rule of Law at Sea: states shall make and clarify their claims based on international law; states shall not use force or coercion in trying to drive their claims; and states shall seek to settle disputes by peaceful means. The FOIP strategy could be regarded as a broader and comprehensive means to diffuse and consolidate the principles.

In terms of national identity, the FOIP had two-level implications. The first is a bilateral partnership with India. In speeches during his visits to India, Abe has often introduced a boyhood episode that his grandfather Kishi talked about how he was impressed by Indian Prime Minister Nehru's warm welcome during his visit to New Delhi in 1957. The introduction of the episode is a way to demonstrate how Abe has a long-term link to India through his grandfather. In advancing the FOIP, Abe regarded India as a key partner. For instance, at the Japan-India summit in September 2016, Abe stated that India was the most important country in terms of linking Asia and Africa, and Japan and India would coordinate closely to make the FOIP strategy a reality. During Abe's visit to New Delhi in September 2017, Abe and Modi issued a joint statement. The FOIP was incorporated into the title of this statement—"Japan-India Joint Statement: Toward a Free, Open and Prosperous Indo-Pacific". This implied that the two leaders shared the value of the FOIP vision, which could be used as a banner for promoting cooperation on maritime security, connectivity development, and stronger ties with the Association of Southeast Asian Nations (ASEAN).

India's importance as Japan's partner in advancing the Indo-Pacific comes from the pragmatic calculation. Both Japan and India have common interests in countering China. Japan was apprehensive about China's aggressive diplomacy and offensive actions regarding the South China Sea in terms of sea-line security and likely impacts on the East China Sea dispute. China's maritime behaviour was growing anxiety for India as well. Beijing extended its footprint in the Indian Ocean littorals with the development of ports in Pakistan, Sri Lanka, Bangladesh, and Myanmar. In the vision statement on the special strategic and global partnership issued at the summit meeting in December 2015, Abe and Modi, "noting the developments in the South China Sea", called on all states "to avoid unilateral actions that could lead to tensions in the region" (MOFA 2015). Japan and India also shared concerns about China's growing economic presence in Eurasia and Africa through the Belt and Road Initiative (BRI). In the November 2016 summit in Tokyo, Abe and Modi agreed to promote collaboration in Africa, particularly the development of industrial corridors and networks under the name of the Asia

Africa Growth Corridor (AAGC). The AAGC concept was announced just after Modi refused to join the BRI international forum in Beijing, accusing the China-Pakistan Economic Corridor (CPEC). This timing could be interpreted as India and Japan's willingness to employ the AAGC as a counterweight to the rising Chinese influence through the BRI.

In addition to geostrategic and geo-economic imperatives, national identity played a crucial role in developing the Japan-India partnership, particularly under the Indo-Pacific vision. Even during the first Abe administration, Abe sought to deepen the relationship with India on the basis of national identity. When Indian Prime Minister Manmohan Singh made a formal visit to Tokyo in December 2006, Singh and his counterpart Abe issued the joint statement towards Japan-India Strategic and Global Partnership. In this statement, the two leaders affirmed that "Japan and India are natural partners as the largest and most developed democracies of Asia", and that the Japanese-Indian relations are "underpinned by a common commitment to democracy, open society, human rights, rule of law and free-market economy" (MOFA 2006). The common national identity assumed a more explicit position in Abe-Modi relations. The two leaders have confirmed a common identity as a democratic nation that pays respect to human rights, the rule of law, and the value of freedom. For instance, the 2015 joint statement contained a phrase that "Japan and India uphold the principles of sovereignty and territorial integrity; peaceful settlement of disputes; democracy, human rights and the rule of law; open global trade regime; and freedom of navigation and overflight".

The second is a multilateral partnership. The FOIP and common values were used as linchpins to develop deeper trilateral cooperation among Japan, India, and the US. When the second Japan-US-India Trilateral Foreign Ministers' Meeting was held in New York in September 2017, the three ministers confirmed that "Japan, the United States, and India are partners in the Indo-Pacific region and share fundamental values such as freedom, democracy and the rule of law, as well as strategic interests" (MOFA 2017a). Such a common value-oriented partnership developed in relation to Australia as well. In June 2015, Japan, India, and Australia held the first trilateral dialogue at the vice-minister level in New Delhi, and afterwards, the trilateral dialogue was organised three times in February 2016, April 2017, and December 2017. During the meetings, the three vice-ministers confirmed that shared basic values and strategic interests would lead to cooperation to secure a free and open order based on the rule of law in the Indo-Pacific. More significantly, Japan proposed the establishment of a quadrilateral security dialogue among Japan, the US, India, and Australia; and this proposal was realised through the holding of the first Australia-India-Japan-US Consultations on the Indo-Pacific on an occasion of the 12th EAS in the Philippines in November 2017. The senior officials discussed "measures to ensure a free and open international order based on the rule of law in the Indo-Pacific" (MOFA 2017b).

The quadrilateral partnership is based on Abe's long-term vision of common values. As already explained, Abe had a strong desire, even during the first administration, to establish a strategic partnership among the US, Japan, Australia, and India, all of which are democratic nations. Abe fostered the importance of the quadrilateral framework further, which was shown in "Asia's Democratic Security Diamond", a strategic idea that Abe showed in an article on the website of the non-profit Project Syndicate in late December 2012. This article collected interests as it represented Abe's balancing strategy against China with the passage that "the South China Sea seems set to become a 'Lake Beijing' ". Abe himself and his entourage did not hope to pursue the democratic diamond concept further because they feared that the concept might serve to create a hawkish image of the second Abe administration and narrow the diplomatic latitude of the administration (Suzuki 2017: 138–139). Five years later, Abe moved the idea with the banner of the FOIP.

After the emergence of the Trump administration in the US, the Abe administration revised its regional strategy. In order to counter the protectionist policy adopted by the Trump administration, the administration pursued the early conclusion of the Comprehensive and Progressive Agreement for Trans-Pacific Partnership (CPTPP) and the Japan-EU Economic Partnership Agreement. These commitments were derived from Abe's determination to maintain a liberal economic regime with countries that share open and liberal principles in the Asia-Pacific and Europe. In relation to China, Abe moved to re-establish stable political relations with Beijing, proposing collaboration between the FOIP vision and China's BRI. The new developments stemmed from Abe's pragmatic calculation to hedge against uncertainty and unpredictability in the Trump administration's diplomatic postures. It is less likely to change the perception of relational identity regarding the US and China.

Abe's Discourses on Asian Identity

As the previous sections confirmed, Abe has adhered to universal values in its diplomacy from his first administration in 2006–2007, and sought to embed the values into a diplomatic vision towards Asia. The FOIP is an advanced regional vision that incorporated a universal value of "free and open". The quadrilateral security dialogue on the basis of the FOIP is Western value-based cooperation. In this sense, Japan's national identity as a democratic nation constituted the base for the FOIP and the quadrilateral partnership.

An interesting aspect in relation to national identity as a democratic nation is that Abe, in partnership with Modi, pushes forwards the importance of Asian values with universal applicability. The 2015 India-Japan joint statement includes a phrase that "the peoples of Japan and India are guided by common cultural traditions including the heritage of Buddhism, and share commitment to the ideals of democracy, tolerance, pluralism and open society" (MOFA 2015). The 2018 joint statement mentions that "the universal values of freedom, humanism, democracy, tolerance and non-violence, which have been shared between Japan and India ... underscore the principles for the two countries to work together for the benefit of the Indo-Pacific region and the world at large". Thus, Abe and Modi have incorporated the Asian elements of tolerance and non-violence as key components of values that developed in Asia and have universal applicability.

Abe's successful prime ministership is contrasted to another Prime Minister Yukio Hatoyama's leadership who advocated the ill-fated EAC (Yoshimatsu 2018). Hatoyama's EAC vision was based on the recognition of a common cultural identity among Asian nations. This point was revealed in his statement at an international conference on the Future of Asia in May 2010 that "one characteristic of Asians is that we do not perceive ourselves and others or humans and the environment in a Western dualistic manner, but rather attach importance to the sameness between the two ....This will surely also serve as a launching point for a 'cultural community'" (Hatoyama 2010). Hatoyama repeated distinctive characteristics in Asia's common culture even after he resigned from the prime ministership. At the Asian Leadership Conference held in Seoul in March 2012, Hatoyama stated that "while the West achieved economic growth on the basis of competitive dualism between nature and human beings, Asia traditionally kept respectful, not adversarial, relations between nature and human beings" (Hatoyama 2012). Hatoyama considered that Asia's holistic approach that contrasts to the West's dualistic approach can constitute the base for a harmonious relationship among the people and the building of a community. Abe is regarded as a realist in contrast to Hatoyama, an idealist who regarded *yuai* (fraternity) as the key political belief (Hatoyama 2009). Importantly, Abe is less explicit in advocating the Asian cultural tradition than Hatoyama, but he also recognises cultural commonality in Asia.

Abe and Modi's stress on Asian values has much to do with the perception of a democratic nation. In 2015, Abe and Modi agreed to hold a regular symposium called the "Samvad" series of dialogue to discuss conflict-avoidance and the philosophical and cultural heritage of Buddhism and Hinduism, the two dominant religions in Asia.[2] Significantly, Abe envisions an Asian-style democracy. At the second Samvad Conference in January 2016, Abe stated that "Be it lovingkindness, benevolence, fraternity, or harmony, I believe that in Asia, there extends an underground rootstock of thinking that supports democracy and values freedom and human rights" (2016). At the fourth Samvad Conference in July 2018, Abe stated that "Democracy not as a 'foreign species' introduced from the West. Democracy that is spoken of not in translation, but through our native words and concepts" (2018). Abe clearly recognised that Asian values are in no way undemocratic, and democracy is an evolving concept as Asian values must be taken seriously with so much of growth in Asia (Gupta 2018).

It is unclear how Abe reconciles an individual autonomy-based democracy in Western society and a collectivism-oriented democracy in Asian society. A crucial point is that Abe gradually incorporated Asian flavour into universal values and the concept of a democratic nation. This tendency might produce subtle issues in relation to the US and China. The stress on Japan's identity that has realised an Asian-style democracy might be regarded as an aspiration to raise Japan's autonomy in relation to the US. According to Abe's interpretation, Chinese traditional philosophical thoughts that constitute a crucial pillar of Asian values could be regarded as universal values. This provokes the issue of how Abe regards the national identity of China, a nation that has assumed a central position in East Asia with producing significant cultural impacts on its neighbouring countries including Japan.

Conclusion

In this chapter, I examined the development of the Abe administration's foreign policy towards Asia and its relevance to national identity. It explored the implications of value-oriented diplomacy during the first administration, and the FOIP and discourses at the Samvad conferences during the administration after December 2012.

The study confirmed that the Abe administration has pushed forwards Japan's unique identity as an Asian nation that has realised universal values such as freedom, democracy, rule of law, open and liberal ideals, and fundamental human rights. This identity constituted the base of the advocacy of value-oriented diplomacy. The advocacy of the FOIP was also based on Japan's identity that has developed a free and open society.

Abe's personal identity as a conservative nationalist led to the administration's advocacy of Japan's distinctiveness as a democratic nation that has paid respect to freedom, rule of law, and fundamental human rights. On the basis of the identity of a democratic nation, Abe pursued close partnerships with Australia and India, the two democratic nations that share universal values, and even the quadrilateral partnership among Japan, the US, Australia, and India. A particularly important partner is India. Abe, who developed a favourable image of India from his personal experiences, regarded the country as a key partner to advance the FOIP. Abe's special attention to India was based on the perception of the country as a nation that holds the same identity as Japan in that both countries have realised an Asian-style democracy that combines universal values and Asia-originated values such as tolerance and non-violence.

In Japan's identity politics, relationships with the two great powers—the US and China—are important. The US has been regarded as the key partner that cherishes democratic principles and shared political values. In contrast, China has been considered as a country that represents otherness, a dissenter from democratic principles and liberal political values held by Japan and its security partners. After the emergence of the Trump administration in the US, the Abe administration has strengthened political linkages with China. This policy shift derived from Abe's pragmatism, and it is uncertain to what extent Japan intended to pursue an independent identity from the US.

A crucial issue in relation to national identity is that Abe envisions an Asian-style democracy and stresses Asia-originated values such as tolerance and non-violence. As shown in discourses at the Samvad conferences, Abe considers that Japan's unique national identity lies in the realisation of a stable and peaceful society by integrating universal values and Japanese/Asian traditions. The stress on Asian values and an Asian-style democracy is likely to require the Abe administration to give careful consideration to relations with the US and China.

Notes

1 Abe was unable to deliver this policy speech because he was forced to go back to Tokyo due to a hostage incident involving the Japanese in Algeria.
2 Four conferences have been held in New Delhi (2015), Tokyo (2016), Yangon (2017), and Tokyo (2018).

References

Abe, S. (2006). *Utsukushii Kuni e* [Towards a beautiful nation]. Tokyo: Bungei Shunju.
Abe, S. (2013a). *Abe sori shisei hoshin enzetsu* [Prime Minister Abe's policy speech]. Retrieved from https://www.kantei.go.jp/jp/headline/183shiseihoushin.html#c6.

Abe, S. (2013b). The bounty of the open seas: five new principles for Japanese Diplomacy, January 18, Jakarta. Retrieved from https://japan.kantei.go.jp/96_abe/statement/201301/18speech_e.html

Abe, S. (2013c). "Japan is back", policy speech at the Center for Strategic and International Studies (CSIS), February 22. Retrieved from http://japan.kantei.go.jp/96_abe/statement/201302/22speech_e.html.

Abe, S. (2016). The Symposium "Shared Values and Democracy in Asia. Retrieved from https://japan.kantei.go.jp/97_abe/statement/201601/1215564_10999.html.

Abe, S. (2018). Remarks by H.E. Mr. Shinzo Abe, Prime Minister of Japan, at the Symposium "Shared Values and Democracy in Asia", Hotel Okura Tokyo, Japan, July 5, 2018. Retrieved from https://www.mofa.go.jp/s_sa/sw/page4e_000865.html.

Gupta, A. (2018). *Samvad: The Fourth Symposium held in Tokyo—A report.* Retrieved from https://www.vifindia.org/article/2018/july/samvad-the-fourth-symposium-held-in-tokyo-a-report.

Hagström, L., & Gustafsson, K. (2015). Japan and identity change: Why it matters in international relations. *The Pacific Review*, *28*(1), 1–22.

Hatoyama, Y. (2009, September). *Watashi no seiji tetsugaku: Sofu, ichiro ni mananda 'yuai' to iu tatakai no hatajirushi* [My political philosophy: Fraternity, a banner of fight learned from my grandfather, Ichiro]. *Voice*, pp. 132–141.

Hatoyama, Y. (2010). Speech by H.E. Dr. Yukio Hatoyama, Prime Minister of Japan, on the Occasion of the Sixteenth International Conference on the Future of Asia, Hosted by the Nihon Keizai Shimbun, May 20. Retrieved from http://www.ny.us.emb-japan.go.jp/en/t/2010/100521.html.

Hatoyama, Y. (2012). Speech at the Asian Leadership Conference 2012. Retrieved from http://www.hatoyama.gr.jp/activity/detail.php?id=6.

Hemmings, J., & Kuroki, M. (2013). Tokyo trade-offs: Shinzo Abe's hedging strategy against China. *The RUSI Journal*, *158*(2), 58–66.

Hook, G.D., et al. (2011). *Japan's international relations: Politics, economics and security* (3rd ed.) Abingdon, Oxon: Routledge.

Hoshiyama, T. (2007). "Kachino gaiko" wa nihon no shin sogo anzen hosho senryaku [Value-oriented diplomacy as Japan's new comprehensive security strategy]. *IIPS Policy Paper*, 331J.

Hughes, C.W. (2015). *Japan's foreign and security policy under the 'Abe Doctrine'.* New York: Palgrave Macmillan.

Kolmaš, M. (2020). Identity change and societal pressures in Japan: The constraints on Abe Shinzo's educational and constitutional reform. *The Pacific Review*, 30(2), 185–215.

Kusaka, K. (2014). *Yuisen shiko de sekai ni katsu* [To win in the world with the predominance battle mind]. Kyoto: PHP Kenkyujo.

LDP. (2012). *Nihon koku kenpo kaisei soan; Zenbun* [The draft of Japan's Constitutional amendment]. Retrieved from http://constitution.jimin.jp/document/draft/.

McNeill, D., & Lebowitz, A. (2007). Hammering down the educational nail: Abe revises the Fundamental Law of Education. *The Asia-Pacific Journal: Japan Focus*, *5*(7), 1–8.

Mochizuki, M., & O'Hanlon, M. (1998). A liberal vision for the US-Japanese alliance. *Survival*, *40*(2), 127–134.

Mochizuki, M.M., & Porter, S.P. (2013). Japan under Abe: Toward moderation or nationalism? *Washington Quarterly*, *36*(4), 25–41.

MOFA. (2006). *Joint Statement towards Japan-India strategic and global partnership.* Retrieved from http://www.mofa.go.jp/region/asia-paci/india/pdfs/joint0612.pdf.

MOFA. (2015). *Japan and India vision 2025 special strategic and global partnership: Working together for peace and prosperity of the Indo-Pacific region and the World*, December 12. Retrieved from https://www.mofa.go.jp/s_sa/sw/in/page3e_000432.html.

MOFA. (2017a). *Japan-U.S.-India trilateral foreign ministers' meeting*, September 19. Retrieved from http://www.mofa.go.jp/s_sa/sw/in/page3e_000752.html.

MOFA. (2017b). *Australia-India-Japan-U.S. consultations on the Indo-Pacific*, November 12. Retrieved from http://www.mofa.go.jp/press/release/press4e_001789.html.

Nilsson-Wright, J., & Fujiwara, K. (2015). Japan's Abe administration: Steering a course between pragmatism and extremism. *Chatham House Asia Programme Research Paper*, September.

Park, G., & Vogel, S. (2007). Japan in 2006. *Asian Survey*, *47*(1), 22–31.

Pyle, K. B. (2018). Japan's return to great power politics: Abe's restoration. *Asia Policy*, *13*(2), 69–90.

Rix, A. (1993). Japan and the Region: Leading from Behind. In R. Higgott, R. Leaver, & J. Ravenhill (Eds.), *Pacific economic relations in the 1990s: Cooperation or conflict?* St. Leonards, NSW: Allen & Unwin.

Ryu, Y. (2018). To revise or not to revise: The 'peace constitution', pro-revision movement, and Japan's national identity. *The Pacific Review*, *31*(5), 655–672.

Sankei Shimbun (2018). *Abe shusho rainen wa Nihon no ashita o kiri hiraku 1-nen ni* [PM Abe: The next year will open Japan's new tomorrows], December 25. Retrieved from https://www.sankei.com/politics/news/181225/plt1812250031-n1.html.

Suzuki, M. (2010). The politics of coordination and miscoordination in the post-Cold War United States-Japan alliance: From a Japanese perspective. *International Relations of the Asia-Pacific*, *10*(3), 491–514.

Suzuki, S. (2007). The importance of 'Othering' in China's national identity: Sino-Japanese relations as a stage of identity conflicts. *The Pacific Review*, *20*(1), 23–47.

Suzuki, Y. (2017). *Nihon no Senryaku Gaiko* [Japan's strategic diplomacy]. Tokyo: Chikuma Shobo.

Togo, K. (2015). *Abe Shinzo's "Sengo rejimu kara no dakkyaku": bunka to dento no shiten kara* [Abe Shinzo's 'Getting out from Post-War Regime': From the perspectives of culture and tradition]. *Kyoto Sangyo Daigaku Sekai Mondai Kenkyujo Kiyo*, *30*, 3–12.

Yoshimatsu, H. (2012). Identity, policy ideas, and Asian diplomacy: Japan's response to the rise of China. *International Area Studies Review*, *15*(4), 359–376.

Yoshimatsu, H. (2018). Japan's role conception in multilateral initiatives: The evolution from Hatoyama to Abe. *Australian Journal of International Affairs, 72*(2), 129–144.

Yoshimatsu, H. (2019). The Indo-Pacific in Japan's strategy towards India. *Contemporary Politics, 25*(4), 438–456.

2. *Ideational Factors behind the Erosion of Japan's Pacifism*

Yoshinori Kaseda
Ritsumeikan Asia Pacific University

Introduction

After its devastating defeat in World War II, Japan underwent a significant transformation during the occupation effectively by the United States (U.S.), from an authoritarian, militaristic state to a democratic, pacifist state. The transformation resulted largely from its adoption of a new constitution in 1946, which had been drafted mostly by the U.S. and became effective in 1947. The new regime based on the constitution came to be called the "postwar regime (*sengorejīmu*)."

The new constitution made the Japanese government peace-oriented externally, in its relations with other countries, and internally, in its relations with the Japanese people, by preventing it from making military aggression at another country and from violating the human rights of the Japanese people. Thus, the postwar Japanese pacifism consisted of external and internal pacifism. Although it was drafted mostly by the U.S., the new, democratic, pacifist constitution received strong support from the Japanese people, who had suffered "the horrors of war through the action of government" of imperial Japan as stated in the preamble of the new constitution.

However, the postwar Japanese regime with the new constitution started with an internal contradiction because of the change in the U.S. policy toward Japan. Although it had disbanded Japan's armed forces, in response to the breakout of the Korean War in June 1950, the U.S. made Japan rearm itself through the establishment of the National Police Reserve (NPR) in August 1950 and the Coastal Safety Force (CSF) in April 1952, which were merged into the National Safety Forces (NSF) in October 1952 and then reorganized into the Self-Defense Forces (SDF) in July 1954. Meanwhile, Japan regained its sovereignty in April 1952 when the San Francisco Peace Treaty and the Japan-U.S. Security Treaty, both signed in September 1951, went into effect.

The Japanese government regarded the SDF as constitutional, arguing that the constitution did not forbid Japan from exercising the right to individual self-defense and therefore did not prohibit Japan from possessing forces exclusively for self-defense, protecting itself when it is attacked by external forces. On the other hand, the Japanese government long held that the constitution did not allow Japan to exercise the right to collective self-defense. Hence, the Japanese government called its security policy "exclusive defense." This exclusive defense policy has been the foundation of Japan's external pacifism and was the essence of the so-called "Yoshida Doctrine" of giving priority to expanding Japan's economic power over military power.

The second Shinzo Abe administration (December 2012 to the present) significantly weakened this external pacifism of Japan, first by adopting a new interpretation of the constitution in July 2014 that it does not prohibit Japan from exercising the right to collective self-defense to deal with the situations that gravely threaten Japan's national security and then by enacting new laws to legalize the new interpretation in September 2015. Furthermore, the Abe administration has deviated from the long-held exclusive defense policy by strengthening Japan's offensive capabilities.

Prime Minister (PM) Abe named his policy "*sekkyokuteki heiwashugi*," whose direct translation is "proactive pacifism," apparently to disguise its deviation from the long-held "pacifism" based on the constitutional ban on "the threat or use of force as means of settling international disputes." The government translates the Japanese expression to "proactive contribution to peace." Yet, "proactive military contribution to international peace" would be more accurate. Thus, Abe's policy has departed from the Yoshida Doctrine and could be called the Abe Doctrine (Hughes 2015: 1–7). Not surprisingly, the erosion of Japan's external pacifism under the Abe administration has attracted strong attention of international observers (Hughes, 2015; Maslow, 2015; Oros 2017; Smith 2019). In contrast, much less international attention has been paid to the erosion of Japan's internal pacifism. However, Japan's internal pacifism has been seriously eroded as well by the Abe administration. It implemented changes, such as the enactment of a new secrecy law in 2013 and the revision to the anti-organized crime law in 2017, and thereby significantly increased the power of the government over the people and weakened the democracy and human security in Japan.

One can think of different factors affecting public policy. Abe's policies to weaken the constitutional constraints on Japan's military operations, to enhance Japan's offensive capability, and to strengthen its alliance with the

U.S. can be seen partly as its response to changes in international conditions, such as the rise of the military power of China and North Korea and the U.S. demand for Japan's greater military role in the international order led by the U.S. Against the backdrop of these changes, Japan has gradually expanded its military operations overseas as can be seen from: its dispatch of minesweepers to the Persian Gulf in 1991; the participation of the SDF in UN Peace Keeping Operations (PKO) since 1992; the dispatch of the SDF to the Indian Ocean to provide logistical support (from November 2001 to January 2010) for the U.S.-led multinational forces engaged in the War on Terrorism; another dispatch of the SDF to Iraq for similar operations (from December 2003 to February 2009) after the onset of the Iraq War in March 2003; and a yet another dispatch of the SDF to the Gulf of Aden to join international anti-pirate operations (from March 2009 to the present) that accompanied construction of an overseas base in Djibouti. Therefore, Abe's military policy can be seen as just a recent development of Japan's military transformation that had already started since the end of the Cold War (Hughes 2009) and appears to be consistent with structural realism.

However, structural realism has difficulty in explaining Japan's international security policy under the Hatoyama administration (2009–2010) that adopted a policy to improve Japan's relationship with China and other East Asian countries in order to create an East Asian Community. Prime Minister Yukio Hatoyama, who had long advocated a Japan-U.S. alliance without continuous stationing of U.S. forces in Japan (Hatoyama 1996: 126–127), attempted to relocate the U.S. Futenma base out of Okinawa despite the bilateral agreement to relocate it within Okinawa made by PM Ryutaro Hashimoto of the LDP in 1996 and kept by the succeeding premiers all from the LDP. Thus, there is no denying that the personal views of policy-makers, particularly the head of the executive branch, can play a crucial role in policy choice.

Needless to say, structural realism and other systemic theories are not good at explaining changes in domestic policies, such as a change in the relative power of the government over the people. Compared to international policy, changes in domestic policy tend to be influenced more by the personal views of policy-makers, particularly the head of the executive branch. Therefore, it is important to examine the impact of the personal views of Prime Minister Abe and other leading LDP lawmakers on the policies of the Abe administration that undermined Japan's pacifism. Hence, this chapter intends to examine the impact of personal views of PM Abe and other leading LDP lawmakers on the erosion of Japan's pacifism with a greater focus on its internal pacifism because much less international attention has been paid to its erosion than to the erosion of its external pacifism.

My basic contention is that PM Abe and other LDP lawmakers have been critical of the three pillars of the current constitution—external pacifism, the sovereignty of the people, and fundamental human rights—and have attempted to undermine them. This chapter first explains the concrete policy measures taken by the first and second Abe administrations (September 2006–September 2007 and December 2012–the present) that eroded Japan's external and internal pacifism. Then, it examines the underlying personal views held by Abe and other LDP lawmakers on which their criticism is based. Those views will be identified from their personal remarks and writings as well as official documents. In the process, particular care will be taken to distinguish between their real opinions and their political rhetoric.

One can think of intervening variables such as various domestic actors and factors that influence the causal relations between the independent variables (the policy preferences of the prime minister and other policy-makers) and the dependent variables (the concrete policy measures implemented in such a form as the enactment of a new law and military operations). In fact, it is hard to find those works that examine this kind of political process concerning the erosion of Japan's pacifism under the Abe administration, while there are more works of this kind concerning Japanese politics in general. However, this chapter does not intend to clarify such a domestic political process. Instead, it focuses on clarifying the personal views of PM Abe and other LDP lawmakers that underlie their policy preferences, for instance, their personal views underlying their preference to make Japan militarily normal. Other actors are deemed influential in the erosion of Japan's pacifism, such as the ministry of foreign affairs and conservative groups such as Nippon Kaigi (Asahi Shimbun Seijibu Shuzaihan 2015; Hirata 2017; Sugano 2016). However, this chapter limits its focus primarily on PM Abe and secondarily on other leading LDP lawmakers because of their greater influence on policy making than other actors.

An Overview of Japan's Pacifism

This section presents a brief overview of Japan's pacifism before explaining how it has been eroded by the Abe administration in the succeeding sections.

As mentioned above, the pacifism of the postwar Japan is founded on its constitution adopted during the occupation period and had two aspects: external and internal pacifism. Its external pacifism consists primarily of its self-imposed prohibition of offensive use of force at an external entity; that is, the self imposed limitation that permits use of force only for self-defense in response to attacks by an external entity, which is called "exclusive defense." This self-imposition is based on the constitutional renunciation of the threat or use of force as a means of settling international disputes. Until 2004, the Japanese government took that the position that the constitution only allows Japan to exercise the right to individual self-defense in response to attacks by external forces but prohibits it from exercising the right to collective self-defense. Japan's internal pacifism consists of protection of fundamental human rights through democratic governance based on the sovereignty of the people.

The external pacifism founded on the constitution led not only to the policy of the exclusive defense but also to other policies: (1) peaceful use of space based on the Diet resolution of 1969 that limited the use of space only for peaceful purposes; (2) prohibition of arms exports adopted by the Eisaku Sato administration in 1967 and then strengthened by the Takeo Miki administration in 1976; (3) prohibition of possessing and producing nuclear weapons and that of accepting foreign nuclear weapons into Japan (the three non-nuclear principles); and (4) the policy not to use Japan's official development assistance (ODA) for military purposes based on the ODA Charter adopted by the Kiichi Miyazawa administration in 1992.

The internal pacifism founded on the constitution was augmented by the Basic Act on Education (*Kyōiku Kihonhō*) of 1947 that replaced the Imperial Rescript on Education (*Kyōiku Chokugo*) of 1890 in which the Emperor gave his subjects (Japanese citizens) an instruction: "should an emergency arise, offer yourselves to the state loyally and bravely and thus support Our Imperial Throne coeval with the Heavens and the Earth." The imperial Japanese government required the students to memorize it (Suzuki 1999: 47–61) and made them willing to sacrifice themselves for imperial Japan. Besides, it required each school to enshrine a copy of the Imperial Rescript together with a photo of the Emperor and the Empress in a special small building called *Hōanden*. In June 1948, both houses of the Diet adopted a resolution to nullify and discredit the Imperial Rescript.

Erosion of External Pacifism

As explained above, the erosion of Japan's external pacifism started in the early 1990s at the latest. However, the extent of erosion under the Abe administration is particularly significant.

Exclusive Defense

At a cabinet meeting in July 2014, the Abe administration adopted a new interpretation of the constitution that it does not prohibit Japan from exercising the right to collective self-defense to deal with the situations that gravely threaten Japan's national security. It argued that the policy change was necessary to deal with the fundamental transformation in the security environment surrounding Japan due to the shift in power balance, rapid technological advancement, and the threat posed by weapons of mass destruction (WMDs) (Kantei 2014: 1). Essentially, the administration justified the policy change as a necessary measure to deal with the threat posed by China and North Korea.

Then, in September 2015, it enacted new laws to legalize this new interpretation, and in September 2016, it agreed with the Obama administration to revise the Japan-U.S. Acquisition and Cross-Servicing Agreement (ACSA) of 1999 (which revised the original 1996 version), which enabled the SDF to provide the U.S. forces with materials such as munitions and fuels even if Japan is not directly attacked. Furthermore, two days after North Korea's threat to launch several missiles around Guam on August 8, 2017, then-Defense Minister Onodera stated at a Diet meeting that such a missile attack could be regarded as a national emergency that would legally permit the SDF's Aegis destroyers to launch intercepting missiles (Sankei News 2017a), which means exercising of the right to collective self-defense.

Offensive Capability

In December 2018, the Abe administration adopted the new National Defense Program Guidelines (NDPG) and the Midterm Defense Buildup Program (FY2019-FY2023), in which it made public its policy to strengthen Japan's offensive capabilities, for instance, by transforming the existing two Izumo-class helicopter carriers into full-fledged aircraft carriers and purchasing eighteen F-35B STOVL for them (totally forty-two in the long run), doubling the number of airborne refueling aircraft from four to eight, and deploying long-range missiles.

Use of Space

The policy of peaceful use of space was eroded by the Keizo Obuchi administration's decision in November 1998 to develop information gathering satellites (IGS), de facto spy satellites in response to North Korea's launch of Taepodong over Japan in August 1998. During the Yasuo Fukuda administration, the Diet resolution of 1969 was replaced by the Basic Act on Space (*Uchū Kihonhō*) in May 2008, in which contribution to Japan's national security was included as one of the primary objectives of Japan's space development. The Taro Aso administration compiled Japan's first Basic Plan on Space in June 2009. The Abe administration revised it three times in January 2013, in January 2015, and in April 2016, strengthening the policy of using space for security and commercial purposes, for instance, by deploying more spy satellites and conducting research for future deployment of early-warning satellites.

Arms Exports, Nuclear Weapons, and ODA

In April 2014, the Abe administration adopted a policy of promoting arms exports and nullified the long-held arms export ban. With regard to the three nonnuclear principles, the administration has not changed them, but in the context of North Korea's nuclear development, leading LDP lawmakers, such as former defense minister Shigeru Ishiba, started arguing the need to consider redeploying U.S. nuclear weapons in Japan (Sankei News 2017b). Ishiba was a leading candidate for the next prime minister. As far as the ODA policy is concerned, in February 2015, the administration revised the ODA Charter of 1992, making contribution to Japan's national security a primary objective of its ODA and enabling the use of ODA for the military development of recipient countries.

Erosion of Internal Pacifism

Under the Abe administration, Japan's internal pacifism has been significantly eroded as well.

Democratic Decision-Making

The Abe administration implemented other security policies that weakened the democratic decision-making on Japan's basic security policy and military actions. First, in January 2007 the first Abe administration (2006–2007) transformed the Defense Agency to the Ministry of Defense. Then, in December 2013 the second Abe administration (2012–the present) reorganized the Security Council into the National Security Council (NSC), concentrating the decision-making power to four ministers (prime minister, defense minister, foreign minister, and chief cabinet secretary) in order for the government "to make quick response to diplomatic and national security matters under strong political leadership" (as explained by PM Abe) (Kantei 2013). However, discussions at four-minister meetings have been undisclosed, and no minutes have been made for future disclosure. In addition, the administration revised the Act for Establishment of the Ministry of Defense in June 2015 in such a way as to weaken the civilian control of the SDF and thereby enabled more rapid deployment of the SDF. To be more concrete, before the revision, high-ranking civilian officials had been placed between the Defense Minister and the four top officers of the SDF (the Joint Chief of Staff and the Chiefs of Staff of Ground, Maritime, and Air SDF). Yet, the revision lowered the position of the civilian officials and enabled the top SDF officers to directly discuss military strategies, plans, and operations with the minister. Consequently, the revision enabled the minister to decide how to mobilize the SDF without any consultation with the top civilian officials.

Government Transparency

In December 2013, the second Abe administration enacted a new special secrecy law called the Act on the Protection of Specially Designated Secrets (SDS Protection Act). Reportedly, the law was in response to the U.S. demand for Japan's stricter protection of the military secrets provided by Washington based on the Japan-U.S. General Security of Military Information Agreement (GSOMIA) that the first Abe administration had concluded in August 2007 (Huffington Post 2013). The new law enabled government agencies to classify a wide range of national security-related information as "specially designated secrets (SDS)" and obliged the court to severely penalize those who leaked or stole the secrets (the jail sentence of up to 10 years or a fine of up to 10 million yen). After its introduction to the Diet for deliberation, the legislation met strong objections by the opposition and the public, including the Japan Federation of Bar Associations, because of the lack of transparency and objectivity in the classification of SDS (Nihon Bengoshi Rengōkai, n.d.a). The new law also received international criticism. For instance, Morton Halperin, who worked for the U.S. National Security Council, maintained that the law deviated from the Tshwane Principles in many ways and was the worst among the equivalent laws of the U.S. allies and those countries close to the U.S. (Halperin and Hofsommer 2014; Kanagawa Shimbun 2014). In effect, the law enabled the government to hide important information from the public, thus weakening democratic control over the government, particularly its national security policies.

Power of the Police and Intelligence Agencies

Furthermore, in June 2016, the Abe administration revised the Wiretap Law in such a way as to expand the scope of wiretapping. Then, allegedly to prevent terrorist acts, in June 2017, it revised the Law on Punishment of

Organized Crimes. By creating "the offense of preparing terrorist acts and so forth" (*Tero tō junbi zai*), it enabled the government to arrest and prosecute a group of people who plan and prepare to commit any of the designated 277 offenses, many of which are unrelated to terrorist acts, such as copyright violation, capturing endangered species, and violating the Consumption Tax Law (Nihon Keizai Shimbun 2017). The two revised laws have significantly increased the ability of the police and intelligence agencies to collect personal information and criminalize suspects of a wide range of offenses unrelated to terrorist acts (Nihon Bengoshi Rengōkai, n.d.b). Not surprisingly, both laws met strong criticism from the public, including the Japan Federation of Bar Associations. Critics called the revised Law on Punishment of Organized Crimes a modern version of the prewar Maintenance of the Public Order Act (*Chian Iji-hō*) abused by the government to oppress those who were deemed critical of the government (Shibata 2017).

In this connection, in his official blog on November 29, 2013, Shigeru Ishiba, then the secretary-general of the LDP and the defense minister between 2007 and 2008, called the popular demonstrations against the bill for the SDS Protection Act, "not so different from terrorist acts in nature." Those demonstrations were peaceful and very different from violent protests such as the "yellow vest protests" in France that started in November 2018. Ishiba was a member of the LDP committee that drafted the revised constitution of 2012 and, as mentioned above, a leading candidate for the next LDP president and prime minister.

Nationalistic Education

In December 2006, the first Abe administration revised the Basic Act on Education of 1947, which was the first revision since its enactment. Together with the current constitution, PM Abe had regarded it as a symbol of the postwar regime imposed on Japan during its occupation by the U.S. (Abe 2013: 32). The revision added development of morality and the attitudes of contributing to the society based on public spirit and "respecting for Japan's tradition and culture and loving our country and regions that have nurtured them" to the existing goals of education (for more detailed analysis of the revision, see Ouchi 2017). Then, in March 2015, the administration changed the status of moral education from a special subject without evaluation of students to a regular subject with evaluation of what they learned in the subject. It was also decided that this new moral education would start in AY2018 at the elementary schools and AY2019 at the junior high schools. One of the stated objectives of the renewed moral education is to nurture the mind of loving "our country and regions." It should be noted that the promotion of love for Japan is one of the objectives included in the LDP's founding policy platform of 1955.

This could be seen as a revival of the prewar moral education, based on the Imperial Rescript on Education of October 1890, which aimed at fostering nationalism in the minds of the students and making them willing to sacrifice themselves for imperial Japan. Just before the change to moral education, at a meeting of the Committee on Education, Culture and Science of the House of Councilors held on April 8, 2014, Education Minister Hakubun Shimomura, a well-known nationalist politician close to PM Abe, revealed a new stance of his ministry to allow schools to use the Imperial Rescript on Education, saying that it was no problem for schools to use it because it contained something universal and applicable today. On March 31, 2017, PM Abe himself made public his position that the Imperial Rescript could be used as a foundation of education, by stating that although it would be inappropriate to regard the Imperial Rescript as the only foundation of education in our country, it was permissible for schools to use it as an educational material in such a way as not to contradict the Constitution and the Basic Act on Education (Shugiin 2017). Not surprisingly, the Abe administration allowed schools to require their students to memorize the Imperial Rescript, which was widely practiced in the moral education of imperial Japan.

As another measure to foster a nationalistic mind, the Abe administration strengthened the policy of urging schools to hoist the national flag (*Hinomaru*) and let their students sing the national anthem (*Kimigayo*) at commencement ceremonies and other occasions, which had started after 1998 when a law had been enacted to designate Hinomaru as the national flag and Kimigayo as the national anthem. The administration first targeted elementary schools, junior high schools, and senior high schools. Then, in June 2015, Education Minister Shimomura urged the national universities (86 in total) to hoist Hinomaru and let their students sing Kimigayo at commencement ceremonies. Then, in March 2017, the Abe administration revised the guidelines for nursery schools and kindergartens, requiring them to familiarize their pupils with Hinomaru and Kimigayo.

The Role of Universities

In a democratic society, intellectuals perform an important role in critically reviewing government policies. In fact, intellectuals in Japan, particularly university professors and students in the fields of education, humanities, and social sciences, led the public criticism and protests against the special secrecy law of 2013 and the security laws of 2015 when they were under deliberation at the Diet because they were deemed threatening to Japan's external and internal pacifism.

Against this backdrop, in June 2015, the Abe administration made public a new education policy of urging national universities to abolish undergraduate and graduate programs in education, humanities, and social sciences or reorganize them into other programs that are socially in greater demand by using the stick and carrot of selectively allocating government subsidies depending on the progress of implementing the new policy. It is conceivable that the real intention of this policy is to weaken the social role of the universities to critically review public policies and educate people to develop critical thinking. It should also be noted that this is a revival of the failed proposal of abolishing non-science programs by the education minister of the Kishi administration in 1960 (Mainichi Shimbun 2015).

Military Research

Furthermore, in 2015, the Abe administration initiated a new grant scheme for universities and other research institutes. Under the scheme, the Ministry of Defense allocates the grant to the researchers who conduct basic research on state-of-art technologies that can be militarily exploited. The grant amount was 300 million yen in FY2015 and 600 million in FY2016, but it rose to 11 billion yen in FY2017. The public subsidies for public and private universities have continued to decline over the years as government debts have expanded. In such dire financial straits, the new grant is attractive to many of them. If more and more Japanese universities become reliant on it, they would feel more reluctant to critically evaluate various public policies.

Personal Views behind the Erosion of Pacifism

The previous sections clarified the extent of erosion of Japan's external and internal pacifism by the policies implemented by the Abe administration. This section examines the personal views of PM Abe and other leading LDP lawmakers that led to those policies. The basic contention presented here is that PM Abe and other major LDP lawmakers have implemented those policies because they are critical of the three pillars of the current constitution—external pacifism, the sovereignty of the people, and fundamental human rights. This section substantiates this contention and looks into their fundamental views that underlie their critical views.

Escape from the Postwar Regime

Generally speaking, the erosion of Japan's external and internal pacifism under the Abe administration can be ascribed to its political objective of "escape from the post-war regime" (*sengo rejīmu karano dakkyaku*). The postwar regime is the political regime based on the current constitution drafted by General Headquarters (GHQ), which was approved by the Imperial Diet in October 1946 and then went into effect in May 1947.

PM Abe has maintained that "escape from the post-war regime" is the most important task for Japan (Abe 2013: 254). The LDP has shared this objective. In fact, its party platform adopted at the time of its formation in 1955 (Jiyuminshuto 1955) calls for developing an independent regime by revising the constitution and reviewing various laws adopted during the occupation period. Thus, "escape from the post-war regime" primarily means creating a new legal system by revising the current constitution and reviewing various laws created during the occupation period. There are different reasons why PM Abe and the LDP want to do so.

Reasons for the Escape from the Postwar Regime

One reason for PM Abe and other LDP lawmakers' desire to escape from the postwar regime is their view that a country should make its constitution independently. In the words of PM Abe, "The Japanese citizens themselves should create the framework of their country from scratch. Thereby, Japan can truly restore its independence" (Abe 2013: 33). However, if they are satisfied with the content of the constitution, then they would not make such an argument. Therefore, one can infer that PM Abe and other LDP lawmakers have been unhappy with the constitution and can ask why.

In fact, they have criticized the three pillars of the constitution: external pacifism, the sovereignty of the people, and fundamental human rights. For instance, at the 3rd study session of Sosei Nippon held in Tokyo on May 10, 2012, Jinen Nagase, who was the Justice Minister of the first Abe administration (September 2006–August 2007) and a graduate of the University of Tokyo's law department, argued that "the sovereignty of the people, and fundamental human rights, and [external] pacifism are the essences of the post-war regime that had been forced upon Japan by MacArthur and must be abolished in a truly independent constitution" (Sosei Nippon 2012). This remark was made in front of Shinzo Abe, the LDP president, and many other well-known LDP lawmakers such as Hakubun Shimomura, Seiichi Eto, and Shoji Nishida, and Hirofumi Nakasone, all of whom were members of the LDP committee that compiled the draft constitution in April 2012, which revised the previous draft compiled in October 2005, fifty years after the LDP's foundation. The following subsections explain why they are critical of pacifism, the sovereignty of the people, and fundamental human rights.

Discontent with External Pacifism

The pacifism the LDP has criticized is the external pacifism based on renunciation of the threat or use of force as a means to settle international disputes, which has prevented Japan from possessing normal armed forces and limited the operations of the SDF to the exclusive defense of protecting Japan when attacked by external forces.

Their desire to make Japan militarily normal clearly manifested itself in the draft constitution of 2012, which allowed Japan to possess regular military forces called the National Defense Forces (NDF, *kokubōgun*). The LDP's party platform (*Tō no seikō*) of November 1955 calls for developing armed forces to protect the national independence and the liberty of the Japanese citizens in expectation of withdrawal of the U.S. forces in Japan (Jiyuminshuto 1955).

One could easily posit that this view that armed forces are necessary to protect Japan's national security, particularly its national independence, has been a driving force behind the series of security policies of the Abe administration that undermined Japan's external pacifism. This belief in the crucial importance of military forces to protect Japan's national security has been held by the LDP as can be seen from policy documents issued by LDP-led administrations, such as the National Defense Program Guidelines (NDPG) of 2004, 2013, and 2018 and the National Security Strategy (NSS) of December 2013, and PM Abe's statement in 2015 to commemorate seventy years since the end of World War II.

In the statement, PM Abe held that the threat of Western imperialism had prompted Japan to modernize itself and that its success had enabled it to maintain its independence. Needless to say, Japan's modernization took place, particularly in the economic and military spheres. In fact, the view that Japan's successful economic and military modernization enabled Japan to maintain its independence is widely held by the Japanese but, probably, more strongly so by conservative politicians such as Shinzo Abe, as can be seen from this statement. Thus, the crucial role that armed forces played in maintaining Japan's independence in the age of imperialism and making Japan the first non-Western imperial power appears to be an important reason why LDP lawmakers generally think that military power is indispensable for a country to protect its independence and its people.

The LDP lawmakers' predominant perception of world politics, which is based partly on their understanding of Japan's modern history, seems similar to that of neo-realists. Their perception may well have been consolidated by unilateral actions made by major military powers during the Cold War era and the post-Cold War era, such as the U.S. military attacks on North Vietnam, the Russian military invention in Czechoslovakia in 1968, and the U.S. attacks on Afghanistan in 2001 and Iraq in 2003, China's use of military force over the South China Sea territorial disputes, and Russia's annexation of Crimea in 2014.

During the Cold War era, Japan under LDP-led administrations regarded the Soviet Union as its primary security threat and adopted the policy of relying on the U.S.-extended nuclear deterrence. After the Cold War, Japan has increasingly come to see the growing power of China and the nuclear and missile development of North Korea as threatening to its national security (Abe 2013: 4; Ishiba 2013: 100–112) and, consequently, has regarded the U.S.-extended nuclear deterrence and its forces stationed in Japan as more important. Identification of China and North Korea as major threats to Japan's national security and the importance attached to its alliance with the U.S. can be seen from the National Defense Program Guidelines (NDPG) issued after the Cold War (in 2004, 2010, 2013, and 2018) and the National Security Strategy (NSS) of 2013.

Considering the importance PM Abe and other LDP lawmakers have assigned to nuclear deterrence and Japan's alliance with the U.S., it could be said that they have given precedence to enhancing Japan's national security by strengthening its alliance with the U.S. over increasing the degree of Japan's national independence by reducing its reliance on the U.S. Their logic is: (1) nuclear deterrence is needed for Japan's national security; (2) yet, Japan does not have nuclear weapons; (3) therefore, Japan has little choice but to rely on the U.S.-extended nuclear deterrence; and (4) in order to maintain the credibility of the U.S.-extended deterrence in the face of the Chinese and North Korean threat, Japan should strengthen its alliance with the U.S. and refrain from taking policies that may damage the alliance. In the words of Hisahiko Okazaki in 2014, a leading conservative intellectual who was a career diplomat and a long-time security advisor of PM Abe, "Japan's national security is unthinkable without its collaboration with the U.S. in defending Japan from China, and we have to think about East Asia's security in terms of the balance of power between China and the Japan-U.S. alliance" (Nagano 2014).

The greater importance attached to strengthening Japan's alliance with the U.S. than enhancing its independence can also be seen from the following facts. First, there have been very few political efforts to reduce the U.S. military presence in Japan after the end of U.S. occupation in 1952, although that is an essential part of the postwar regime from which PM Abe and the LDP have allegedly tried to escape in order to restore Japan's independence. Second, the Japanese government has hardly attempted to revise the Japan-U.S. Status of Forces Agreement (SOFA) of 1960, which succeeded the Japan-U.S. Administrative Agreement of 1952 and has given U.S. forces and soldiers extraterritorial privileges and rights, although there have been strong demands from Japanese people, particularly the Okinawans who have suffered from various problems resulting from an excessive concentration of U.S. forces in Okinawa, such as the crimes committed by U.S. soldiers, the noise pollution near U.S. military bases, and the environmental contamination by U.S. forces. In fact, the Japan-U.S. SOFA has never been amended, unlike the SOFA between the U.S. and its other allies such as Germany (Yanagisawa, Isezaki and Kato 2017: 149–181).

It is pointed out that Japanese policy-makers have lingering distrust with the U.S. military support for Japan in the case of Chinese seizure of the Senkaku islands (Hughes, 2015: 70–71). It is conceivable that their concern has strengthened the view of PM Abe and other LDP lawmakers that normal armed forces are necessary to protect Japan's national security and their eagerness to militarily normalize Japan and enhance Japan's own military capabilities. However, it should be noted that their concern has not resulted in a rapid buildup of independent military capabilities, as can be seen from its policies to enlarge import of U.S. weapons and to promote greater interoperability between the SDF and U.S. forces.

PM Abe and other LDP lawmakers, who strongly believe that normal armed forces are necessary to protect Japan's national security, also share the view of Carl von Clausewitz that war is the continuation of politics by other means and therefore hold that it is permissible for Japan to use its military force outside its territory in order to protect and advance its national interest even when it does not face a military attack by another country or its imminent danger. The presence of this view can be seen, for instance, in the National Defense Program Guidelines (NDPG) of 2018, which states that the first objective of national defense is "to create a security environment desirable for Japan by using all the capabilities of the country" and that Japan will strengthen its own defense capability and its alliance with the U.S in order to successfully achieve its national defense objectives (MOD 2018: 7). Another example is the immediate support of the Junichiro Koizumi administration for the Bush administration's decision to attack Iraq in 2003 and its rapid enactment of a special law on the Iraq War that enabled the government to dispatch the SDF to Iraq.

The view that it is permissible for a country to use its military forces outside of its territory to protect its national interests in the absence of the military attacks by another country is closely associated with the view that resultant civilian sufferings are acceptable collateral damages. This view could explain why PM Abe and other LDP lawmakers were not very regretful for Japan's strong support for the U.S. attack on Iraq in 2003 although it caused massive damages to the Iraqi people. While, after the fall of the Saddam Hussein regime, the military attack on Iraq was critically reviewed in the U.S., the U.K., and other countries that had sent troops to Iraq, no extensive official review has been conducted by the successive LDP-led administrations. In the case of Prime Minister Abe, at the Budget Committee of the House of Representatives on May 28, 2014, he held that the U.S. attack on Iraq was justifiable and blamed Iraq for its failure to prove the absence of WMDs in Iraq. His positive evaluation of Japan's dispatch to Iraq can also be seen from the fact that in November 2015, his administration conferred a national decoration, a Grand Cordon of the Order of the Rising Sun, to Donald Rumsfeld and Richard Armitage, Secretary of Defense and Vice Secretary of State of the Bush administration at the time of its decision to attack Iraq. Both of them urged the Koizumi administration to dispatch the SDF to Iraq. As for Armitage, he has long urged Japanese administrations to enable Japan to play a greater military role in the Japan-U.S. alliance by exercising the right to collective self-defense in his co-authored policy reports known as the Armitage-Nye reports issued in 2000, 2007, 2012, and 2018 (Armitage, Bob, Campbell, Green, Harrington, Jannuzi and Wolfowitz 2000; Armitage and Nye 2007, 2012, 2018).

The view that the civilian sufferings resulting from the use of force by a country to protect its national interest are acceptable collateral damage could also explain why PM Abe and other LDP lawmakers do not recognize the need of the Japanese government to clearly admit its responsibility for the human sufferings caused by the imperial Japanese army, such as those of comfort women and the Okinawans who were urged to die rather than surrender themselves to the U.S. forces. Instead, they have been eager to downplay those human sufferings, as can be seen from their effort to reduce descriptions of such sufferings in history textbooks.

Furthermore, PM Abe and other LDP lawmakers' view that military power is an important diplomatic tool to advance its national interests is also attributable to their desire to expand Japan's economic and military power. In his speech at the Center for Strategic and International Studies (CSIS) on

February 22, 2013, PM Abe said, "Japan is not, and will not be, a second-tier country. That is what I wanted to say the most here" and "[Japan] must be strong in its economy, and strong in its national defense" (Abe 2014: 13) (the author's direct translations from the Japanese version).

Discontent with the Sovereignty of the People and Fundamental Human Rights

As mentioned above, PM Abe and other LDP lawmakers have criticized not only Japan's external pacifism but also the sovereignty of the people and fundamental human rights that constitute Japan's internal pacifism. A vivid example is the aforementioned remark of a former Justice Minister, Jinen Nagase, at a meeting of Sosei Nippon in 2012 that the sovereignty of the people, and fundamental human rights, and pacifism are the essences of the postwar regime that had been forced upon Japan by MacArthur and must be abolished in a truly independent constitution.

Sosei Nippon is an association of conservative politicians that succeeded in 2010 the Genuine Conservative Policy Research Association (*Shin Hoshu Seisaku Kenkyukai*) founded in 2007 and has been chaired by Shinzo Abe since 2009. Nagase was an acting chairman of Sosei Nippon. The major activities of the Genuine Conservative Policy Research Association and Sosei Nippon were preventing the government from: (1) establishing an independent human rights protection organization following Japan's acceptance of the recommendation by the UN Commission on Human Rights in 2008, (2) allowing foreign permanent residents to participate in local elections, and (3) allowing all people to retain their surname after marriage if they so choose.

Abe and other LDP lawmakers' criticism of the sovereignty of the people and fundamental human rights could be attributed to their elitist views that they are superior to ordinary people and capable of leading them and that ordinary people should follow the state they run. In the case of PM Abe, his elitism can be found in his positive evaluation of the revision to the Japan-U.S. Security Treaty of 1951 by his grandfather, PM Nobusuke Kishi, and his negative view that the nation-wide opposition of the general public, intellectuals, and media to the revision was based on their ignorance, irrationality, and misjudgment (Abe 2013: 23–28). Furthermore, their criticism of the sovereignty of the people and fundamental human rights can also be ascribed to their nationalistic and authoritarian view. From their standpoint, the existence of the people is based on the existence of the state to which they belong. Their rights are not by birth but guaranteed by the state. Therefore, people should follow and serve the state. Thus, these two different views can be seen as underlying their criticism of the sovereignty of the people and fundamental human rights and their belief that the people should follow the state. This belief in the state's superiority over the people can be seen as a driving force behind the Abe administration's policies that undermined Japan's democratic rule and internal pacifism, which were discussed above. Their belief in the state's superiority is observable from several pieces of evidence, including the LDP's draft constitution of 2005 and 2012, their remarks and writings, the orientation of the political associations to which they belong, and the policies they promoted.

The LDP's draft constitution of 2005 and 2012 gives precedence to the public interests and the public order over individual freedom and rights. Clause 12 of the 2012 draft, titled "The Duty of the Citizens," obliges the citizens "to be aware that freedom and rights come with responsibility and duties" and "never to violate the public interest and the public order."

PM Abe and other LDP lawmakers prioritize the public interest and the public order over individual freedom and rights since they reject the theory of natural rights. Satsuki Katayama, who was the Minister of State for Special Missions of the second Abe administration and was a member of the LDP's committee that had compiled the 2012 draft constitution, tweeted on December 7, 2012, "Our [the LDP's] basic stance is to stop accepting the theory of natural rights that prompts the people to think that their rights are given by the heaven and that they do not need to carry out their duties. We drafted a preamble that prompts all the people to think about what they can do to maintain their country rather than what their country would do for them." She graduated from the Law Department of the University of Tokyo and worked for the Finance Ministry for twenty-two years before becoming a Diet member in 2005.

The LDP argues that human rights have been gradually generated in the context of the history, tradition, and culture of a community and holds that it is necessary to define human rights based on Japan's history, tradition, and culture (Jiyuminshuto Kenpō Kaisei Suishin Honbu 2013: 13). Therefore, its conception of human rights is different from that of the Universal Declaration of Human Rights of the United Nations as stipulated in Article 1, which goes: "All human beings are born free and equal in dignity and rights." From the LDP's perspective, human rights are socially defined and granted to the citizens by the state. This view was reflected in its draft constitution of 2012: "Freedom of thought and conscience is guaranteed" (Clause 19), whereas "Freedom of thought and conscience shall not be violated" in the current constitution (Clause 19). Likewise, "All of the citizens shall be respected as people" (Clause 13), while "All of the citizens shall be respected as individuals" in the current constitution (Clause 13). These changes strongly indicate that the LDP is unwilling to respect each people as an individual. It follows from it that the LDP does not want to recognize the fundamental human rights of individuals. Respect for individuals derives from the theory of natural rights. Since the LDP does not accept this theory, it is not surprising that it does not respect individuals.

Besides, the belief of PM Abe and other LDP lawmakers in the superiority of the state over the citizens can also be seen from the new obligation of the people that the LDP created in the final clause, Clause 99, of its draft constitution of 2012, which goes: "All the citizens must respect this constitution." In the LDP's perspective, the constitution is the foundational legal document whose primary role is to oblige the Japanese citizens to follow it rather than prevent the abuse of power by those in power. This is clearly stated by Hidetsugu Yagi, a professor of law at Reitaku University and a well-known advisor for PM Abe (Minetoshi 2018). Moreover, PM Abe himself said, "The view, which is often expressed in the discussion over the constitution, is that the role of the constitution is to constrain the power of the state. However, this is, in a way, a very old-fashioned view. It is true that the constitution played the role of constraining the power of the power-holder in the era when absolute monarchies existed" (Abe and Hyakuta 2013: 44). Thus, he does not seem to recognize that preventing the abuse of power by the power-holders is its fundamental role. In fact, Yoichi Masuzoe, who used to be an LDP lawmaker and led the LDP to make the draft constitution of 2005, doubted that the 2012 version was based on constitutionalism and criticized that it had been drafted by those who did not understand the basic nature of a constitution (Masuzoe 2014: 3–8).

The critical view of PM Abe and other LDP lawmakers toward the sovereignty of the people and fundamental human rights is observable also from the newly created chapter on a state of emergency, Chapter 9 of the 2012 draft constitution, which enables the government to mobilize the citizens just like the imperial Japanese government did in the 1940s. This new chapter allows the prime minister to declare a state of emergency at the time of armed attacks on Japan, internal disorders, natural disasters, and other situations specified by law, without prior approval by the Diet to do so. The chapter also enables the cabinet to issue government ordinances that are equivalent to laws. It also obliges the citizens to follow all those ordinances even if they infringe upon their fundamental human rights.

The belief of PM Abe and other LDP lawmakers in the superiority of the state over the people can also be seen from their policies. One recent example is the disregard of the Abe administration of the clear opposition of the Okinawans to the construction of a new U.S. base in Henoko, Okinawa, which was demonstrated repeatedly and most recently by the Okinawa prefectural referendum on February 24, 2019. The administration had expressed in advance its intention to continue the construction regardless of the result of the referendum and then actually did not even halt it after the negative result had come out.

The view of PM Abe and other LDP lawmakers that individual rights originate from the existence of a state can be seen as underlying their views that the citizens must protect their country, that the citizens should love and respect their country, and that the citizens should follow the state. The preamble of the LDP's draft constitution of 2012 states that Japanese citizens protect their country by themselves with pride and mettle. The draft has no reference to conscription. However, the government could use this preamble as a justification to institute it. Tomomi Inada, who used to be a lawyer before becoming an LDP lawmaker in 2005 and was the defense minister (2016–2017) under the second Abe administration, said to the audience at an anti-*Minshuto* (Democratic Party of Japan [DPJ]) gathering on December 1, 2010, "Each citizen, each of you, needs to defend one's own country, and must be ready to shed one's own blood to defend one's own country" (SakuraSo TV 2011). It can be said that the priority PM Abe and other LDP lawmakers give to the state over fundamental human rights enables them to make such a demand without much hesitation and underlies their aforementioned view that human sufferings as a result of the military actions by the state are acceptable collateral damage.

Concerning their view that the citizens should love and respect their country, the word "love" does not appear in the 2012 draft constitution. However, the aforementioned preamble expects the citizens to take pride in their country. Besides, their view that the citizens should love and respect their country can also be found in a newly created article (Article 3) on the national flag and anthem, which designates Hinomaru and Kimigayo as the national flag and anthem, respectively, and obliges citizens to respect them, although there have been those citizens who regard them as symbols of the totalitarianism and militarism of imperial Japan.

It should be noted that, from the viewpoint of PM Abe and the LDP in general, love of one's own country is crucial for national security, as can be seen from the content of the National Security Strategy (NSS) compiled in December 2013. The NSS included the policy of promoting the Japanese citizens to have the mind of loving their own country and regions in order to strengthen the domestic basis of national security (Kokka Anzen Hoshō Kaigi 2013: 32).

Besides, the LDP's view that the citizens should follow the state because their existence is based on the existence of the state to which they belong could be seen as a basis for the policy of the LDP administrations to follow the U.S., on which the LDP sees Japan's existence has highly depended. Another basis could be the realist evaluation that Japan's alliance with the U.S. is indispensable to Japan's national security in countering the threat posed by China and North Korea.

Reasons for Promoting Patriotism

As explained above, the view that the citizens should love and respect their country can be attributed to the view that the existence of a state is the origin of individual rights. In addition to this, another origin is conceivable, which is: the view of PM Abe and other LDP lawmakers that Japan is a wonderful country that the people should be proud of. Their positive evaluation of Japan can be seen from the books authored by two prime ministers: *Utsukushii kuni e [Towards a Beautiful Country]* by Shinzo Abe (2006) and *Totetsumonai Nippon [An Extraordinary Japan]* by Taro Aso (2007).

Reasons for this evaluation can also be found in the LDP's draft constitution of 2012 and PM Abe's statement in 2015 to commemorate seventy years since the end of World War II. In the preamble of the 2012 draft constitution, there are such sentences and expressions as: "Japan is a state that possesses a long history and indigenous culture and is headed by the emperor who is a symbol of national integration" (which is the first sentence in the preamble), "Japan now occupies an important place in the international society, having overcome the devastation of the previous world war and numerous big disasters," "its beautiful land and natural environment," and "our good tradition."

In the 2015 commemorative statement, PM Abe held that Japan's success to modernize itself enabled it to prevent Western powers from colonizing it and that "the Russo-Japanese War encouraged many people in Asia and Africa under the colonial rules," while he totally disregards Japan's invasion of Korea during the war. PM Abe and other LDP lawmakers highly evaluate or even glorify the Meiji era (1865–1912) probably because they can feel proud of Japan's great achievement of transforming itself from a feudal, peripheral state to a major power in the world. This positive evaluation led to an official ceremony hosted by the Abe administration in 2018 to celebrate the 150th anniversary of the onset of the Meiji era.

Among the reasons for their positive view of Japan being a wonderful country to be proud of, the emperor and his household are of particular importance. That can be seen from the above sentence in the preamble and also from the remarks made by LDP lawmakers. It is well known that in May 2000 Prime Minister Yoshiro Mori said that Japan is a divine state (*kamino kuni*) centered on the emperor. Minoru Kiuchi stated, at the third study session of Sosei Nippon held in Tokyo on May 10, 2012, that what is most important for Japan is the imperial household and Japan's fundamental national character (*kokutai*) (Sosei Nippon 2012). After graduating from the University of Tokyo, he became a career diplomat and later a Diet member. He was the Vice Foreign Minister (September 2014–October 2015) of the second Abe administration. Besides, in 2017, Shigeru Ishiba, an LDP heavyweight and a leading candidate for the next LDP president, said, "when the imperial household ends, that is when Japan ends" (SAPIO 2017).

The special importance LDP lawmakers assign to the emperor and the imperial household can be ascribed to their recognition that the Japanese emperor and his household are particularly unique to Japan. This recognition in turn derives from their belief that the emperor is a descendent of a Shinto god, *Amaterasu Ōmikami*, and that the Japanese imperial household has continued since the first emperor, *Jinmu*, who assumed the position on February 11, 660 B.C. according to the imperial Japanese government that designated the date as the national foundation day. The day was abolished in 1948 by the Diet, but was revived in 1966 by the administration led by PM Eisaku Sato, a younger brother of PM Nobusuke Kishi, who is PM Abe's grandfather. In the eyes of the LDP lawmakers, the divineness of the emperor and the continuity of the imperial household over 2,000 years make the Japanese emperor and his household particularly special and unique to Japan, unlike other aspects of the Japanese culture, which were strongly influenced by other cultures, particularly, Buddhism and the Chinese culture.

Therefore, they regard the emperor and his household as a primary source of "Japanese-ness." The emperor system is "the foundation of Japan's national character" in the words of Prime Minister Abe (2013: 105), while the imperial household is "the foundation of Japan" in the words of Keiji Furuya, who is a member of Sosei Nippon and was a member of the LDP committee that made the draft constitution of 2012. PM Abe also sees the emperor as the social foundation of Japan, claiming that the unwavering existence of the emperor has enabled the postwar Japanese society to maintain its stability since his tenure is much longer than that of the head of the executive branch (Abe 2013: 105).

However, it should be noted that the emperor did not dictate the imperial Japanese regime. Although the imperial constitution gave him the status of the supreme leader, the regime was controlled by political elites (including top military officers). Basically, the political elites governed the country by exploiting the emperor's authority, which had been a long tradition of Japan. In this sense, the imperial Japanese regime was very convenient for them. Of course, neither Prime Minister Abe nor other LDP lawmakers publicly express their preference for reviving the prewar emperor system because of its exploitability. However, we cannot deny the possibility that they actually have such a preference and that this preference is one of the reasons why the LDP's draft constitution of 2012 gives the emperor a clear and greater role of the head of state in contrast with the ambivalent and limited role of a national symbol in the current constitution.

Conclusion

This chapter has examined the personal views that prompted the Abe administration to implement various policies that eroded Japan's external and internal pacifism. Those policies have been driven by its overarching objective of "escape from the post-war regime," that is, creating a new legal system by revising the current constitution and reviewing various laws created during the occupation period. PM Abe and other leading LDP lawmakers have criticized the three pillars of the current constitution: external pacifism, the sovereignty of the people, and fundamental human rights. External pacifism is based on the renunciation of the threat or use of force as a means to settle international disputes. In contrast, the sovereignty of the people and fundamental human rights are the foundations of Japan's internal pacifism.

Their criticism of Japan's external pacifism is based on their view that Japan should be a militarily normal country, just like other countries, in order to protect its national security and advance its national interest. Their criticism of the sovereignty of the people and fundamental human rights originates from their view that the state is superior to the people, which in turn derives partly from their elitist view that ordinary people should follow the state led by them who are superior to ordinary people and partly from their view that human rights are not by birth but granted by the state. Their view of state superiority led the LDP to make the draft constitution of 2012 that obliges the Japanese people to respect, love, and protect Japan and refrain from disturbing the public interest and the public order.

In December 2006, the first Abe administration succeeded in revising the Basic Act on Education of 1947, which PM Abe and other LDP lawmakers had regarded as a pillar of the postwar regime, and included nurturing of the love for Japan as one of the primary objectives of education. Yet, it seems that the success in nurturing patriotism has been limited so far, and there is still a very long way to go (Kolmaš 2018: 12–16). In fact, only 11% of the Japanese respondents expressed their willingness to fight for their country to the international comparative polls conducted in 2014, which was the lowest among the sixty-four countries polled (Gallup International 2015). In May 2007, the first Abe administration also passed the law to carry out a national referendum to revise the current constitution. Nevertheless, the constitution has not been revised yet despite the second Abe administration's strong effort since 2012 due to multiple obstacles (Kolmaš 2018: 21–26), which strongly suggests continuing difficulty in revising it.

However, in July 2014, the Abe administration adopted a new interpretation that the constitution does not prohibit Japan from exercising the right to collective self-defense. Then, in September 2015, it succeeded in enacting new laws to legalize the new interpretation and enable the SDF to conduct military operations overseas even if Japan has not been attacked. It further undermined the long-held policy of exclusive defense by enhancing Japan's offensive capabilities. Consequently, Japan's external pacifism was seriously eroded. Moreover, allegedly as a measure to cope with external threats such as North Korean terrorist attacks, the Abe administration passed the special secrecy law in December 2013 and the revised anti-organized crime law in June 2017, which, respectively, enabled the government to hide a wide range of information from the public and to arrest and prosecute those who plan and prepare anti-government activities, thereby significantly expanding the power of the government over the people and undermining the democracy and human security in Japan. In these ways, the Abe administration seriously weakened Japan's external and internal pacifism without amending the constitution.

In stark contrast, the Abe and other LDP-led administrations made few efforts to review the U.S. military presence in Japan, although it is a pillar of the postwar regime that Abe and other LDP lawmakers have criticized and have attempted to change. In fact, the Abe administration has made it a core security policy of Japan to strengthen its alliance with the U.S., which includes its continuous support for U.S. military presence in Japan, particularly in Okinawa, despite the strong demand of the Okinawans to reduce its excessive presence on the small island of Okinawa. PM Abe said, "Japan remains unable to protect its national security by itself" and "the Japan-U.S. alliance is indispensable, considering nuclear deterrence and the stability of the Far East, and is the best choice, given the U.S. influence in the international society, its economic power, and its supreme military power" (2013: 133). One can read between the lines and can posit that PM Abe and other LDP lawmakers think it necessary to continue to host and financially support U.S. forces in

Japan, import U.S. weapons in large quantity, and accept other U.S. military demands not only for Japan's national security and interest but also for them to maintain their status as power-holders (Magosaki 2012).

The various policies that eroded Japan's internal pacifism discussed earlier in this chapter could also be seen in this light. That is, those policies could be ascribed to the desire of PM Abe and other LDP lawmakers to maintain and strengthen their status as power-holders by increasing the power of the government over the people. Therefore, their strong attachment to their position could be the common denominator of the international and domestic policies of the Abe administration that eroded Japan's external and internal pacifism.

Their strong attachment to their status could also explain PM Abe's pragmatic political stance of avoiding risky policies that could shorten his tenure. For instance, his aforementioned reluctance to reduce U.S. military presence in Japan and review the Japan-U.S. SOFA, in contrast to PM Hatoyama's attempt at its reduction, could be ascribed to his concern about the backlashes from the U.S. and the largely pro-U.S. Japanese elites. Another example is his visit to the Yasukuni Shrine, which was only once in December 2013 compared to PM Koizumi's annual visits during his six-year tenure from 2001 to 2006, although Abe is widely seen as very nationalistic, more so than Koizumi. This could be attributed to Abe's concern about Japan's economic damage resulting from China's retaliation and the opposition from Japan's business circles to his repeated visit for fear of this damage.

It may be that PM Abe and other LDP lawmakers themselves think that their desire to maintain and strengthen their status as a power-holder is selfish. However, it may be that they think otherwise. Earlier in this chapter, the author pointed to the possibility that they have elitist views that they can lead ordinary people and that ordinary people should follow the state they run. If that is the case, they may think that maintaining and strengthening their status as power-holders/political leaders is not at all selfish but socially preferable. However, history shows that this kind of elitism and self-righteousness of power-holders is a major source of abuse of power. In fact, one has to conclude that PM Abe has already reached this stage of abuse of power, considering his administration's policies that have undermined the constitutionalism and democracy in Japan.

References

Abe, S. (2006). *Utsukushii kuni e [Towards a Beautiful Country]*. Tokyo. Bungeishunju.

Abe, S. (2014). *Nippon no ketsui [Japan's Determination]*. Tokyo: Shinchosha.

Abe, S., & Hyakuta, N. (2013). *Nippon yo, sekai no mannaka de sakihokore [Japan! Be proud of yourself in the "center of the world"].* Tokyo: WAC.

Armitage, R.L., & Nye, J. S. (2007). The U.S.-Japan alliance: Getting Asia right through 2020. *CSIS Report*, February.

Armitage, R.L., & Nye, J. S. (2012). The U.S.-Japan alliance: Anchoring stability in Asia. *CSIS Report*, August.

Armitage, R.L., & Nye, J. S. (2018). More important than ever: Renewing the U.S.-Japan alliance for the 21st century. *CSIS Report*, October.

Armitage, R.L., et al. (2000). The United States and Japan: Advancing toward a mature partnership. *INSS Special Report*, October 11.

Asahi Shimbun Seijibu Shuzaihan. (2015). *Abe seiken no urano kao [The Other Face of the Abe Administration].* Tokyo: Kodansha.

Aso, T. (2007). *Totetsumonai Nippon [An Extraordinary Japan].* Tokyo: Shinchosha.

Gallup International. (2015). WIN/Gallup International's global survey shows three in five willing to fight for their country. *Gallup International.* Retrieved from http://gallup-international.bg/en/Publications/2015/220-WIN-Gallup-International%E2%80%99s-global-survey-shows-three-in-five-willing-to-fight-for-their-country.

Halperin, M.H., & Hofsommer, M.M. (2014). Japan's secrecy law and international standards. *Japan Focus, 12*(37), 1.

Hatoyama, Y. (1996). Minshutō, watashino seiken kōsō [My plan for the administration led by the Democratic Party]. *Bungeishunju*, pp. 112–130.

Hirata, K. (2017). Japanese nationalism and foreign policy. In H. Sakai & Y. Sato (Eds.), *Re-rising Japan: Its strategic power in international relations* (pp. 71–92). New York: Peter Lang.

Huffington Post. (2013). Tokutei-himitsu-hogo-hō wa 'nichibei dōmei no kyōka' no tameni tsukurareru? [Is the SDS Protection Act for a stronger Japan-U.S. alliance?], *Huffington Post,* October 14. Retrieved from https://www.huffingtonpost.jp/2013/10/04/japan-nsc_n_4041820.html.

Hughes, C.W. (2009). *Japan's Remilitarisation.* Oxon: Routledge.

Hughes, C.W. (2015). *Japan's Foreign and Security Policy under the 'Abe Doctrine'.* New York: Palgrave Macmillan.

Ishiba, S. (2013). *Nippon wo, torimodosu. Kenpō wo, torimodosu [Recover Japan, Recover the Constitution].* Tokyo: PHP.

Jiyuminshuto [the Liberal Democratic Party]. (1955), *Tō no seikō [Party Platform],* November 15. Retrieved from https://www.jimin.jp/aboutus/declaration/#sec03.

Jiyuminshuto Kenpō Kaisei Suishin Honbu [The Headquarter of Promotion of Constitutional Revision, the Liberal Democratic Party]. (2013). *Kaikenan Q&A Zōhoban [Q&A on the Draft Constitution, Expanded Edition].* Tokyo: Jiyuminshuto Kenpō Kaisei Suishin Honbu.

Kanagawa Shimbun. (2014). Tokutei himitsu hogohō wo tou (20) "Hitsuyōsei naku saiaku no mono" Morton Halperin san [Questioning the SDS Protection Act (20) "Needless and the worst thing" Mr. Morton Halperin], *Kanagawa Shimbun,* May 15. Retrieved from https://www.kanaloco.jp/article/entry-47322.html.

Kantei. (2013). *Kokka Anzen Hoshō Kaigi no sōsetsu ni kansuru yūshikisha kaigi, Dai 1 kai kaigō, Giji yōshi [Proceedings of the 1st meeting of the Expert Council on the establishment of the National Security Council]*, February 15. Retrieved from www.kantei.go.jp/jp/singi/ka_yusiki/dai6.

Kantei. (2014). *Cabinet decision on development of seamless security legislation to ensure Japan's survival and protect its people.* July 1. Retrieved from https://japan.kantei.go.jp/96_abe/decisions/2014/__icsFiles/afieldfile/2014/07/03/anpohosei_eng.pdf.

Kokka Anzen Hoshō Kaigi [National Security Council]. (2013). *Kokka Anzen Hoshō Senryaku [National Security Strategy].* December 17.

Kolmaš, M. (2018). Identity change and societal pressures in Japan: the constraints on Abe Shinzo's educational and constitutional reform. *The Pacific Review.* doi: 10.1080/09512748.2018.1540497.

Magosaki, U. (2012). *Amerika ni tsubusareta seijikatachi [The Politicians Crushed by the U.S.]*, Tokyo: Shogakukan.

Mainichi Shimbun. (2015). 'Ronten' Kiro ni tatsu, kokuritsu bunkei [Opinion: Non-science programs of the national universities at a crossroad], *Mainichi Shimbun*, July 24. Retrieved from https://mainichi.jp/articles/20150724/org/00m/070/013000c.

Maslow, S. (2015). A blueprint for a strong Japan? Abe Shinzō and Japan's evolving security system. *Asian Survey*, 55(4), 739–765.

Masuzoe, Y. (2014). *Kenpō kaisei no omote to ura [The Front and Back of the Reform to the Constitution].* Tokyo: Kodansha.

Minetoshi, I. (2018). Abe shushō burēn jyogen no dōtoku kyōkasho mo gōkaku, Yagi Hidetsugu kyōju [Abe administration moral textbooks, Professor Hidetsugu Yagi]. *Asahi Shimbun*, March 28. Retrieved from https://www.asahi.com/articles/ASL3R3FLYL3RUTIL00K.html.

Ministry of Defense (MOD). (2018). *National Defense Program Guidelines for FY 2019 and beyond.* December 18, https://www.mod.go.jp/j/approach/agenda/guideline/2019/pdf/20181218_e.pdf.

Nagano, Tomoko (2014). 'Jieitai wa sensō suru guntai ni nari masuyo' Abe shushō no burēn Okazaki Hisahiko shi ni kiku shūdanteki jieiken [The SDF will become military forces that will engage in a war. An interview with Mr. Hisahiko Okazaki, a brain of PM Abe on the right to collective self-defense]. *The Huffington Post*, May 19, https://www.huffingtonpost.jp/tomoko-nagano/okazaki-hisahiko_b_5349355.html.

Nihon Bengoshi Rengōkai [Japan Federation of Bar Association]. (n.d.a). *Himitsu hogohō no mondaiten wa* [*What are the problems with the secret protection act?*]. Retrieved from https://www.nichibenren.or.jp/activity/human/secret/problem.html.

Nihon Bengoshi Rengōkai [Japan Federation of Bar Association]. (n.d.b). *Nichibenren wa kyōbōzai-hō no haishi wo motomemasu* [*Nichibenren demands repeal of the conspiracy law*]. Retrieved from https://www.nichibenren.or.jp/activity/criminal/complicity.html.

Nihon Keizai Shimbun. (2017). 'Kyōbōzai' no taishō hanzai 277 [277 crimes of 'Conspiracy'], *Nihon Keizai Shimbun*, June 15. Retrieved from https://www.nikkei.com/article/DGXLASFS14H4C_U7A610C1000000/.

Oros, A.L. (2017). *Japan's Security Renaissance: New policies and politics for the twenty-first century*. New York: Columbia University Press.

Ouchi, H. (2017). Kyōiku kihon hō 'kaitei' to sonogo ['Revision' to the Basic Act on Education and its aftermath]. In H. Tsukada (Ed.), *Tettei kenshō Nihon no ukeika [In-depth Examination of Japan's Shift to the Right]* (pp. 148–167). Tokyo: Chikumashobo.

SAPIO. (2017). Ishiba Shigeru shi 'Kōshitsu ga owaru toki wa nihon ga owaru toki to omotteiru [Mr. Shigeru Ishiba, 'I think that Japan ends when the imperial household ends']. *NEWS Post Seven*, March 30. Retrieved from https://www.news-postseven.com/archives/20170330_500888.html.

SakuraSo TV. (2011). *2/4 [Kanzenban] 12.1 Minshutō (Kan) naikaku tōkaku sengen! Kokumin daishūkai [2/4 Complete edition: December 1 National Grand Convention to bring down the DPJ (Kan) Cabinet]. YouTube*, January 4. Retrieved from https://www.youtube.com/watch?v=QXBbzl94UTc.

Sankei News. (2017a). Kita misairu, Shūdanteki jieiken de geigekika [North Korean missiles: Possible to intercept based on the right to collective self-defense], *Sankei News*, August 10. Retrieved from http://www.sankei.com/politics/news/170810/plt1708100037-n1.html.

Sankei News. (2017b). Beigun kaku no kokunai haibi giron wo. Ishiba Shigeru shi [Redeployment of nukes of the U.S. forces in Japan should be discussed. Mr. Shigeru Ishiba], *Sankei News*, September 6. Retrieved from https://www.sankei.com/politics/news/170906/plt1709060030-n1.html.

Shibata, T. (2017). 'Terotō junbizai' to Chian Ijihō, Suzuki Yasuzo ['Crimes for preparing terrorist acts and so forth' and the Maintenance of the Public Order Act, Suzuki Yasuzo]. *The Huffington Post*, April 16. Retrieved from https://www.huffingtonpost.jp/tetsuo-shibata/anzo-suzuki_b_16028904.html.

Shugiin (House of Representatives). (2017). *Shugiin Tōben dai 114 gō [House of Representatives, Reply No. 114]*. March 31.

Smith, S.A. (2019). *Japan Rearmed: The Politics of Military Power*. Cambridge: Harvard University Press.

Sosei Nippon (2012). *Sosei Nippon dai 3 kai Tokyo kenshū kai 3 [Sosei Nippon, the 3rd study session 3]*, May 10. Retrieved from http://www.sosei-nippon.jp/default_015.html.

Sugano, T. (2016). *Nippon Kaigi no kenkyū [The Research on Nippon Kaigi]*. Tokyo: Fusosha.

Suzuki, R. (1999). Kyōiku chokugo anki anyō no keii [Survey about the memorizing of the Imperial Rescript on Education]. *Kyōiku Kagaku*, *56*, 47–61.

Yanagisawa, K., Isezaki, K., & Kato, A. (2017). *Shin-Nichibei anporon [A New Japan-US security Doctrine]*. Tokyo: Shueisha.

3. *Japan-UK Relations before and after the Brexit Referendum*

Utpal Vyas
Ritsumeikan Asia Pacific University

Introduction

Despite their geographical separation, Japan and the UK have a long history of international relations. Although there have been times of enmity and distrust, in the post-war era they have built up good economic and political relations which have increasingly been characterised by a mutual respect and even appreciation of each other's cultures and interests. There are some (perhaps more commonly in Japan than in the UK, see Taida 2007) who maintain that they have many cultural similarities due to geographical and geopolitical situations as island nations facing strong continental powers (Akimoto 2017), although these assertions can often be used as a cover for sometimes deep differences which result from philosophies and cultures separated by half the globe, as well as the legacy of conflict in the Second World War (Dobson and Kosuge 2009; Towle and Kosuge 2007).

In recent years, relations between the two have been increasingly amicable as Japan has sought to deal with China's rise and Japan's own internal economic problems, while the UK has been dealing with the European Union (EU) and its own post-financial crisis problems. However, the Brexit referendum in the UK, which resulted in the government pronouncing that it would leave the EU due to the popular vote in favour of leaving, has created confusion and surprise in a Japan which craves stability and reliable international partners outside its own tense region.

This chapter will use a framework of national identity to consider how Japan is dealing with the sudden change in its perceptions of its relations with the UK. The following sections will explicate how interaction in and change in national identities can help us to understand how nations relate to each other. After considering the historical aspects of Japan's national identity in the modern period, the chapter goes on to explain how Prime Minister Shinzo Abe has tried to use aspects of Japan's national identity and change it for his own purposes. The changes in Japan's national identity in part encouraged by Abe are shown to be relevant to understanding its relations with the UK, and in particular Japan's response to the Brexit referendum in terms of economic and security relations. The chapter finally argues that Japan's identity is gradually becoming more independent of the US security alliance, and its confidence has allowed it to pursue diversification of its international partners and economic and security options.

National Identity and Japan

National identity is an important factor to consider when analysing the interactions between nation states. There is no doubt that it is a difficult concept to grasp and may not be susceptible to positivist methods of analysis, but this does not preclude its importance in international relations. Diplomats, politicians and experts judge other countries and carry out negotiations and analyses based on their perceptions of the relevant national identities of the countries involved (Wendt 1994). Thus, the perceptions of national identities and the interactions between national identities can give us a strong idea of how nation states are interacting and how their international relations are changing (Checkel 1999; Triandafyllidou 1998).

National identities are constantly evolving, but it is possible to glean some notions about relatively constant aspects of how a nation is perceived and what kind of image it projects. In the case of Japan, national identity has been shaped by three major forces. First, its history of interactions with other nation states in the modern period, second its perceptions of its place in international society, and third by domestic factors such as national culture (Grosvenor 1999) and politics. This section will briefly give an overview of important aspects of these factors in Japan's national identity, before moving on to consider how they affect current Japan-UK relations.

It is clear that, in the post-war period, Japan's attitude towards other nations has primarily been shaped by its relationship with the US and the need to fit into the US global strategy. However, within the constraints of accepting US leadership on general strategic issues, such as anti-communism, Japan has had leeway to form its own national identity in the international arena, for example, in how it deals with the UN (Drifte 1998) and international security issues (Inoguchi 2014). In particular since the end of the Cold War, and after the first Gulf War, Japanese governments have become more willing to allow their military forces to take part in peace-keeping operations overseas, and have continued to gradually develop their operational abilities to cooperate with partner countries' military operations overseas. However, despite successive governments' attempts to reinterpret the Japanese constitution in order to allow a more active security policy, Japan's security identity has still mostly been dependent on the US stance.

This national identity strengthening is, however, most obvious in the economic space, where Japan successfully developed a mercantilist style of engagement, in conjunction with its developmentalist outlook (Johnson 1982; Öniş 1991). Successive Japanese governments' basic premise has been to engage with the world on their own terms, encouraging the import of ideas while impeding the advance of foreign goods and capital into their economy and society as far as possible until Japanese firms became globally competitive. This somewhat wary approach, which has been sceptical of neoliberal ideas of free trade and openness to global capital while at the same time taking advantage of a rules-based international trade system, has allowed it to develop a successful international profile and deal with other developed states from a position of strength and equality (Hook et al. 2005).

The 1964 Tokyo Olympics is often considered as a particular milestone in Japan's quest to show a strong national identity. This was when the country unveiled its ground-breaking Shinkansen bullet trains to the world, and when it joined the OECD club of developed economies. It was soon to become a founding member of the G5 group of leading industrialised economies, and later took on prominent roles within the IMF, World Bank and UN among other international organisations. As it developed a strong economic identity, international resistance to its more mercantilist policies of export promotion and import barriers grew, and in response Japanese administrations increased overseas development assistance (Arase 1995), while Japanese companies increased overseas investment in order to gain diversified production bases (Komiya and Wakasugi 1991), as well as to gain trust in local communities in its trading partners by providing employment and furthering cultural exchanges.

Although the image of national economic strength took a blow after the bursting of its economic bubble in 1989, Japan has managed to maintain its identity as a nation which other developed countries must deal with on a basis of mutual respect, and which can be trusted; one strong indicator of this is its global number one ranking on the Henley Passport Index, which measures the number of countries to which visa-free access is allowed for a country's passport (Henley and Partners 2019).

This international identity construction has been complimented by Japan's own internal changes which, while keeping aspects of cultural sovereignty, protection of traditions and so on, have gradually leaned towards a stronger emphasis on democratic values and human rights in the last 20 years. There has been an increasing recognition of diversity within Japanese society, and many local campaigns against discrimination of minority groups in the country such as *burakumin*, ethnic Korean and Chinese Japanese, and disabled people demonstrate some recognition of international liberal human rights norms (Chapman 2006; Flowers 2012). Although the foreign resident population is still small compared with most of its Western partners at 2% of the total population (Urano 2018), the country has gradually started to become more willing to deal with immigrants and has developed ideas about multiculturalism and diversity (Burgess 2008; Kashiwazaki 2013). The one area of diversity where Japan has lagged behind is in women's rights and systematic discrimination against women in society, although here too, the government and society in general have gradually been taking steps to address these issues (Nagase 2018; Takeda 2018). Partly due to these domestic developments in liberal democratic norms, Japanese administrations have become increasingly confident in espousing 'values-based diplomacy' and encouraging the image and soft power of Japan as a strong, liberal democratic country based on the rule of law (Zakowski, Bochorodycz, and Socha 2018).

Japan's National Identity before and during the Abe Years

Shinzo Abe was elected prime minister of Japan for his second time in 2012. Abe's election, however, was partly in response to the domestic electorate's disgust with the manner in which the Democratic Party of Japan (DPJ) had been dealing with the problems in the Japanese economy, in addition to its perceived weakness on issues such as the denuclearisation of North Korea and the rise of China (Asahi Shimbun 2012). Abe campaigned on a platform which promised to reform Japan's domestic economy, as well as to increase its international assertiveness. The country was still recovering from the combined disasters of the Tohoku earthquakes, subsequent tsunami and the meltdown in the Fukushima nuclear reactor which had all occurred in 2011. Subsequent gradual disclosure of cover-ups, incompetence among the authorities involved, and perceived lack of crisis management by the national government led people to yearn for stronger leadership, in addition to deal with the ongoing economic malaises of deflation and negligible nominal growth.

Abe promised stimulus of the economy as well as structural reforms, and despite their scepticism of his right-wing views and the corruption among elite bureaucrats and businesses, his promises seemed to be welcomed by the majority of Japanese and outside observers. Abe had correctly calculated that Japanese people's confidence in the national economy, as well as in Japan's international position, was low. The multiple disasters had only added to a feeling that Japan's position was weakening on all fronts; as a result of continued deflation and weakness in growth, companies had been continuously restructuring over the previous decade, to the point where more and more employees were on lower paid temporary or contract jobs even in larger companies. Inequality in society was increasing due to these deep and long-term changes, and the lack of job security for many people was feeding into lower consumption and hence a cycle of continuing deflation, despite many attempts by the government to inject money into the economy, and by the central bank to print money through quantitative easing. Compounding these problems was the related problem of ageing and population decline (Yoshikawa 2007; Esteban-Pretel, Tanaka, and Meng 2017).

The lack of confidence in the domestic economy had led many companies to reduce capital investment in Japan, further deepening the problems. However, after the global financial crisis of 2008, Japanese companies were in a stronger position than other global companies due to their lower exposure to risky international assets and higher capital ratios, as well as higher productivity due to the painful restructuring (Ogawa, Saito, and Tokutsu 2017); in addition to this, the Japanese yen was still seen as a 'safe haven' currency in foreign exchange markets, and strengthened due to the crises elsewhere. Hence Japanese companies and banks were able to increase their foreign direct investment—a sign of strength for the large companies involved, but weakness in the domestic economy.

In short, it can be said that Japan's identity before Abe's second term began was rather inward-looking and reflected a very negative atmosphere of low expectations, low growth, and increasing domestic and international challenges (Ozawa 2001). Abe's major project was to talk up Japan's prospects, and introduce a positive feeling of Japan's future prospects and place in the world. To some extent, this project has had successes which can be seen in the short-term boost to consumer confidence, business confidence, and international perceptions of Japan's identity (Harding 2017), especially due to Abe's enthusiasm for pursuing free trade agreements (FTAs), such as the Trans-Pacific Partnership and the EU-Japan Economic Partnership Agreement. He also made a strong point of showing the Japanese public that he was energetically pursuing foreign diplomacy initiatives (Shimada 2018);

his repeated efforts to create a good relationship with President Trump immediately after his election were seen by many in Japan as a positive for Japan (Reynolds 2017). There has nevertheless been an underlying scepticism of any real change in Japan's position among some parts of the voting public, as well as among some experts (Stokes and Devlin 2018).

In particular, the situation of Japan's international partners and growing competition with China in economic as well as security fields has fed into uncertainty about Japan's international position. The election of Abe was seen as potentially disastrous for relations with its East Asian neighbours, although the results have not been as bad as perhaps many expected. However, the election of the Abe administration was seen to be a positive development for relations with Western allies, due to his prior focus on values diplomacy, that is, creating stronger relations with democratic allies (Zakowski, Bochorodycz, and Socha 2018).

Japan's relations with the UK should be seen in the context of the domestic and international aspects of Japan's national identity as described above. The next part of the chapter will briefly consider how Japan-UK relations have developed in the post-war era, and then investigate more deeply the situations before and after Brexit.

Japan-UK Relations in the Post-War Period

In the immediate post-war period, relations between Japan and UK were marred by their opposing positions during the war, as well as humiliation of prisoners of war by the Japanese during the conflict (Lowe 2007: 103). On the Japanese side, there has been a deeply rooted recognition of Western domination as a fact. This was reinforced by its designation as an enemy state in the UN Charter, and the resistance by Western nations to admit it as an equal partner in the major international organisations until decades after the war ended (Drifte 1998). The UK has not generally supported Japan's wish to be admitted as a permanent member of the UN Security Council until more recent times (Drifte 2009), and together with other prominent European states was reluctant to cede influence in the major Breton Woods international economic institutions, such as the GATT (Kosuge 2007: 171) and the IMF (Rapkin, Elston, and Strand 1997: 179) despite Japan's growing economic clout in the 1960s and 1970s.

However, as the Second World War veterans' pressure groups' influence waned in the UK (Dobson 2009: 163), and pragmatic economic concerns became more important, Japanese overtures to invest in the UK were welcomed (Toyoda 2014); and Japanese companies have gradually worked their way into British society, first becoming accepted and even admired household names in electronics and other industries (Kosuge 2007: 178), and then becoming important local employers in important clusters around the UK. In common with their actions in other countries (Vyas 2010), Japanese government agencies have invested in cultural relations with the UK, and in particular in supporting a small but strong contingent of researchers, business people, and policy experts to maintain a good base for bilateral communication and understanding (Cortazzi 2016: 395).

After Japan's economic bubble burst in 1989, Japanese companies were spurred on to globalise further and more deeply. At the same time, the UK had become an important base for Japanese producers and other companies to sell to and invest in other EU markets, taking advantage of the single market and other common regulations which had developed across the bloc; between 1990 and 2000, Japanese companies' investments in the UK accounted for 53% of all EU investment by Japan (Lee 2007: 139).

Although there have been occasional disagreements on international issues, statements by Japanese foreign policymakers were in general positive about Japan's relations with the UK, and its position as a strong base for Japanese investment in the future. In fact, it is clear that the deepening relationship was complimenting Japan's gradual moves towards a more diversified international identity, and setting the stage for future changes of its identity in a more independent direction. There is no doubt that Japan had intended the UK to be a key part of its relationship with the EU as a part of these moves.

This situation continued until the Brexit referendum result, which clearly surprised Japanese policymakers as much as most other observers. In the next sections, this chapter will consider the situation of Japan's relations with the UK before and after the Brexit referendum in more detail.

Japan-UK Relations before Brexit

Economic Relations

From Figure 3.1 we can see that foreign investment from Japan to the UK increased rapidly from 2010 onwards; this is especially evident in comparison to Germany and France. As Japanese companies decided to take advantage of depressed prices around the world after the US subprime mortgage and Eurozone financial crises, the UK was seen as a key market to invest in for the longer term, partly due to their already relatively strong base there; in 2014 the ambassador to Japan mentioned that 'about 140,000 jobs in the UK come from Japanese investment' (British Embassy Tokyo 2014). Japanese

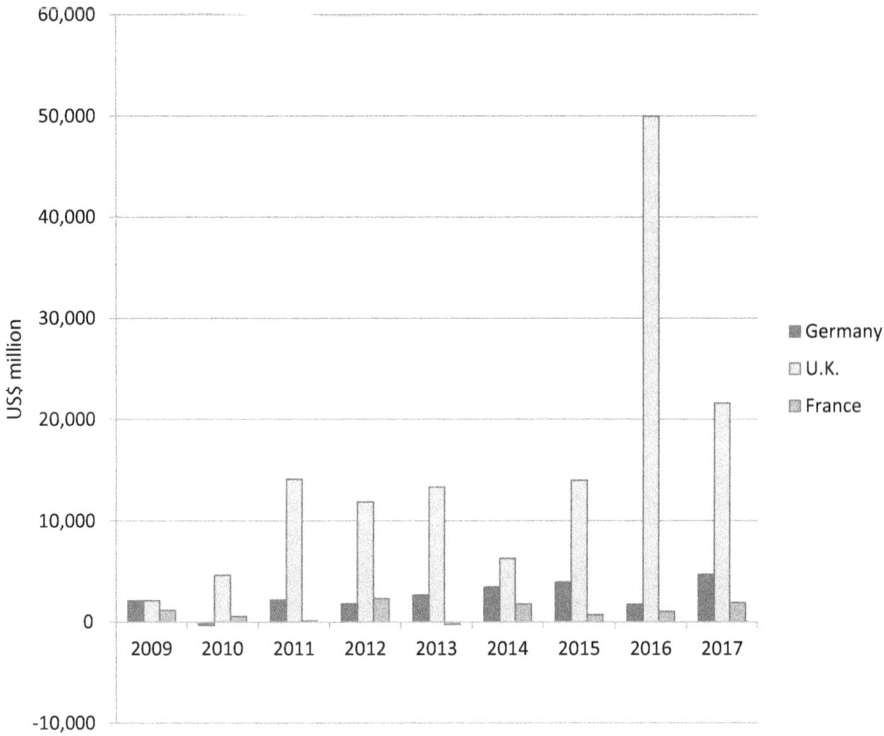

Figure 3.1. Japan's outward FDI. Source: compiled by author from data source JETRO (2018)

investment rose from US$1.61 billion in 2009 to a peak of $49.9 billion in 2016 (JETRO 2018).

The UK was also seen as a strong base for trading with other countries in the EU (Suzuki 2017). A large proportion of Japanese products manufactured in the UK was destined for export to EU markets. In particular, complex items such as cars are important for the broader UK economy. Examples of large car manufacturing plants in the UK are the Nissan plant in Sunderland, a Toyota plant in Derby and a Honda plant in Swindon (Perez and Ma 2019). These not only generate export income for the UK and provide jobs directly, but have become an important part of the local economies where they are based, attracting Japanese and other parts and service suppliers to their areas. These Japanese investment and trading networks have been built up over decades, and decisions to reinvest, upgrade or move are not taken lightly, but with a view to the long-term benefits over ten0 to twenty years.

This increasing investment and trade between Japan and the UK was an important part of the long negotiations over an EU-Japan FTA. The UK has been one of the top two destinations for Japanese exports among EU countries between 1979 and 2017, and is also an important source of imports (MOF 2018).

The large scale of Japanese investment in the UK, not only in cars but many other industries (Nikkei Shimbun 2014, 2012), was in large part a result of increasingly warm relations between the two countries in recent years. Partly due to Japanese companies wanting to have good access to the EU, but also because of the links and clusters which had been built up by Japanese companies in the UK, and the importance of globally competitive manufacturers in Japan, Japanese companies had been planning for further investment in the UK before the Brexit referendum.

In addition to the investment and trade ties, Japanese policymakers and experts have often shown interest in new ideas and innovations from the UK. For example, in relation to Tokyo's 2020 Olympics bid, and execution organisation, there has been significant interest in studying the London Olympics in 2012 (Yamaguchi 2014).

One worry for Japanese government officials during the Cameron administration was the manner in which the UK seemed to be trying to improve its connections with China, to the extent that the UK was the first US ally to declare support for the China-led Asian Infrastructure Investment Bank (AIIB). The Obama administration had tried to dissuade its allies from supporting the venture, and Japan had agreed with that stance (Dyer and Parker 2015). However, Prime Minister Cameron was keen to gain economic advantage through engagement with China; and once he had declared support, most other EU member states and Western allies followed, except for Japan and the US. Soon afterwards news that a Chinese state-owned enterprise was due to build and operate a new nuclear power plant in the UK caused further concern in Japan (Nikkei Asian Review 2015).

Therefore, along with worries about the UK's continuing arguments with the EU, and Cameron's stated intentions to hold a referendum on the UK's membership of the EU (Asahi Shimbun 2013), these developments were another reason for the Japanese government to try to cultivate a strong relationship with the UK in order to deal with its strategic issues in East Asia.

Regarding Japan's goal to strengthen its independent international identity, until the Brexit referendum the UK was being cultivated as an important economic base for Japanese companies within the EU, while economic ties with the EU as a whole were to be strengthened through the EU-Japan FTA negotiations.

Security Relations

One of Prime Minister Abe's most cherished goals has been to change Japan's identity as a pacifist nation which has renounced the right to wage war, into a 'pro-active' peace state which can join its partners in security and defence operations around the world (Oros 2015; Hughes 2015). Clearly, for Japan in general the relationship with the US is the main factor in deciding how to proceed on international security issues, but Abe and his nationalist allies have long wanted to emerge from US protectorate status, and allow Japan to maintain a more independent foreign policy and security stance (Inoguchi 2014). One way in which he has done this is to try and build security relationships with non-US partners, and in particular US allies with which Japan shares many interests (Hemmings and Bew 2017). He has accordingly advanced the security relationship with Australia, increased intelligence sharing with South Korea, and he has also been pursuing deeper security cooperation with the UK.

Moves towards deeper cooperation on security issues had been taking place since before Abe came to power for the second time (Drifte 2009). In April 2013, Prime Ministers Noda and Cameron, meeting in Tokyo, decided to pursue deeper strategic cooperation on a range of security and defence issues (Swire 2013). Soon afterwards, in 2014 the Abe and Cameron administrations released a formal statement on their 'strategic partnership' which included commitments to military exchanges and joint exercises, cooperation in international security issues and information sharing (FCO 2014). In keeping with Abe's focus on 'values diplomacy' the joint statement noted pointedly that it is 'based on shared values of democracy, rule of law, human rights and open and transparent markets'. In the case of Japan, this phrasing is usually used to highlight the contrast between relations with Japan and relations with China. This was particularly pertinent as the Cameron administration had made a special effort to show that it was being friendly towards China, and in fact Cameron had made an extended tour of China together with an entourage of businessmen in December of the previous year (Swire 2014).

In May 2014, the UK and Japan agreed to set up a '2 plus 2' institutionalised meeting of foreign and defence ministers between the two countries, and at the first meeting in January 2015, the ministers discussed the British interest in the new Kawasaki P-1 anti-submarine marine patrol aircraft, as well as joint research on anti-chemical weapons suits and cooperation on civilian evacuation (Tajima 2015). The P-1 aircraft was later to make a demonstration appearance at the Royal International Air Tattoo air show in the UK in July 2015, the first time a Japanese military aircraft had ever been displayed in a European air show (Royal International Air Tattoo 2015). In the end, the

Royal Air Force decided to buy US aircraft, but the expressions of interest and serious consideration of Japanese aircraft marked a significant deepening of the security relationship between Japan and the UK.

Taken together, the evidence shows that Japan's interest has been in strengthening relations on the economic and security sides with the UK, notwithstanding the Cameron administration's overtures towards China. This has been an important part of Abe's, and his predecessors', moves towards a more independent international identity for Japan.

Japan-UK Relations after Brexit

Economic Relations

Japan-based experts, along with businesses, were mostly unpleasantly surprised by the result of the Brexit referendum. The Japanese government, along with many others, had repeatedly urged the UK and its government to stay in the EU. The initial reaction to the vote reflected in the Japanese media was a kind of grim disbelief in the attitude of British politicians to such a serious event (Kunisue 2016), a search for reasons and possible consequences (Asahi Shimbun 2016a, c), and finally a certain fatalistic acceptance that the world was becoming more uncertain for Japan (Nikkei Shimbun 2016a) and its companies (Asahi Shimbun 2016b). It has to be said that this sequence of reactions was not unique to Japan.

The Japanese government mostly reflected its companies' desires at first, while trying to convey that 'Japan respects the will of the British people as demonstrated in the referendum' (MOFA 2016) to separate from the EU. Its initial response was to support the many Japanese companies which stood to be affected by the turmoil (Nikkei Shimbun 2016b) while paying lip service to British government ministers' hopes of a bilateral free trade deal between the UK and Japan (Nikkei Shimbun 2016c).

Japanese businesses first tried to extract promises from the British government to protect their free access to the EU market even in the event of a full UK exit. For example, the then boss of Nissan, Carlos Ghosn, tried to place pressure on the UK government to give Nissan assurances in order to make a long-term investment decision in its Sunderland factory (Farrell 2016). The government response was not disclosed, due to fear that other companies would complain of unfair treatment. However, subsequent reports intimated that Nissan had received assurances that its business would not be adversely affected by Brexit (Ruddick, Mason, and Kollewe 2016); the UK government would not admit that any monetary promise had been made until a letter to Nissan was leaked in 2019, which made clear that up to £80m had been promised if Nissan were to invest further in its UK production (Campbell and Pickard 2019, Clark 2016). The Japanese government also wrote a detailed letter from the Japanese ambassador to the UK government in which it made clear, in an unusually direct manner, that Japanese companies required free trade and free financial flows in order to remain committed to staying in the UK (MOFA 2016). Apart from this, the letter emphasised the problems which would result from uncertainty during the negotiation process, and asked to be kept informed in a transparent way, citing the danger to 440,000 jobs which had been created by Japanese companies in the EU.

It later became clear that Prime Minister May's idea of Brexit was quite far removed from the EU27's vision, and also in fact from the wishes of the Japanese government and its companies. Led by Germany, the EU made clear that it would not give the UK free access to the EU market if freedom of movement was not also preserved; however, the UK administration under Prime Minister Theresa May continued to insist that the British people had voted to restrict freedom of movement for EU citizens, and so the UK needed to be able to control immigration from the EU.

While these conflicting positions were becoming clearer during 2017, several Japanese companies, such as Secom (Nikkei Shimbun 2017c), Hitachi (Nikkei Shimbun 2017a) and JR East (Iwamoto 2017), were making investments in the UK, although the companies said that their decisions would not be affected greatly by Brexit.

Nevertheless, the Brexit process faced further uncertainty when Theresa May called a surprise general election in June 2017 in order to gain support for her position on Brexit. The result was that she lost her majority in the House of Commons, and had to enter into an agreement with the small, conservative Democratic Unionist Party of Northern Ireland in order to continue in government. Japanese companies' wish for more certainty was becoming less and less likely to be fulfilled. Accordingly, Japanese companies whose businesses were more reliant on smooth transactions across the EU, notably investment banks and other financial institutions, were the first to actively consider moving their headquarters and other important operations out of the UK, and on to the continent. The three large banks, Mitsubishi UFJ, Sumitomo Mitsui and Mizuho, had all begun planning to move their operations from London, while Daiwa Securities was also considering establishing a base in Frankfurt (Nikkei Shimbun 2017d). While these and other companies had established bases in the UK for decades, they had also gained familiarity with EU markets and through their operations. The fact that they were ready to move to bases in Germany, Amsterdam and Paris reflected this confidence in their ability to thrive outside London. In addition to this, the EU and Japan had been negotiating an FTA since 2013, the EU-Japan Economic Partnership Agreement, which was finalised in 2017, and ratified by both sides' parliaments in 2018. The wide-ranging agreement came into force on 1 February 2019 (European Commission 2019). The agreement represents a clear step forward in understanding and relations between Japan and the EU, and to some extent represents a broadening of Japan's global interests beyond the US and East Asia, in line with its more confident, independent identity.

The confidence has been further reflected in the subsequent events; in 2018, Panasonic decided to move its Europe HQ from the UK to Amsterdam (Fukao 2018); Sony has more recently followed suit, and Norinchuokinko (an important investment cooperative) and Daiwa Securities added to the investment banks which had announced plans to move their trading operations from London to Frankfurt or other EU bases (BBC 2019; Martin 2018). Japanese investment banks have been at the forefront of international companies' plans to relocate due to Brexit concerns.

In the meantime, seemingly worried about potential economic impacts, the UK government decided to pursue talks with Japan about the possibility of joining the Trans-Pacific Partnership, an FTA between Japan and ten other Asia-Pacific countries. While this seemed to many experts to be unlikely, the Abe administration welcomed Trade Secretary Liam Fox's overtures and offered to help the UK join (Japan Times 2018b). Nevertheless, and for obvious reasons, Japan, along with most other countries, has been reluctant to give any concrete assurances of FTA talks while the UK's own future relationship with the EU is still unclear (Nikkei Shimbun 2016c). In fact, at the current time in view of the weak position of the UK in any bilateral trade negotiations, the Japanese government has stuck firmly to its intention to negotiate strongly for its own advantages in any post-Brexit bilateral FTA deal (Lewis 2019).

The trends in Japan's economic engagement with the UK have therefore been disrupted to a certain extent by the Brexit vote and subsequent drawn-out process. Japan's own interest has been to continue to strengthen its own independent identity; therefore, rather than hope the UK could establish a strong position after Brexit, Japanese companies' and the government's priority has been to diversify their economic positions within the EU in order to try to establish a more stable and secure position for themselves. In this case, therefore it can be seen that economically, the relationship between Japan and the UK has been damaged significantly, and that Japan's own independent identity and stability in its global economic networks is much more important for it than supporting an economic partner through instability.

With the implementation of the EU-Japan EPA, it is likely that this economic move away from the UK towards other EU countries will continue in the near future, whatever the final outcome of Brexit.

Security Relations

The situation regarding security relations has been in notable contrast to the negative economic news. In part because of Abe's desire to diversify Japan's security relations and lead Japan's foreign and defence policy on to a more independent path, and in part because the May administration wishes to show that the UK is still an important power in the world, and will continue to be so even if it leaves the EU, there has been renewed effort between the two governments to cooperate on security issues.

There was new impetus given to UK-Japan defence cooperation agreements by the Brexit vote (Hemmings and Bew 2017). From Japan's point of view, this was a good opportunity to put its new more independent security identity focus into practice and diversify its partnerships (Akimoto 2017). At the same time, both the UK and Japan have been careful to place their agreements in the context of their alliances with the US. This is why the cooperation was announced at the Pentagon as a trilateral cooperation agreement in October 2016 by the chiefs of the three countries' navies. The purpose of this was to ensure further deepening of the partnerships in various areas of defence, including freedom of navigation operations (FONOPs) in the South China Sea (Stashwick 2016).

Beyond both Japan and the UKs' need to cooperate closely with the US, the two countries have accelerated their plans for deeper defence cooperation in the light of their mutual interests and changing identities.

In January 2017, it was announced that the UK and Japan had signed a Defence Logistics Treaty (also known as an Acquisition and Cross Servicing Agreement), the main purpose of which is to work jointly to ensure that each country's defence systems have a high level of interoperability, and to allow for sharing of services and equipment (FCO 2017).

In November 2017, the two governments decided to jointly develop an air-to-air missile system. The system was planned to incorporate a missile system from European manufacturer MBDA, and a radar system developed by Mitsubishi Electric (Nikkei Shimbun 2017b). This was touted as the first time for Japan to develop a weapons system with a non-US partner. Abe has been clear on his desire to encourage Japanese defence companies to collaborate on defence projects, and to even try to export weapons systems to its military allies in the future. This became possible after his administration loosened post-war restrictions on arms exports in 2014. The UK, being a fellow US security ally, falls under the remit of the new rules, and so is a potentially key defence collaboration partner.

Further cooperation was apparent in the joint military exercises which were agreed on in December 2017, when Foreign Minister Kono and Defence Minister Itsunori met with their UK counterparts Boris Johnson and Gavin Williamson in London, for the so-called 'two-plus-two' talks. Joint army, navy and air force drills were envisaged, and joint positions were established regarding North Korea denuclearisation and with regard to freedom of passage in the South China Sea, which is being challenged by China's assertions of sovereignty over the area (Hayashi 2017; Madden 2018). The joint army exercises actually took place in October 2018 (*Japan Times* 2018a).

In August 2018 it was reported that Japan and the UK were in talks to collaborate on another long-term project, a sixth-generation stealth fighter aircraft, although the chances of Japan choosing a non-US company for joint development were still seen as low (Gady 2018).

A final, significant new area of cooperation is on cybersecurity. With the increasing importance of hybrid warfare, including strategic internet-based campaigns to destabilise democracies which have been carried out by Russia and China, the UK's expertise in the area of information technology and communications intelligence is highly valued by Japan, and joint statements and cooperation agreements between the UK and Japan have been clear on the need to cooperate in these areas. With Japan hosting the Rugby World Cup in 2019, and the Olympics in 2020, the UK has been able to use its recent experience in holding these events to offer cooperation on cybersecurity and counter-terrorism techniques with Japan (*The Economist* 2019).

It can be seen, therefore, that developments in security relations between Japan and the UK fit nicely into Abe's, and successive Japanese administrations', efforts to carve out a more independent security policy, while at the same time trying to not jeopardise its vital alliance with the US. Arguably, the UK's ability to project military power around the world, its expertise in communications and IT systems, and its deep interoperability with the US and NATO are much more valuable for Japan's purposes than its waning economic influence in the EU and in the world more generally. Hence, the Abe administration has been using the uncertainty of Brexit to present itself as a strong and reliable security partner for the UK at a time of increasing security competition in Europe as well as in Asia. It seems likely that security relations will continue to strengthen, and Japan's pursuit of an independent security policy will reinforce the trend.

Japan's Identity and Changes in Japan-UK Relations

This chapter has outlined a framework of national identity, in Japan's case consisting of historical international relations, its perception of its place in the contemporary international arena and its own domestic developments. It has then investigated how Prime Minister Shinzo Abe has tried to use and change this national identity, and how this process has affected the manner in which Japan has approached its relationship with the UK before and after the events of the Brexit referendum in 2016. It has argued that the Japanese administration of Shinzo Abe has used the changing relations with the UK in order to proactively further its goal of strengthening Japan's independent international identity and diversifying its network of close alliances and partners beyond its reliance on the US. Not only has it been able to work with the UK more closely in security issues, but it has been able to gradually work towards reducing its dependence on the UK in its financial and trading relations with the EU, using the Brexit referendum as an opportunity in both respects.

The change in Japan's perception of the UK due to the Brexit vote and subsequent negotiations has been to some extent dependent on the Brexit events themselves, and this seems particularly clear on the economic side. However, it is clear that the manner in which Japan has approached diplomacy towards the UK, in many ways showing support for an ally during a difficult time while at the same time considering ways in which Japan can use the situation to further its own strategic goals, is based on the longer-term gradual changes in Japan's identity towards a more independent security and foreign policy and diversification of its alliances.

The two events of Brexit as well as the Trump presidency in the US have given Abe an unprecedented chance to pursue these goals in the face of a Japanese public reluctant to support a more assertive international stance. The Abe administration would no doubt have been delighted by the UK defence minister's statement that it was prepared to send an aircraft carrier to the South China Sea to defend against countries which 'flout international law' (Parker and Mance 2019), an obvious reference to China's claim on sovereignty over the area. The Japanese government is under no illusions as to the UK's lack of real influence in the Asia-Pacific region; however, international moral support, and the support of another close US ally which has access to valuable intelligence and skills, is of much more importance regarding its pressing needs to put a brake on China's expanding influence in East Asia and beyond.

From Japan's perspective, this is a part of the overall strategy which includes improving security relations and integration with other US allies, such as Australia, New Zealand as well as developing relationships with other Asian countries to strengthen the Indo-Pacific trade routes. While Japan wishes to reduce its dependence on the US, the growing pressure from China has meant that it has not been able to do this in practice; and the alternative goal of diversifying its security relations to achieve similar aims has been emphasised.

References

Akimoto, C. (2017). *Senryaku no chiseigaku: rando pawa vs shi pawa* [Geopolitics of strategy: land power vs sea power]. Tokyo: Wedge.

Arase, D. (1995). *Buying Power: The Political Economy of Japan's Foreign Aid.* London: Rienner.

Asahi Shimbun (2012). *Jiminto taisho, Abe seiken e, chi ni ashi no tsuita seiji o* [LDP win towards an Abe administration - looking for well-grounded politics]. 17 Decemeber.

Asahi Shimbun (2013). *Ei, kasoku suru EU banare, Kameron shusho, asu kankei minaosu enzetsu* [UK accelerating divergence with the EU: Prime Minister Cameron to give speech on restructuring the relationship]. 17 January, p. 11.

Asahi Shimbun (2016a). *Ei EU ridatsu, shosha no mikata* [Various commenters' opinions on UK leaving the EU], 27 June.

Asahi Shimbun (2016b). *Ei shinshutsu kigyo ni kogeki Toyota, Mitsui Bussan, EU ridatsu e* [Shock to companies invested in UK—Toyota, Mitsui Bussan, Hitachi, leaving the EU], 25 June.

Asahi Shimbun (2016c). *Ridatsu no kogeki—datsu EU, unerizuyoku, Ei, keizai risuku yori dokuritsu iko* [Leave shock—strong waves, leaving the EU—UK chooses independence over economic risk], 25 June.

BBC. (2019). *Sony to move Europe headquarters to avoid Brexit disruption*, 23 January. Retrieved from https://www.bbc.com/news/business-46968720.

British Embassy Tokyo. (2014). *Japan is Back, Britain is Back,* 5 February. Retrieved from https://www.gov.uk/government/news/japan-is-back-britain-is-back.

Burgess, C. (2008). Celebrating 'multicultural Japan': Writings on 'minorities' and the discourse on 'difference'. *Electronic Journal of Contemporary Japanese Studies.* Retrieved from https://www.japanesestudies.org.uk/articles/2008/Burgess.html

Campbell, P., & Pickard, J. (2019). UK government vowed to shield Nissan from Brexit fallout, *Financial Times*, 5 February. Retrieved from https://www.ft.com/content/01191c5e-287b-11e9-a5ab-ff8ef2b976c7.

Chapman, D. (2006). Discourses of multicultural coexistence (Tabunka Kyosei) and the 'old-comer' Korean residents of Japan. *Asian Ethnicity*, *7*(1), 89–102.

Checkel, J.T. (1999). Norms, institutions, and national identity in contemporary Europe, *International Studies Quarterly*, *43*(1), 83–114.

Clark, G. (2016). *Letter to Carlos Ghosn of Nissan Motor Company*, 21 October. London: BEIS. Retrieved from https://www.gov.uk/government/publications/nissans-investment-in-the-uk.

Cortazzi, H. (2016). Britain and Japan: a survey of recent books in English dealing with aspects of Anglo-Japanese relations. *Japan Forum*, *28*(3), 394–412.

Dobson, H. (2009). Reporting the fiftieth and sixtieth anniversaries of the end of World War II: Less fear and loathing in the UK press towards Japan? In H. Dobson & N. Kosuge (Eds.), *Japan and Britain at war and peace* (pp. 151–165). Abingdon: Routledge.

Dobson, H., & Kosuge, N. (2009). Introduction. In *Japan and Britain at war and peace* (pp. 1–8). Abingdon: Routledge.

Drifte, R. (1998). Japan's quest for a permanent seat on the Security Council. *Asia-Pacific Review*, *5*(2), 87–109.

Drifte, R. (2009). Japan-UK relations in the global context. In H. Dobson & N. Kosuge (Eds.), *Japan and Britain at war and peace* (pp. 166–177). Abingdon: Routledge.

Dyer, G., & Parker, G. (2015). US attacks UK's constant accommodation with China, *Financial Times*, 13 March. Retrieved from https://www.ft.com/content/31c4880a-c8d2-11e4-bc64-00144feab7de.

Esteban-Pretel, J., Tanaka, R., & Meng, X. (2017). Changes in Japan's labor market during the Lost Decade and the role of demographics. *Journal of the Japanese and International Economies*, *43*, 19–37.

European Commission. (2019). *EU-Japan agreement enters into force*. Brussels: European Commission. Retrieved from http://trade.ec.europa.eu/doclib/press/index.cfm?id=1976.

Farrell, S. (2016). Nissan demands Brexit compensation for new UK investment. *The Guardian*, 30 September. Retrieved from https://www.theguardian.com/business/2016/sep/30/nissan-hard-brexit-compensation-new-uk-investment-tariffs.

FCO. (2014). *UK-Japan Joint Statement*. Retrieved from https://www.gov.uk/government/news/uk-japan-joint-statement.

FCO (2017). *UK and Japan strengthen defence ties*, 26 January. Retrieved from https://www.gov.uk/government/news/uk-and-japan-strengthen-defence-ties.

Flowers, P.R. (2012). From kokusaika to tabunka kyosei. *Critical Asian Studies*, *44*(4), 515–542.

Fukao, K. (2018). *Panasonikku, Oshu honsha oranda ido, Ei EU ridatsu ni sonae* [Panasonic moves its Europe HQ to Holland, prepares for Brexit]. *Nikkei Shimbun*, 30 August.

Gady, F.-S. (2018). Will Japan and the UK collaborate on sixth generation Tempest future fighter aircraft? *The Diplomat*, 2 August. Retrieved from https://thediplomat.com/2018/08/will-japan-and-the-uk-collaborate-on-sixth-generation-tempest-future-fighter-aircraft/.

Grosvenor, I. (1999). 'There's no place like home': Education and the making of national identity. *History of Education*, 28(3), 235–250.

Harding, R. (2017). Japanese business conditions strongest in a decade, Tankan shows. *Financial Times*, 2 October. Retrieved from https://www.ft.com/content/65cfc8f6-a707-11e7-ab55-27219df83c97.

Hayashi, S. (2017). Japan and UK to expand joint military exercises. *Nikkei Shimbun*, 15 December.

Hemmings, J., & Bew, C. (2017). America, Japan and the UK: A new three-way alliance against China? *The National Interest*, 4 April. Retrieved from https://nationalinterest.org/feature/america-japan-the-uk-new-three-way-alliance-against-china-20019.

Henley and Partners. (2019). Passport Index. Retrieved from https://www.henleypassportindex.com/global-ranking.

Hook, G.D., Gilson, J., Hughes, C.W., & Dobson, H. (2005). *Japan's international relations: Politics, economics, and security*. London: Routledge.

Hughes, C.W. (2015). *Japan's foreign and security policy under the 'Abe Doctrine': New dynamism or new dead end?* Basingstoke: Palgrave.

Inoguchi, T. (2014). A call for a new Japanese foreign policy: the dilemmas of a stakeholder state. *International Affairs*, *90*(4), 943–958.

Iwamoto, K. (2017). JR East starts operations in UK—'birthplace' of railway. *Nikkei Shimbun*, 29 December.

Japan Times. (2018a). *Japan and Britain hold joint military exercise in central Japan*, 8 October. Retrieved from https://www.japantimes.co.jp/news/2018/10/02/national/japan-britain-hold-joint-military-exercise-central-japan/.

Japan Times. (2018b). *Japan OK with Britain joing the TPP*, 31 July. Retrieved from https://www.japantimes.co.jp/news/2018/07/31/business/japan-ok-britain-joining-tpp/.

JETRO (2018). Japan's Outward FDI by Country/Region (Balance of Payments basis, net and flow). Retrieved from https://www.jetro.go.jp/en/reports/statistics.html.

Johnson, C. (1982). *MITI and the Japanese miracle: The growth of industrial policy*. Stanford: Stanford University Press.

Kashiwazaki, C. (2013). Incorporating immigrants as foreigners: Multicultural politics in Japan. *Citizenship Studies*, *17*(1), 31–47.

Komiya, R., & Wakasugi, R. (1991). Japan's foreign direct investment. *The ANNALS of the American Academy of Political and Social Science*, *513*(1), 48–61.

Kosuge, N. (2007). The pressure of the past on the Anglo-Japanese relationship. In P. Towle & N. Kosuge (Eds.), *Britain and Japan in the twentieth century: One hundred years of trade and prejudice* (pp. 166–179). London: I B Tauris.

Kunisue, N. (2016). *Baibai Eikoku deru mo nokoru mo, itashikayushi* [Bye bye Britain, leave or stay, a painful dilemma]. *Ashahi Shimbun*, 23 June.

Lee, S. (2007). Bilateral stability, gobal instability: The political economy of contemporary Anglo-Japanese economic relations. In P. Towle & N. Kosuge (Eds.),

Britain and Japan in the twentieth century: One hundred years of trade and prejudice (pp. 106–115). London: I B Tauris.

Lewis, L. (2019). UK-Japan trade talks sour after letter from Hunt and Fox. *Financial Times*, 18 February. Retrieved from https://www.ft.com/content/9cd62bde-32ba-11e9-bd3a-8b2a211d90d5.

Lowe, P. (2007). Britain and the recovery of Japan post-1945. In P. Towle & N. Kosuge (Eds.), *Britain and Japan in the twentieth century: One hundred years of trade and prejudice* (pp. 97–106). London: I B Tauris.

Madden, P. (2018). *Kiko, Maden junichiei taishi, anpo ya keizai renkei shinka* [Contribution by British Ambassador to Japan Madden: Deepening partnership on security and the economy]. *Nikkei Shimbun*, 30 August.

Martin, K. (2018). Japan's Daiwa trading unit shifts to Frankfurt as Brexit looms. *Financial Times*, 11 October. Retrieved from https://www.ft.com/content/2f695a7c-cd38-11e8-b276-b9069bde0956.

MOF. (2018). *Yearly Trade Statistics*, 21 November. Retrieved from www.customs.go.jp/toukei/suii/html/time_e.htm.

MOFA. (2016). *Japan's Message to the United Kingdom and the European Union*. Retrieved from https://www.mofa.go.jp/files/000185466.pdf.

Nagase, N. (2018). Has Abe's Womanomics Worked? *Asian Economic Policy Review*, *13*(1), 68–101.

Nikkei Asian Review. (2015). *Economic benefits take front seat amid warmer Sino-UK ties*, 29 October.

Nikkei Shimbun (2012). *Itochu buys UK clothing firm to expand Asian ops*, 15 July.

Nikkei Shimbun (2014). *Tepco to enter UK wholesale power market*, 26 June.

Nikkei Shimbun (2016a). *Furueru sekai Ei EU ridatsu, kaikokugata seicho moderu ni shiren* [Shaking world, UK leaves EU, a test of the open country model of growth], 25 June, p.1.

Nikkei Shimbun (2016b). *Japan fears UK lacks experience needed to seal trade deals*, 28 June.

Nikkei Shimbun (2016c). *Japan will weigh trade pact with UK: foreign minister*, 30 June.

Nikkei Shimbun (2017a). *Hitachi enters Europe elevator market with UK acquisition*, 28 April.

Nikkei Shimbun (2017b). *Japan and UK to collaborate on missile development*, 24 November.

Nikkei Shimbun (2017c). *Secom broadens UK foothold via Northern Ireland acquisition*, 4 June.

Nikkei Shimbun (2017d). *UK election surprise adds to Japanese Brexit worries*, 10 June.

Ogawa, K., Saito, M., & Tokutsu, I. (2017). Did divine wind rescue Japan out of the lost decade? *Journal of the Japanese and International Economies*, *44*, 39–51.

Öniş, Z. (1991). The Logic of the Developmental State, *Comparative Politics*, *24*(1), 109–126.

Oros, A.L. (2015). International and domestic challenges to Japan's postwar security identity: 'Norm constructivism' and Japan's new 'proactive pacifism'. *The Pacific Review*, 28(1), 139–160.

Ozawa, T. (2001). The "hidden" side of the "flying-geese" catch-up model: Japan's dirigiste institutional setup and a deepening financial morass. *Journal of Asian Economics*, 12(4), 471–491.

Parker, G., & Mance, H. (2019). 'Gunboat diplomacy' dispute upsets UK trade mission to China. *Financial Times*, 15 February. Retrieved from https://www.ft.com/content/f38cc1d4-306e-11e9-8744-e7016697f225.

Perez, I.G., & Ma, J. (2019). Honda to shut U.K. factory in latest blow as Brexit looms. *Bloomberg*, 18 February. Retrieved from https://www.bloomberg.com/news/articles/2019-02-18/honda-is-preparing-to-shut-u-k-car-plant-by-2022-sky-says.

Rapkin, D.P., Elston, J.U., and Strand, J.R. (1997). Institutional adjustment to changed power distributions: Japan and the United States in the IMF. *Global Governance*, 3(2), 171–196.

Reynolds, I. (2017). Abe's golf diplomacy with Trump scores on the home front. *Japan Times*, 22 February. Retrieved from https://www.japantimes.co.jp/news/2017/02/22/national/politics-diplomacy/abes-golf-diplomacy-trump-scores-home-front/#.XNoJYI5LhjU.

Royal International Air Tattoo. (2015). Japan makes Air Tattoo history, 7 July. Retrieved from https://www.airtattoo.com/news/2015/jul/07/japan-makes-air-tattoo-history.

Ruddick, G., Mason, R., & Kollewe, J. (2016). No cheque book' involved in Nissan pledge, says minister. *The Guardian*, 28 October. Retrieved from https://www.theguardian.com/business/2016/oct/27/new-nissan-super-plant-hopes-for-tariff-free-eu-access.

Shimada, G. (2018). Abe's fourth arrow—diplomacy. *Nikkei Asian Review*, 26 January. Retrieved from https://asia.nikkei.com/Spotlight/Cover-Story/Abe-s-fourth-arrow-diplomacy.

Stashwick, S. (2016). US, UK, and Japan navies sign first-ever trilateral cooperation agreement. *The Diplomat*, 1 November. Retrieved from https://thediplomat.com/2016/11/us-uk-and-japan-navies-sign-first-ever-trilateral-cooperation-agreement/.

Stokes, B., & Devlin, K. (2018). Despite rising economic confidence, Japanese see best days behind them and say children face a bleak future, 12 November. Pew Research Center. Retrieved from http://www.pewglobal.org/2018/11/12/despite-rising-economic-confidence-japanese-see-best-days-behind-them-and-say-children-face-a-bleak-future/.

Suzuki, H. (2017). The new politics of trade: EU-Japan. *Journal of European Integration*, *39*(7), 875–889.

Swire, H. (2013). *Speech at UK-Japan Global Seminar.* Retrieved from https://www.gov.uk/government/speeches/hugo-swire-speech-at-uk-japan-global-seminar.

Swire, H. (2014). *The UK in the Asian Century*, 15 July. Retrieved from https://www.gov.uk/government/speeches/the-uk-in-the-asian-century.

Taida, H. (2007). Anglo-Japanese economic relations since the 1970s. In P. Towle & N. Kosuge (Eds.), *Britain and Japan in the twentieth century: One hundred years of trade and prejudice* (pp.119–127). London: I B Tauris.

Tajima, Y. (2015). *Nichiei boeisobi de kyoryoku kakudai, sho no 2 purasu 2, shokaiki yushutsu nado kento* [Japan-UK cooperation on defense procurement increases: First 2 plus 2 meeting, export of marine patrol aircraft considered]. *Nikkei Shimbun*, 22 January.

Takeda, H. (2018). Between reproduction and production: Womenomics and the Japanese Government's approach to women and gender policies. *Jenda Kenkyu [Gender Research], 38*(21), 49–69.

The Economist. (2019). Shinzo Abe visits Britain to firm up security ties, 10 January. Retrieved from https://www.economist.com/britain/2019/01/10/shinzo-abe-visits-britain-to-firm-up-security-ties.

Towle, P., & Kosuge, N. (2007). Introduction. In P. Towle & N. Kosuge (Eds.), *Britain and Japan in the twentieth century: One hundred years of trade and prejudice* (p. xiii). London: I B Tauris.

Toyoda, S. (2014). British hospitality. *Nikkei Shimbun*, 5 August.

Triandafyllidou, A. (1998). National identity and the 'other'. *Ethnic and Racial Studies, 21*(4), 593–612.

Urano, N. (2018). Number of foreign residents hits record 2.63 million in June. *Asahi Shimbun*, 20 September. Retrieved from http://www.asahi.com/ajw/articles/AJ201809200060.html.

Vyas, U. (2010). *Soft power in Japan-China relations: State, sub-state and non-state relations.* London: Routledge.

Wendt, A. (1994). Collective identity formation and the international state. *The American Political Science Review, 88*(2), 384–396.

Yamaguchi, D. (2014). The British way of winning. *Nikkei Asian Review*, 14 August.

Yoshikawa, H. (2007). Japan's lost decade: What have we learned and where are we heading?, *Asian Economic Policy Review, 2*(2), 186–203.

Zakowski, K., Bochorodycz, B., & Socha, M. (2018). New pillar of Japan's foreign policy: Arc of freedom and prosperity and values-oriented diplomacy. In K. Zakowski, B. Bochorodycz, & M. Socha (Eds.), *Japan's foreign policy making: Central government reforms, decision-making processes, and diplomacy* (pp. 117–136). Cham: Springer.

4. *Industrial Policies, the East Asian Miracle, and Regional Integration after the 2008 Global Financial Crisis*

YOICHIRO SATO
Ritsumeikan Asia Pacific University

Introduction

In the process of implementing Japan's doctrine of "following the West" and the subsequent industrialization which began in the Meiji period, the government led a trend toward "state capitalism." This can be identified, for example, in the construction of government-operated steel and textile factories. Even though the ensuing economic development, private capital growth, industrial diversification, and political democratization worked to weaken the state's industrial control, economic control which accompanied the start of the Sino-Japanese War again strengthened the state's involvement in the economy. The approach of economic and regional integration devised during the construction of the Greater East Asian Co-Prosperity, which merged the public and the private sectors (Akamatsu 1937), was continued in the process of postwar Japanese economic recovery and regional economic integration with East Asia. Published by the World Bank in 1993, the report titled "The East Asian Miracle" (World Bank 1993) attracted attention of researchers and policymakers in Japan as well as abroad as a development paradigm, an alternative to the American-style liberal capitalism doctrine. While developing countries positively evaluated the role of the state in suppressing the "exploitative" aspect of globalized capitalism, the United States criticized Japanese-style capitalism due to its perceived "unfair" advantage from the point of view of international competition (Wade 2003).

The 1997–1998 Asian economic crisis and the subsequent response of each of the affected countries was a major challenge to the "East Asian model." Taking advantage of IMF emergency loans, Korea, which had already stopped receiving official development assistance (ODA) from Japan, performed an extensive deregulation and liberalization of the system. Thus, Korea was ahead of Japan's "Koizumi reforms" in the selection of economic "winners" and "losers." In China as well as in many other East Asian countries, the so-called tied aid in the form of Japanese ODA funds flowing directly back through purchasing capital goods from Japan was largely eliminated. Nevertheless, there was continuous close negotiation between the ODA plans and Japanese businesses' plans of overseas investment, production relocation, and parts trade (Hatch and Yamamura 1996).

The large-scale relocation of manufacturing from Japan to Asia due to the appreciation of the Japanese yen that originated from the Plaza Accord was a step toward Japanese economy's shift of focus toward the service sector. Japan's economy increased the amount of earnings from financial services and intellectual property and as a result increasingly shared interests with Western countries in terms of the elimination of regulations impeding business development or the promotion of stricter intellectual property protection in developing countries. While income from overseas investment increased, Japan's trade surplus has shrunk and has even fallen into deficit in some recent years. Japan has come to possess an economic structure similar to Western countries. In the area of setting up investment rules it has established an identity of a developed investing country (Sato 2011).

The 2008 global financial crisis revealed the negligence in the U.S. supervision of its own financial companies, which were the center of the globalized financial business. Thus, a reconsideration of the U.S.-style liberal capitalism, which was becoming the global standard, was about to begin. With regards to the liberalization of world trade, multilateral negotiations at the WTO had been in a deadlock even before the 2008 crisis, accelerating the signing of bilateral or regionally limited free trade agreements (FTAs) (Sato 2006). Neither the making of investment rules was actively pursued through multilateral agreements. Instead it has remained centered on bilateral agreements. Japan decided to participate in the Trans-Pacific Partnership (TPP) negotiations, however, as the U.S. barriers left in the automotive industry handicapped the Japanese exporters, while domestic political resistance in Japan toward liberalization of the agricultural sector limited U.S. and other exporters' potentials.

China has overtaken Japan in terms of GDP and now occupies a larger part of the East Asian economy, through a mercantilist economic model formerly adopted by Japan. This model rests on making a large surplus in trade with and drawing investments from developed countries. It puts restrictions on free transnational business activities, promoting inward transfer of technology while protecting and fostering domestic enterprises and regulating capital movements. Governments with this model also tend to overlook the theft of intellectual property by domestic companies and are reluctant to open the service industry market. FTAs with developed countries are only established with small economies, in order to maximize negotiation leverage to force many exceptions to liberal trade. China differs from Japan due to the lack of regional economic planning beyond its national boundary and a large cumulative investment in other countries. Chinese FTAs with developing countries focus on procuring material resources and food for its own country, while a heavy focus is placed on selling its domestic industrial products. In this respect, Chinese leaving of development of neighboring countries to pure market forces is no different from the U.S.-style liberal capitalism model.

Japan has internationally projected development ideologies such as the former "Japanese model" and "the East Asian miracle," but can they play a central role in the process of regional integration? (Sato and Hirata 2008) In contrast to the previous model centered on regionalization of the production network in the manufacturing industry, can Japan present a comprehensive new model that includes the service industry and agriculture? Furthermore, what are the conditions for the model presented by Japan to be accepted in East Asia or the wider Asia-Pacific region? These points will be considered in this chapter.

Japanese-Style Capitalism

The Origins of State-Led Capitalism

After abolishing the isolationism of the Edo period, one of the pressing issues of the Meiji Restoration Government was to open up Japan to Western countries and to develop and strengthen industrial and military power. Japan did not have enough private capitalists, and in order to compete with advanced Western countries it was therefore necessary to force the concentration of capital on the state scale. In the process of transition from light industry to heavy industry, state-operated factories (e.g., Tomioka Silk Mill, Yawata Steel Works) were first constructed and later sold off to the private sector. In the wartime economy following the start of the Sino-Japanese War, military control was again strengthened. The post-WW2 process of dissolution and liberalization of *zaibatsu* (mega industrial conglomerates) was reversed after the Occupation ended by the Ministry of International Trade and Industry (MITI) and its directions (Johnson 1982).

Industrial Policies in the Period of High Growth

In the postwar reconstruction period, Japan aimed to catch up with and overtake the industries which were already led by the Western capitalist countries. Compared to the remarkable diversification and quick innovations of today's economy, the economy at that time was much more uniform and the competition there was also unilinear. In order to catch up, the policies MITI designed were a combination of capital concentration, investment in priority technologies, preferential research and development while incorporating foreign advanced technologies, and protection from external competition in the domestic market for a limited duration (Johnson 1982). The Ministry of International Trade and Industry was, however, not omnipotent. Occasional successful examples of businesses such as Sony and Honda in defiance of the MITI policy attest to this point. Nevertheless, in general, until the mid-1970s oil crisis and capital liberalization, the industrial policies of MITI spearheaded the development of the Japanese manufacturing industry. However, MITI's industrial policy repeatedly failed in the subsequent economic transition to the service industry, software development or information system administration, and lost its previous prestige before the period of further economic diversification in the twenty-first century.

Socialist Protection Policies

While the export-oriented economic development of Japan was mainly led by large businesses which accounted for a large part of the GDP, a large part of Japan's domestic employment has been occupied by small- and medium-sized enterprises as well as the primary sector. The gap between companies that are able to compete internationally and the ones that are not (winners and losers) widened during the economic liberalization under the Koizumi administration. The liberalization policy was reversed against the market trends by the "resisting forces," Japan's employment policy tended to protect and maintain employment in industries where competitiveness declined. The main reason for this is the so-called iron triangle, which consists of the close relationship of the supervisory authorities and the supervised industry groups, and the involvement of *zoku* (special interest) politicians within the Diet affiliated with special interest groups (Sato 1995).

At the same time, national subsidies to municipal governments and public works expenditure have slowed the depopulation of agricultural and fishing villages and contributed to social stability by preventing the increase of unemployment. Therefore, the policies have retained wide support even in recent years. The introduction of a tax-exempted donation scheme known as the "hometown tax," which allows taxpayers to choose municipalities to donate to, is also based on this national sentiment. Yet, not only due to rapid changes in the industrial structure, but also because of demographic changes (e.g., the declining birth-rate and the rapidly aging society), motorization, proliferation of the Internet, and the change in consumption behavior, the existing economic regulations are no longer able to fulfill their original purpose of maintaining social harmony. Moreover, as the financial burden of maintaining such regulations has reached its limits (Grimes 2002; Mabuchi 1994), bold liberalization has become an urgent policy issue.

Administrative and Financial Reform

More than thirty years have passed since the proclamation of the "administrative reform" by the Nakasone administration in the 1980s, but there is still a long way to go. There are examples of different administrations fulfilling their priority tasks (e.g., Nakasone's privatization of national railways or Koizumi's privatization of the Japan Post); however, liberalization has not progressed enough to revitalize the entire Japanese economy. The Koizumi administration temporarily arrested the increasing of the cumulative national debt per GDP. After that, however, the cumulative debt continues to increase, today due to the financial policies under Prime Minister Abe's policy of inflation-targeting known as Abenomics. The increase of the consumption tax rate has hampered economic recovery, trapping the country in a vicious cycle.

Collapse of the Bubble Economy

Looking back past the Asian economic crisis, the 1989–1990 collapse of the stock and estate bubble was a forewarning of the global financial crisis in 2008. While the long-term appreciation of the yen after the Plaza Accord and the liberalization of the financial sector attracted overseas funds, domestic and foreign funds allowed for speculation in the stock and real estate markets. Based on the manipulated collateral value of domestic assets, Japanese financial institutions created an unbalanced state of finance, in which further financing for property development was provided based on the inflated value of the property. It was inevitable that the financial economy, which was inflated over the fundamentals of the real economy, would rupture; and the magnitude of the rupture of the resulting crisis would be even larger. This is because in a world of progressing globalization and information technology, no proper measures have been put in place to tackle excessively financialized economic activities (Strange 1998).

The Asian Economic Crisis and Reconsideration of the East Asian Model

The Plaza Accord and Foreign Investment

As trade disputes between Japan and the United States intensified in the late 1980s, the free trade advocating Reagan administration aimed at improving the U.S. trade balance by adjusting foreign exchange rates. At the meeting of G7 Finance Ministries at the Plaza Hotel in New York, the yen together with the Deutsche Mark were revalued, and through the first and (perhaps) the last cooperative intervention between each country's central bank, the yen was significantly appreciated. In about six months after the beginning of the intervention, the yen increased against the U.S. dollar in value from about 240 yen per dollar to approximately 120 yen per dollar, triggering foreign investment by domestic manufacturers who were displeased with the sharp decline in their export competitiveness (Funabashi 1992).

Overseas Infrastructure Development through Official Development Assistance

The driving force behind the miraculous economic growth in East Asia was undoubtedly private investment from Japan. It is worth noting that private investment was preceded by infrastructure development in investment destinations in the form of government ODA. Infrastructure such as transportation, electricity, and water supply are considered public goods; and individual companies considering overseas investment (especially small- and medium-sized enterprises that are the main focus in the initial stage) cannot build the infrastructure themselves. Therefore, attracting businesses is made easier if the target country's government, enterprises considering investment, and the Japanese government jointly work to study each project and develop appropriate infrastructure (Hatch and Yamamura 1996; Kojima 2004). In Japan, government-academia exchange is facilitated by the Institute of Developing Economies, a research organization under the Japan External Trade Organization (JETRO), which is under the supervision of the Ministry of Economy, Trade and Industry (formerly Ministry of International Trade and Industry). It has carried out research on economic assistance to emerging Asian countries, which has also been reflected in ODA policies.

Production Transfer and Parts Trade Network

Taking advantage of the benefits of cheap labor force, but considering the technological gap, the initial overseas relocation of production bases by the

Japanese firms was centered on the final product assembly process. However, as more companies in the same industry relocated overseas, the cost competition further shifted onto the parts manufacturing process; and the total number of *keiretsu* (groups of affiliated companies) and subcontractors relocating overseas rose. The multinationalization of production networks by Japanese companies not only increased the trade between Japan and other Asian countries, but also stimulated the trade between Asian countries and increased the ratio of intra-regional trade in East Asia (Hatch and Yamamura 1996).

The Asian Bubble

As dollar-based fund liquidity was provided in order to repay the debt of countries with major national debt, namely the United States and states of Latin America (Brazil, Mexico, Argentina, etc.), the financial liberalization of Asian countries since the 1990s has lured abundant capital that circulated the world in search of high-yield investment destinations. The growth of Asian economy based on industrial development stimulated housing development in urban areas, and a construction bubble similar to the one in Japan in the late 1980s was observed in major Asian cities. The so-called mismatch problem caused by using money borrowed from short-term funds into the financing of long-term development projects set in motion the eventual burst of the bubble. Furthermore, short-term funds from overseas investors flowed into the deregulated stock market, greatly amplifying fluctuations in market prices. In Thailand where the Asian economic crisis began, the currency depreciation quickly grew into a negative spiral as a result of massive withdrawal of overseas short-term funds (Sakakibara 1998). In an attempt to stop the depreciation, the central bank intervened in the market and depleted its foreign currency reserves. The crisis was finally relieved by the IMF emergency lending. The crisis spilled over to Indonesia, causing a similar negative spiral. This was again relieved by the IMF. Moreover, Malaysia temporarily limited the withdrawal of capital and protected the currency value only with a modest devaluation. As conditions for the relief, the IMF requested structural reforms (deregulation and liberalization) in Thailand, Indonesia, and later South Korea. However, critical voices against the IMF remedies instead cite Malaysia's success.

Currency Pegs and Intra-regional Trade

In the East Asian region, economic division of labor, the transboundary production chain and expansion of intra-company trade, progress in economic integration, and increase in the ratio of intra-regional trade are all connected to the propensity toward currency cooperation which eliminates the risks of exchange rate fluctuation and exchange fees. Although complete currency integration similar to Euro is unlikely, the blueprint for currency cooperation that precedes such integration in the form of the Asian Currency Unit (ACU) modeled on the European Currency Unit (ECU) has already been announced (Sakakibara 1998). Furthermore, the Chiang Mai Initiative aims to foster cooperation for stabilizing the exchange rates. This can also be considered a preceding stage of a monetary union. After the Asian economic crisis, the central banks of Japan, China, and Korea plus ASEAN countries have created a mechanism that allows for the exchange of foreign currency reserves. This mechanism increased the financial defense capabilities of participating currencies against foreign exchange speculators. The Japan-proposed Asian Monetary Fund (AMF) concept did not materialize due to opposition from the US, EU, and China. Yet, as East Asian economic integration further deepens, it is possible that the trend will be reactivated. However, given that the idea of self-defense against the constant long-term depreciation of the dollar was behind the European currency cooperation (Cohen 2000; Eichengreen 2008), Japan's turning to financial easing in order to reflate the economy should hurt credibility of the Japanese leadership. Not only the U.S. dollar, but also the yen has depreciated against emerging market currencies as a result of its reflationary policy. Hence Japan has no more strong leadership that spoke of a "internationalization of the yen." The Chinese Yuan might become the next common currency in Asia instead.

Changes in Japan's Economic Structure and Identity

Changes in Trade Structure

The long-term transformation of Japan's industrial structure has caused a decline in the overall trade surplus for about 15 years, occasionally even leading to a deficit. Japan-U.S. trade friction was hardly mentioned since the year 2000. The mutual importance in trade on a relative term declined, as China has become a more important partner for both Japan and the United States, and Japan's trade surplus with the United States had shrunk significantly. The strong yen and overseas relocation of main industrial production drove a decrease in exports and an increase in imports on a relative term. Export of capital goods to Asia increased, but product import growth was much larger. A part of the import of capital goods that appear in China's trade statistics are due to Japanese companies investing in China, and China's export statistics include various Japanese components assembled in China into final products.

The "service industry" has become the core of the economy, accounting for 60% of the Japanese GDP, but service trade is far below the trade volume of industrial products. Previously, service trade in Japan yielded a deficit. However, in recent years, it has demonstrated a continuous surplus trend with Taiwan since 2003, with the ASEAN region since 2006, and with China since 2010. The service trade deficit with the United States is shrinking, but it remains on a high level.

Reduction of the Trade Surplus in the Current Account Balance and Transition to an Investment Economy

As a country with limited natural resources, Japan was said to have no other choice but to adopt a strategy of a processing trade nation, but nowadays this explanation is only partially correct. The proportion of trade surplus in Japan's international current account balance has shrunk, and since 2005 the income from overseas investments has exceeded the trade surplus. In other words, although many of the globally competitive Japanese businesses are still within the manufacturing industry, the transformation of Japan into a major investment economy has implications for the country's stance toward international investment rules, trade balance, and foreign exchange policies. The parts of the manufacturing industry that remain in Japan are limited to processes with technological sophistication levels not suitable for relocating overseas. Through a period of trade friction in the 1980s and 1990s, the localization of Japanese automobile production in the U.S. market proceeded due to political reasons. In order to secure profits within the framework of voluntary export restriction quota, production inside Japan shifted toward luxury export models. The deepening of investment relations between Japan and the United States, such as the expansion of automobile production bases in the United States, was carried out in accordance with OECD investment-related rules and hence went relatively smoothly despite the highly politicized background of its origin. Also, even though the gap between the contents of intellectual property laws and copyright laws in the two countries still remains, patent laws related to the manufacturing industry have greatly been harmonized. Thus, at least in the manufacturing industry, a mutually free investment environment was established by the 1980s.

On the other hand, under the Chinese mercantilist industrial policy, Japanese companies entering China's labor-intensive industry have often been required to create a joint venture with local businesses or pushed toward forced technology transfers. Compared to local businesses in the same field, they have received discriminatory treatment and have faced restrictions on the transfer of capital and profit. Political subordination of an investment receiving country by the investing country and its businesses (as suggested by Marxist political economy) has proven not to be a case for China with its massive market luring foreign investors. Benefitting from the absence of multilateral rules regarding investment and protection of intellectual property rights, China has skillfully driven wedges between developed countries by bilaterally negotiating with them. While cooperating with other developed countries, Japan as an investor can benefit from improving the investment climate in China. However, such efforts are still lacking. The strong yen boosts overseas investment, and the income from those investments supports a large part of Japan's balance of payments. Abenomics with its massive supply of financial liquidity has the effect of inducing depreciation of yen. In effect, therefore, it follows the traditional paradigm focused on trade surplus, essentially going against the structural reform of the Japanese manufacturing industry.

The Global Financial Crisis and Criticism of American Neoliberalism

The Issue of Leverage

While the balance sheet to assure transparency in the financial economy remains underdeveloped, the financial economy continues expanding. Thus, the gap between the financial economy and the real economy becomes a problem. In transactions between international banks under the BIS (International Settlement Bank) capital adequacy regulations, the risk of bankruptcy can be quantified and restricted. Nevertheless, in case of transactions with financial institutions other than banks, there are many areas where risks are not fully visualized and regulated (Strange 1998). The ratio of security deposits in commodity futures such as foreign exchange, precious metals, grains, crude oil, and the balance between risk and collateral in investment in various financial derivatives such as hedge funds, is the responsibility of each individual company. In most cases, there is no guideline, let alone universal government regulations for the industry. In addition to the risks of the banking and insurance industries, the banking and insurance industry funds are used in such areas where regulation and supervision are weak, creating an invisible state of leverage. As a result, since the 1990s there has been a pattern of frequent unexpected chain failures of financial institutions causing economic crises.

Information Society and the Market—Provision of Trust

In a capitalist market, it is impossible to make an investment decision without assessing future profitability. However, the barrier between the spot market (which handles commodities for immediate delivery) and the futures market becomes lower, and the futures market remains not fully regulated and monitored. Buying and selling is conducted owing to the ability of obtaining more accurate information in superhuman speed. The competition in obtaining accurate information faster has entered the illegal domain of insider trading. Moreover, controlling information per se by disseminating convenient (or even false) information to time buying and selling on the market is commonly practiced. Most of this essentially circumvents the law, since there are no rules enforcing effective control. The trust that underpins regulated economic activity has been secured by the government. Unregulated information competition means that the function of providing trust for economic information is left to free competition. From a long-term perspective, sources providing unobjective and inaccurate information (securities analysts, rating agencies, etc.) might perhaps be weeded out by the principles of the market. However, when information is spread globally in real time through the Internet, the control of competing information with a difference of a few seconds, rather than information quality, is directly linked to profit.

Global Economic Governance—Liberalization and Supervisory Responsibility

In a globalized economy, the role of the state, an entity responsible for regulating and supervising economic activities, has been relatively reduced. Advocating liberal capitalism in the 1980s, the policies of Reagan and Thatcher, who led the United States and the Great Britain, respectively, were ahead of other developed countries. They opened a path for the financial industries of both countries to play an active global role. While there is universal consistency between the Washington Consensus urging liberalization through structural reform in developing countries as conditions of the World Bank and IMF financing, and the United States abolishing its own economic regulations and actively introducing foreign capital, they were indifferent toward the negative impact of unregulated global capital movement on small-scale developing economies.

Chinese Mercantilism and Globalization

Industrial Policies in Industrial Product Trade

Chinese industrialization went through stages of fostering labor-intensive industries and small and medium enterprises in the 1980s and capital-intensive industries in the 1990s, with economic growth owing to large-scale state-owned businesses. Since the 2000s China has aimed to shift its economy toward technology-intensive industries through privatization of state-owned enterprises and technology transfer. China has sought to expand into foreign markets with its mass-produced industrial products, and by joining the WTO in 2001 it has received most favored nation (MFN) treatment from its major trading partners. However, in an attempt to promote domestic production, China's mercantilist trade policy imposes high tariffs on imports of finished products and key parts. Furthermore, the policy of maintaining the exchange rate against the U.S. dollar lower by artificially depreciating the yuan aimed at promoting exports, luring foreign capital in, and fostering domestic production of manufacturing components. China's mercantilist trade policy conflicts with existing international trade rules, as seen in the overwhelming number of cases in which China is sued at the WTO dispute resolution panel. China's mercantilist economic policies are evading the law as much as violating them. In other words, in areas where international rules are not clear, China applies policies based on its convenient interpretations, resisting the efforts of trading partners to create more explicit rules and try to regulate evasive mercantilist policies.

Stagnation of New Multilateral Trade Rules—Intellectual Property and the Service Industry

The most prominent aspect of the Chinese mercantilism is the resistance against the developed countries' effort to strengthen intellectual property protection and liberalize the service industry trade. In line with global market capitalism, a developed country which has moved its industrial production in fields that had lost their competitiveness to newly industrializing countries wants to expand overseas in the newly competitive field of the service industry. But GATT (General Agreement on Trade and Tariffs) trade rules were originally created with industrial products in mind, and the later added GATS (General Agreement on Trade in Services) is not keeping up with a need to expand its scope of rules to govern the rapidly diversifying service industry trade. Furthermore, as the tariff rates on industrial products between developed countries approach zero, the attractiveness of tariff cuts to newly industrializing countries decreases; and it has thus become more difficult for the developed countries to draw concessions from the newly industrializing countries in multilateral negotiations. In the Doha Round, China together with India representing newly industrializing and developing countries resisted comprehensive market-opening demands from economically developed countries.

Bilateral Free Trade Agreements

When the pursuit of multilateral free trade in the WTO came to a deadlock in the 2000s, the trend of forming bilateral free trade agreements accelerated. The three developed economic poles (United States, Japan, and EU) represented large-scale economies with high economic effects. Yet, due to their conflicting domestic interests, politically difficult free trade agreements between them was postponed. They have instead prioritized bilateral agreements with smaller partners that are relatively easy. Due to the difference in bargaining power owing to market size and other factors, the three advanced economies have often made exceptions in liberalization in order to protect domestic producers. Still, the developed countries did not abandon the WTO-based global free trade. In contrast, China's free trade agreements with smaller partners have lower degrees of freedom. As far as the three poles are concerned, free trade negotiations in all bilateral pairs have started, and the bilateral agreement between Japan and the EU and the first-stage agreement between Japan and the United States have been concluded.

At present, Japan appears to be the lynchpin of global free trade. However, the path to its present role as well as the prospect of future global free trade are not smooth. Avoiding bilaterally negotiating free trade with the United States, Japan pursued a two-thronged strategy under the Trans-Pacific Partnership Agreement (TPP) negotiation and the Regional Comprehensive Economic Partnership (RCEP) negotiation, using the existing division of industrial production in East Asia as a pivot. Small economies (New Zealand, Chile, Singapore, and Brunei) willing to embrace a higher degree of trade liberalization but unable to take leadership in the RCEP grouping launched the TPP negotiation. The United States joining the TPP negotiation led Japan to leverage the RCEP against TPP and vice versa.

Trump's withdrawal from the TPP negotiation in 2017 passed the onus of leading TPP in the Japanese hands, while his demand to negotiate a bilateral free trade agreement with Japan under a threat of trade sanction brought back the pre-WTO challenge of more politicized trade relations with the United States (Sato 2019). With China under the same sort of bilateral U.S. pressure (at even a greater extent), Japan and China in late 2018 tactically put aside their political discord and pledged economic cooperation in the first summit meeting in five years. Their joint effort toward an early conclusion of the RCEP ratification, however, is unlikely. India for domestic opposition from both its industrial and agricultural sectors withdrew from the RCEP negotiation in late 2019, and Japan (which wants to renegotiate for India's return) and China (which would happily sideline India) disagree, clouding the prospect of the treaty's ratifications despite its signing in November 2020. The stagnation of the RCEP has robbed Japan of its hope to leverage it in a negotiation vis-à-vis the United States. Japan's effort to accelerate signing of the free trade agreement with EU, on the other hand, succeeded in the wake of the U.S. withdrawal from the TPP (Sato 2019). However, Japan had to accept an illiberal fist-stage free trade agreement with the United States, which completely excluded the automobile sector the United States wanted to protect.

Investment Rules

As industrialized countries de-industrialize, moving their production bases and shifting their economies toward the service industry, expansion of investment rules becomes important. Investment rules created in the 1960s and 1970s, the prime of Marxism, embodied the minimum compromise in the fierce conflict between developed and developing countries which merely banned requisition and nationalization of foreign investment without compensation.

However, within the present globalized economy, the motivation of developing countries for attracting foreign investment has increased. Some large-scale industrializing countries (especially China) have emphasized the strategy of domestic economic growth supported by foreign investment. They have employed skillful political tactics when negotiating with foreign investors and have been able to draw out favorable conditions for themselves, unlike smaller developing countries which cannot leverage their unattractively small domestic markets. Developed countries have also recognized investment rules as one of the mercantilist policy tools of the newly industrializing countries and have aimed to create international rules that favor themselves. Nevertheless, Multilateral Agreement on Investment (MAI) negotiations even only among developed countries came to a deadlock, and agreements with developing countries are bilateral. China has resisted the renewal and expansion of old investment agreements with developed countries, and has continued to enforce technology transfers, restrict repatriation of profits, and favor domestic enterprises. Despite Japan's enthusiasm based on the Japan-Korea agreement that meets the latest developed country standards, the Japan-China-Korea trilateral investment agreement ended with China having its own way by not granting full national treatment to foreign investors (Sato 2011).

China's Belt and Road Initiative and Infrastructure Development

China announced its Belt and Road Initiative (BRI) as a model of economic coprosperity with developing countries in the broad Indo-Pacific littoral and the Eurasian landmass. At the macroeconomic level, the BRI was a way of recirculating the country's growing balance-of-payments surplus, in order to ease upward pressure on the renminbi (RMB). As a means of financing the BRI projects, the Asian Infrastructure Investment Bank (AIIB) was launched with a Chinese control. The U.S.-European-dominated global multilateral financial institutions under their "Washington Consensus" had assigned reduced role to national governments in economic development, and this trend even affected infrastructure development. As a result, the World Bank loans had shifted to poverty reduction and human resource development, while liberalization of building and running basic infrastructure in developing countries was explored under liberalization of service trade and government procurements. The Asian Development Bank (ADB) under heavy Japanese influence did not go to the extreme of the World Bank, but market-based feasibility in decisions for infrastructure development was more rigorously explored than Japan's own domestic infrastructure development (which has been a "pork" issue for the ruling party politicians, Sato 2005).

The United States and Japan declined China's invitation to take part in the AIIB in fear that their money would simply serve China's strategic purposes (Yoshimatsu 2018). The duplication with the ADB missions was another reason. However, they agreed to increase China's share and voting rights in the ADB, and the AIIB agreed to work with ADB in coordinating loan decisions. However, China's BRI projects have not only created pork in the recipient states and promoted corruptions in their domestic politics, but also heavy debt dependency in these countries. In fear that China would exploit such dependency to advance its maritime geostrategic outreach via leasing of port facilities, the United States and Japan in their "Free and Open Indo-Pacific" strategy have started addressing infrastructure development aid to the region. In criticizing China's loans, the United States is in effect moving away from the Washington Consensus, if too slow, too small of a step. The competition among the donors in getting contracts back to their domestic construction industry and service operators will likely promote more sustainable and less predatory aid model.

Is It Possible to Present a New Japanese Capitalist Model?

In the past, there was a unique "Japanese" capitalist economic model, but with the liberalization and changes in the structure of the Japanese economy during the 1990s, convergence with the American-style free capitalism considerably advanced (Kitschelt et al. eds. 1999). At the same time, East Asian economic integration centered on Japan and China, which has adopted the

Japanese model even more skillfully, has deepened. The new model of the Japanese economy promoting increased relative weight of investment income from overseas markets, including the service and knowledge-intensive industries, is neither the previous Japanese mercantilist model nor the U.S.-style free capitalism model with a heavy emphasis on financial services of all sorts of technologically inspired but poorly regulated derivatives. Instead, the Japanese model has to be an eclectic one.

Under the current situation where the creation of economic rules through multilateral processes is stagnating in both trade and investment, it is difficult for Japan to bridge the confrontation between the developed countries and the developing countries. Chinese mercantilism and American free capitalism both promote domestic economic disparity. The fact that they are both concerned with the resulting social unrest suggests the usefulness of policy elements (protection of agriculture and SMEs, securing local employment, etc.) within the old Japanese model that alleviates such problems (Sawa 2000).

However, it is not easy to paraphrase (systematize and utilize as a macro model) Japan's unique experience into universal and previously easily understandable values and principles. Trump's populism-based rise in the United States quickly reversed the U.S. embrace of economic globalism under the three previous presidents between 1993 and 2016. Moreover, the U.S. economic nationalism is not a mere tactical move to bring China into line of the previously U.S.-supported global liberal capitalism. Rather, the United States is reexamining its own economic model, in light of the catching up by China and the growing strategic rivalry with it.

Japan has to cope with two disparate models of political economy (Chinese and American) and a way of realistically maintaining individual relationships with them. For that purpose, it is important to refrain from a unique Japanese "value projection" and visualizing the values' contradiction with the American and Chinese models. Instead, it is necessary to adopt the advantages from both of them. Rather than in multilateral negotiations where agreement is unlikely, the rule-making should use multiple bilateral and regional negotiations as mutual levers while aiming for maximum profits.

Furthermore, elements of "America First" populism contain return to localities. Although a full-scale reversal of globalization in this age of liberal information and communication flows is unlikely, the elite-led and a cookie-cutter-like uniformity of globalization is being revised (Murakami 1992; Sawa 2000). The growing strategic rivalry between China and the United States does not have the kind of ideological bipolarity between Marxism and laissez-faire capitalism. Today's China is internally more elitist and laisse-faire capitalist than Japan, but lacks democratic governance to tame their malaises. Though U.S. populism is misguided in many ways (such as its racist and parochial attitude), it does correctly identify the twin dangers of globalization, which robs social cohesion of the United States for the sake of overall economic efficiency, and China, which robs the United States with its mercantilist and selective engagement with globalization. The lessons the United States are learning are very much found in Japan's history of pragmatically seeking like-minded allies without fully embracing any dogma.

References

Akamatsu, K. (1937). *Sangyo Tousei Ron* 『産業統制論』[Industrial Control]. Tokyo: Chikura shobo.

Cohen, B. (2000). *The geography of money*. Ithaca, NY: Cornell University Press.

Eichengreen, B. (2008). *Globalizing capital: A history of the international monetary system* (2nd ed.). Princeton, NJ: Princeton University Press.

Funabashi, Y. (1992). *Tsuuka Retsuretsu* 『通貨烈々』[Fierce Currencies]. Tokyo: Asahi Shimbunsha.

Grimes, W.W. (2002). *Unmaking the Japanese miracle: Macroeconomic politics, 1985–2000*. Ithaca, NY: Cornell University Press.

Hatch, W., & Yamamura, K. (1996). *Asia in Japan's embrace: Building a regional production alliance*. Cambridge: Cambridge University Press.

Johnson, C. (1982). *MITI and the Japanese miracle: The growth of industrial policy, 1925–1975*. Redwood, CA: Stanford University Press.

Kitschelt, H., Lange, P., Marks, G., & Stephens, J.D. (Eds.). (1999). *Continuity and change in contemporary capitalism*. Cambridge: Cambridge University Press.

Kojima, K. (2004). *Gankougata Keizai Hattenron, Dai ikkan "Nihon Keizai, Ajia Keizai, Sekai Keizai," Dai nikan "Ajia to Sekai no Shinchitsujo"* 『雁行型経済発展論』第１巻「日本経済・アジア経済・世界経済」、第２巻「アジアと世界の新秩序」[The theory of flying geese pattern economic development. Volume 1 "Japanese Economy, Asian Economy and World Economy", Volume 2 "New Order of Asia and the World"]. Tokyo: Bunshindo.

Mabuchi, M. (1994). *Okurasho Tousei no Seijikeizaigaku* 『大蔵省統制の政治経済学』[Political economy of control by the Ministry of Finance]. Tokyo: Chuokoronsha.

Murakami, T. (1992). *Han-Koten no Seijikeizaigaku (Jo)*『反古典の政治経済学』（上）「進歩史観の黄昏」 [Anti-classical Political Economy (Vol. 1). The Twilight of View of Progressionist History]. Tokyo: Chuokoronsha.

Sakakibara, E. (1998). *Kokusai Kinyu no Genba—Shijo Shihon Shugi no Kiki wo Koete.* 国際金融の現場—市場資本主義の危機を超えて [The field of international finance—beyond the crisis of market capitalism]. Tokyo: PHP Kenkyūjo.

Sato, Y. (1995). Dawn of Japanese politics: Evaluating the political changes in Japan through a pluralist perspective. *Japanese Studies Bulletin*, *15*(3), 47–62.

Sato, Y. (2005). Developmentalism, corruption, and marketisation of public policies in Japan. In N. Tarlin (Ed.), *Corruption and good governance in Asia*. Routledge Curzon Studies in the Modern History of Asia, no. 30 (pp. 23–38). New York: Routledge.

Sato, Y. (2006). Japan and the emerging free-trade agreements in the Asia-Pacific: An active leadership? In Y. Sato & S. Limaye (Eds.), *Japan in a Dynamic Asia: Coping with the new security challenges* (pp. 37–68). New York: Lexington Books.

Sato, Y. (2011). Substituting multilateralism, guiding trilateralism: The Japan-ROK investment agreement in the growing East Asian regionalism. In M. Söderberg (Ed.), *Changing power relations in northeast Asia: Implications for relations between Japan and South Korea* (pp. 138–153). New York: Routledge.

Sato, Y. (2019). Japan's Indo-Pacific strategy: The old geography and the new strategic reality. *Journal of Indo-Pacific Affairs*, *2*(4), 107–119.

Sato, Y., & Hirata, K. (2008). Introduction: Constructivism, rationalism, and the study of norms in Japanese foreign policy. In Yoichiro Sato and Keiko Hirat (Eds.), *Norms, interests, and power in Japanese foreign policy* (pp. 3–17). Houndmills: Palgrave-Macmillan.

Sawa, T. (2000). *Shijo Shugi no Shuen—Nihon Keizai wo Dousuru no ka.* 市場主義の終焉—日本経済をどうするのか [The end of marketism: What to do about the Japanese economy?]. Tokyo: Iwanami Shoten.

Strange, S. (1998). *Mad money: When markets outgrow governments.* Ann Arbor: University of Michigan Press.

Wade, R. (2003). *Governing the market: Economic theory and the role of government in East Asian industrialization.* Princeton, NJ: Princeton University Press.

World Bank. (1993). *The East Asian miracle: Economic growth and public policy* (World Bank Policy Research Report). Oxford: Oxford University Press.

Yoshimatsu, H. (2018). New dynamics in Sino-Japanese rivalry: Sustaining infrastructure development in Asia. *Journal of Contemporary China*, *27*(113), 719–734.

5. *National Identity, National Pride, and Armed Force in Japan: How to Verify the Existence of Pacifist Culture in Japan*

Takashi Hosoda
Charles University

Introduction

In the past decades, many scholars have attempted to apply constructivism to explain Japan's postwar antimilitary culture (Katzenstein 1996; Berger 1998), although some point out existence of the Japan-U.S. alliance (Miyashita 2006) or buck-passing to the United States by Japan (Lind 2004) is the major element to explain Japan's low-key postwar security approach.
Over the past several years, due to North Korea's nuclear brinkmanship and the coercive responses from U.S. President Donald Trump, the security environment around Japan worsened dramatically, even though a kind of moratorium works nowadays. In particular, Japan is concerned about North Korea's nuclear program and the prospects for denuclearization. In Neorealist theory, when a country faces a serious security threat, it should arm with a sufficient level of military might to protect its territory and sovereignty. This means Japan should counter the North Korean nuclear threat with nuclear deterrence supplied by its ally or, if that "nuclear umbrella" becomes less reliable, going nuclear itself. According to opinion polls conducted by Genron NPO, however, Japanese people are clearly more hesitant to arm their country with nuclear weapons than the South Koreans (see Table 5.1).

It is natural to suppose that the Japanese don't need to rush indigenous nuclear armament as long as the U.S. continues to supply "extended nuclear deterrence" (a nuclear umbrella) for Japan. However, the Japanese have a much more consolidated consciousness of nuclear weapons due to the

	Japanese				Korean			
	agree	disagree	don't know	no reply	agree	disagree	don't know	no reply
2016	5.1	80.3	14.5	0.1	59.0	36.1	4.9	0.0
2017	9.0	74.7	16.3	0.0	67.2	26.7	6.1	0.0
2018	11.3	65.5	23.2	0.0	43.3	50.3	6.4	0.0

Table 5.1: What do you think about possible nuclear armament by your country? (%). Source: 6th Japan-ROK joint opinion research, Genron NPO, June 2018

country's experiences with atomic bombing. Table 5.2 shows the feelings of ordinary Japanese regarding various approaches to improving Japan's image in the world. Because Japan is the only country ever bombed with nuclear weapons, many Japanese recognize that explaining those experiences will do more to strengthen Japan's position in the world than beefing up the country's Self Defense Forces (SDF).

Improving Japan's position in the world through diplomatic efforts	Strengthening its economic power (influence)	Explaing importance of peace to the world as a state which has experiences of Atomic-bombing	Improving relations with Asian countries	Beefing up the Self Defense Forces
28.2%	21.9%	21.8%	13.3%	1.9%

Table 5.2: What should Japan do to improve Japan's position in the world? (%). Source: Opinion research on seventy years since the end of WWII, NHK, 2015

Over the past three decades, China has been rapidly beefing up its military with no accountability or transparency. According to the *2018 Defense White Paper of Japan*, the official figure for the Peoples Republic of China (PRC)'s military budget in 2018 was almost fifty-one times bigger than it was in 1989. And *China Power* of CSIS points out that China's actual defense spending may have been upward of four times larger than the officially announced figure. In this context, why would Japanese governments, especially the Abe administration, usually described as "hawkish," not drastically increase defense spending to catch up with China's pace? The Japanese people typically respond to this question by asserting that Japan is a pacifist state, or pointing out that Article 9 of its Constitution renounces war, or characterizing the identity of postwar Japan as represented by the so-called Yoshida Doctrine, a strategy for allocating resources that prioritizes *butter* (domestic economic interests and development) over *guns* (increased military spending) with accepting U.S. military presence for defense.

According to *Opinion research on seventy years since the end of WWII* conducted by NHK in 2014, 87% of the respondents were proud of "a peaceful society without engaging in a war" as a feature of postwar Japan, and want to keep it this way in the future. In postwar Japan, Japanese naturally think "war is evil" and prefer to avoid the use of armed force to settle disputes. There clearly is a kind of socially shared culture or ethos of peace in Japan (or at least a sedimented identity, as we call it in the introduction to this edited volume), which influences the choices made by political actors. Thus, it is necessary to tear down the analysis of Japan's pacifist culture from the structural side, because national security is not solely the province of political actors; the discourse shared by ordinary Japanese plays an important role as well.

Theoretical Framework

To analyze the peace sentiment, we should start by understanding what an "idea" is in the popular mind, and what role the idea plays. Schmidt defines "ideas" as the substantive content of discourse. She distinguishes ideas in three main categories: policy ideas, programmatic ideas, and philosophical ideas. Policymakers propose policy ideas for debate and adoption. The programmatic ideas, which are located between policy ideas and philosophical ideas, may be cast as "paradigms" that reflect the underlying assumptions or organizing principles orienting policy. Philosophical ideas operate at a fundamental level, framing the policies and programs with a deeper core of organizing ideas, values, and principles of knowledge and society. Both the policy and programmatic ideas can be seen as occupying the foreground, while the philosophical ideas sit in the background as underlying assumptions (Schmidt 2008). In this context, it is possible to place the peace sentiment among the philosophical ideas.

Boswell and Hampshire point out two distinct roles that ideas play in political science: as strategic tools mobilized by agents (actors) to achieve predetermined preferences, and as structures imposing constraints on what is considered legitimate or feasible (Boswell and Hampshire 2016). They acknowledge the former as an instrumentalist approach, in which political agencies consciously use definition, framing, valence, and other rhetorical devices to mobilize support and activate new constellations of interests in order to promote policy preferences. They characterize the latter as an institutionalist approach, which utilizes ideas as structural constraints on agents as paradigms or frames, limiting what is seen as feasible or legitimate. Following on these definitions, they point out that theories of "discursive institutionalism" are a reconciliation of these two approaches, suggesting that while public philosophies and programmatic ideas can constrain political action, they also "provide resources that can be selectively deployed to advance political goals" (Boswell and Hampshire 2016). In this context, I define pacifist elements such as the war-renouncing Constitution, the Exclusively Defense-Oriented Policy, and the Three Non-Nuclear Principles as governmental tools for mobilizing the support of the nation. It is possible to call these "instruments for peace." I also define the peace sentiment of the nation as an "institution for peace" in its constraint on agents.

On the one hand, Boswell and Hampshire focus on the instrumentalist approach of strategies by agency—in other words, Agent Constructivism (AC)—and identify three discursive strategies through which policy actors can selectively mobilize ideas. First, they may foreground one level over others; second, exploit ambivalence in public philosophies; and third, link program ideas over time by invoking "policy legacies." On the other hand, Wendt and Kauppi emphasize the importance of the Structural Constructivist (SC) approach, which focuses on how structure, which is to say the norms of society, shapes the behavior of actors (Wendt 1999; Kauppi 2006).

There are various reasons why we need to analyze the pacifist culture with SC. First, the core of Japan's pacifist culture is basically the fears of war and the military shared by the Japanese public. Second, it is necessary to recognize that political actors often pretend to share norms in order to win support from the electorate. That is why there is a high necessity to evaluate the existence of a peace sentiment from the public side. Thus, I focus on this sentiment as an "institution for peace," which imposes constraints on what is considered legitimate or feasible for political actors. While political actors have some autonomy to influence and change the structure, basically the structure constrains the actions of actors (Schmidt 2008; see also Kolmaš 2019). In other words, if the institution has enough resilience to resist structural change by political actors, the ideas can be maintained and passed on to the next generation. Thus, SC is required to analyze the validity of the pacifist culture in Japan.

Peace Sentiment of the Japanese

For the Japanese, the horrific experience of World War II (WWII) and fears of the army function as a collective memory (which we understand as a social construction, see Rothstein 2000) that political entrepreneurs can utilize for their political purposes. Therefore, the war experience is a core of shared postwar memory in Japanese society and a placenta of the country's pacifist culture, even though political actors utilize only suitable narratives of the war experience for strengthening their political legitimacy. Education, war films, TV programs, and animation have also played essential roles in shaping and fostering pacifist sentiment. Here, I mainly focus on the education at school.

Of course, the collective memory of the war is not mono memory. It contains many memories, often composites of direct experience and narratives heard from others. The horrors of the war, such as 3.1 million casualties; the sadness of losing family members and relatives; oppressed daily life under the military regime; shortage of food and other commodities; the terror of air raids on major cities; group evacuations of children from major cities to the country; the destruction of Hiroshima and Nagasaki by atomic bombs; the experiences of war prisoners in the Soviet Union, and so on, are all part of the nation's shared experience. To illustrate this point quantitatively, I will use the number of articles in the Citation Information database of the National Institute of Informatics: CiNii (keywords searched on November 1, 2018) as one of the indicators to measure each element of collective memory (see Figure 5.1).

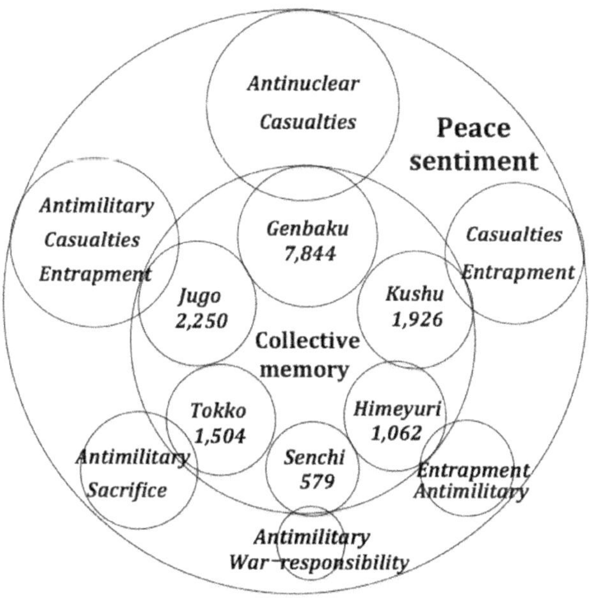

Figure 5.1: Image of collective memory and peace sentiment in Japan. Source: Author

The biggest number of articles (7,844) records the atomic bombings of Hiroshima and Nagasaki, with the main Japanese keywords *Genbaku* (atomic bomb) and *Hibaku* (being exposed to radiation). In second place (2,259 articles) are the experiences of wartime life, such as food shortages and the social pressures of war, told with keywords *Jūgo* (home front) and *Senji-ka* (wartime). Third place (1,926 articles) is occupied by the experience of air raids (*Kūshu).* Then, narratives of kamikaze attacks are told with the keyword *Tokubetsu kōgeki: Tokkō* (special attack). Next, at 1,062 articles, is the misery of the battle on Okinawa with *Himeyuri* (Lily Princesses girls' junior high school student corps). The smallest number of articles records the experiences of Japanese soldiers in *Senchi* (the front).

It is understandable that the narratives about *Genbaku* occupy the biggest portion of Japan's collective memory, because the grisly devastation of the nuclear attacks and their radioactive aftereffects marked the first time these were experienced by humanity. According to Halbwachs, the audience as members of the same community can share narratives and make them self-experienced stories (Rothstein 2000). Therefore, narratives of *Genbaku* and *Hibakusha* (atomic bomb survivors) in Hiroshima and Nagasaki became the core of postwar antinuclear sentiment and the social atmosphere in Japan.

The experiences of wartime life and the social pressures imposed by military rule are a deep part of the core of Japan's wartime experience, especially in shaping fears of entrapment and distrust of the military (Katzenstein 1996; Berger 1998). As a result, people worry about becoming involved in war again. Air raids were also a seminal war experience for ordinary Japanese. There are many books and movies related to this topic, especially in peace education programs at public schools in Japan, which offer a lot of material about *Kūshū* (air raid). This memory forms part of the foundation of pacifism, which also includes a fear of casualties shaped by the deaths of family members and relatives. Almost all members of the wartime generations had these experiences.

Narratives of kamikaze attacks are a special case of war memory. 3,948 pilots lost their lives in kamikaze attacks, many of them former university students conscripted after 1943, when a shortage of personnel forced the government to strip the students of their immunity from conscription (Ogawa 2001). Why did less than 0.5% of 750,000 casualties (total of Imperial Japanese Army and Navy) become one of the top narratives in postwar Japan? It is because of a book titled *Kike Wadatsumi no Koe (Listen to the voices from the sea).* The book, collections of letters written by kamikaze pilots before they departed on their suicide missions, became very popular in the 1950s because many letters contain criticism of the war and the military authorities. Conservatives tend to admire the pilots' noble patriotism and glorify their sacrifices, but most readers responded to the antimilitarist tone and distrust of the military. In addition, the Japanese felt sympathy for students who were forced to give up their intellectual lives at university and die in suicide attacks, even though the students also supported the idea of the Greater East Asia Co-Prosperity Sphere. Fukuma points out that through sharing their narratives, the Japanese recognized them as sacrificial victims and felt some catharsis about the war as well (Fukuma 2009).

It is curious that only a relatively small number of articles tell about the battle of Okinawa and the sad stories of the *Himeyuri gakuto*, female junior high school students who took part in battles as field nurses. Many of them were killed or committed suicide. This reflects the fact that interest in narratives about Okinawa is relatively small compared to the air raids and atomic bomb attacks, which took place on Japan's main part *Hondo*. Another reason is that Okinawa was under U.S. military control until 1972. After it was returned to Japan, Okinawa became a destination for school trips, and the miserable stories of the *Himeyuri gakuto* helped shape fear of entrapment.

Narratives about Japanese soldiers, including *Senchi* (battlefield) and *Hikiage* (evacuation from external territories after the war), are surprisingly small in number. This means that ordinary Japanese have very limited knowledge of fighting at the front outside Japan, contributing to a lack of consciousness about war responsibility. As Masayasu Hosaka points out, another reason is invisible but solid—pressure from *Senyu-kai* (war veterans associations). In many associations, the military hierarchy remained intact after the war ended, even though the Imperial Army and Navy were defeated and destroyed. Former officers advised former soldiers not to speak much about their experiences at *Senchi* (Hosaka 2015). Other evidence verifies this stricture as well. At the beginning of the postwar period, former generals and high-ranking officers started talking and writing about their experiences. As a result, the people who once played important roles in the highest positions of military authority, leading the war operations, controlled the narratives and nobody was allowed to speak differently. Once those people began to die off, middle- and low-ranking officers and soldiers started talking and writing about their war experiences. The narrative shifted, and now almost all soldiers' experiences are portrayed as atonement, including the memories of both victims and assailants.

From quantification of elements in the articles, five themes emerge: (1) antinuclear atmosphere; (2) fear of suffering casualties; (3) fear of entrapment; (4) antimilitarism; and (5) war responsibility. The outcome of this analysis is similar to the conclusion of Izumikawa. He points out three elements—pacifism, antitraditionalism, and the fear of entrapment—to explain the functions of Japan's antimilitarist norms. He characterizes Japan's antimilitarist culture as multidimensional, with varying tendencies depending on these three elements (Izumikawa 2004). These five elements can reasonably be identified as the fundamental elements of Japan's collective memory about the war. They are the key ingredients of peace sentiment and discourse, with each element influencing the process of shaping policies not only independently but also in combination with others. In particular, the antinuclear weapon atmosphere is very solid, strengthened by narratives of *Dai Go Fukuryū Maru*, a contamination accident caused by a U.S. nuclear test in 1954, and civilian nuclear accidents such as the Tōkaimura JCO nuclear accident in 1999, and the Fukushima Daiichi nuclear power plant accident in 2011.

Consciousness of War Responsibility

Teaching deep remorse about the past and consciousness of war responsibility should be essential elements for postwar peace education. However, the sense of war responsibility remains relatively weak, because it has not been taught very much in the postwar period due to a perception gap between generations (Akazawa 2000; Hosaka 2015; Murakami 2009).

This insuperable gap exists between the generations with direct war experience and the postwar generations with no direct experience. The direct war generations (including *Senzen-ha*, those educated before 1938, when the regime started that led Japan into war, and *Senchu-ha*, who were educated with militarism under the war regime, and many of whom were conscripted into the Imperial Army or Navy and killed during the war) have a "sense of ownership" of the war. But they tend not to accept Japan's war responsibility, because that would mean not only taking on personal responsibility, but denying the sacrifices made by their relatives and friends during the war (Hosaka 2005). After the war, many of them who were teaching or became teachers avoided talking about war responsibility, either for emotional reasons or just to avoid acknowledging their own responsibility in encouraging students to go to the battlefield. Instead, they used the excuse "we were deceived by the military" to dodge responsibility, and shifted the blame to the class-A war criminals (Ienaga 1985).

On the other hand, the postwar generations—especially *Sengo-ha*, those born during the war and educated in the new postwar era—have pointed out the responsibility of the direct war generations for supporting the war (Akazawa 2000; Fukuma 2009; Hosaka 2005). In 1960, the *Sengo-ha* were the main participants in *60 nen ampo toso* (demonstrations by university students who opposed renewal of the security treaty between the U.S. and Japan in 1951, motivated largely by their negative feelings toward war criminal Nobusuke Kishi rather than the treaty itself). *Senmu-ha*, those born after the war, tend to recognize that "war is evil" but feel no sense of ownership of the war, nor responsibility for it, because they know so little about the issues.

After the conclusion of the Tokyo military trials, the issue of war responsibility faded from the consciousness of ordinary Japanese. It surfaced again among ordinary Japanese after diplomatic relations between Japan and the PRC were established in 1972, and many atrocities caused by the Japanese army in China become known to the public. War responsibility also became more widely recognized in the 1980s, when controversies about history textbooks created diplomatic issues between Japan and its neighbors, making the Japanese conscious of their responsibility (Akazawa 2000; Akazawa 2003)

Peace Education

Heiwa Kyōiku (peace education) in postwar Japan has played an important role in creating "collective memory" from some individual war experiences and shaping the peace sentiment among the Japanese. This education focuses on teaching and sharing wartime experiences that emphasize the misery and horror of *Taiheiyō Sensō* (the Pacific War), grooming students with an "anti-war" attitude. This helps foster a peace sentiment among ordinary Japanese, who recognize emotionally that "war is wrong and evil" and believe that peace means the absence of not only war, but "any kind of military strength." In other words, they abhor war and believe that denial of the military brings peace. However, they don't know about the "mechanisms and reasons why states fight" or "how to prevent war," because they were simply taught that "war is wrong," based on the wartime experiences of relatives and media accounts that emphasize the misery and horrors of the war. In contrast, educators from the *Senzen-ha* and *Senchu-ha* generations have taught students little about Japan's war responsibility. This is why the education about Japan's wartime experience has been criticized for portraying the war only from a victim's standpoint rather than accepting responsibility. These older generations also neglect to tell students about the indivisible ties between the Three Non-Nuclear Principles and the "nuclear umbrella," and between the "Exclusively Defense-Oriented Policy" and the presence of U.S. Forces in Japan.

In general, peace education can be seen as a type of socialization process, because its objectives are concerned with the internalization of specific worldviews, as defined by the society in question. Peace education is always related to particular conditions prevailing in the society that carries out this educational mission (Bar-Tal 2002). During the Cold War, social conditions in Japan were shaped by the so-called 1955 system, dominated by the conservative Liberal Democratic Party (LDP) in the Diet, which had close relations with the bureaucracy and the business sector. The LDP was in ideological conflict with the Social Democratic Party (SDP), which insisted on *Hibusō Chūritsu* (unarmed neutrality) as the grand strategy of Japan. In particular, the *Nikkyōso* (Japan Teachers Union), which cooperated with SDP, had strong influence over the emotional peace education in postwar Japan. Through peace education, the Japanese learned the negative aspects of war on an emotional level. However, this education was conditioned by left-wing parties such as SDP and an overemphasis on the misery and horrors of the war, which ironically reduced people's interest in the war or even made it a taboo.

The Fundamental Law of Education was set as a basic principle in March 1947, with the ideas of democracy, pacifism, and denial of militarism emphasized as the foundation of the law. However, there were no official guidelines for peace education at that time, because the country was still digging out from the ruins of war, and everybody knew well the misery and sadness from direct experience. Therefore, it is not surprising that there was no anti-nuclear weapons education in Hiroshima and Nagasaki until 1951, when "Genbaku no Ko" (*Atom-bombed Children in Hiroshima*), a collection of notes by students who were exposed to atomic bomb radiation, was published. Arata Osada, an editor of the book, was himself exposed to radiation in Hiroshima. He insisted on the importance of grooming students with peace-oriented attitudes using four steps: (1) teaching the inhumane cruelty of the war; (2) teaching students to abandon all the prejudices which are psychological factors in causing war; (3) teaching correct knowledge to avoid war; and (4) fostering sensitive, strong-willed students. His peace education style became an archetype of postwar peace education in Japan, which aims to shape a "collective memory" by teaching and sharing the experiences of misery and horror of the war (Murakami 2009).

However, since the Korean War broke out and started Japan's rearmament, the Japan Teachers Union, cooperating with SDP, developed a critical stance against the Japan-U.S. security treaty, U.S. military bases in Japan, and SDF. The ruling LDP and the Ministry of Education tightened official control over compulsory education by screening school textbooks. The confrontation was a clear reflection of the 1955 system. The LDP preferred to keep close relations with Washington to secure security guarantees, including a "nuclear umbrella" for Japan during the Cold War, even though the campaigns against the Japan-U.S. Security Treaty and the U.S. war in Vietnam had massive support in Japanese society. In the high economic growth period of the 1960s, in the wake of increasing pressure from LDP to reduce peace education in schools, many experts started to worry about the fading memory of wartime experiences. They foresaw a pessimistic future for peace education, with little sharing of emotional memory due to the dwindling population of people with direct wartime experiences (Maruki 1965). Therefore, how to revive the memory of wartime experiences for peace education was a major item on the agenda of educators in the 1970s. During the 1970s and 1980s, as the number of people with direct war experiences declined, a growing consciousness about Japan's war responsibilities began to develop. In 1972, Okinawa's reversion to Japan brought wide attention to the inhumane atrocities committed by Japanese soldiers against the local population during the battle of Okinawa. A series of articles on the atrocities committed by Japanese soldiers during WWII called "Chūgoku no Tabi" (Travels in China) by Katsuichi Honda also raised awareness about the war responsibilities of Japan, even though the articles contained many factual mistakes. As a result, some educators started to point out problems with an emotional peace education. They criticized an approach that told students only the misery of the war, with no assailant perspective or accounting of Japan's war responsibilities (Adachi 1987). The history textbook controversies of the 1980s also increased public awareness of Japan's war responsibilities.

With the end of the Cold War and the 1955 system—especially after Tomiichi Murayama, a prime minister of the Social Democratic Party Japan (SDPJ) coalition government with LDP and the New Party Sakigake, accepted the SDF as constitutional and supported the Japan-U.S. Security Treaty for the first time in July 1994—ideological confrontation ended, and broader questions were raised about what peace education in post-Cold War Japan should be. In response, during the 2000s, issues such as structural violence, environmental concerns, and human rights abuses were included in a more comprehensive peace education program. This included the Holocaust, with the Auschwitz concentration camp as an example, and the Vietnam War. However, as Murakami points out, increasing the comprehensiveness of the peace education curriculum blurs "the war," including the Second Sino-Japanese war and the Pacific war, into a general image of "wars," and reduces the time and resources available for a traditional "peace education" that draws on Japan's wartime experiences, which had been the central measure of the peace education effort (Murakami 2009).

Fujioka criticizes postwar peace education in Japan for promoting "military allergy," a special feeling that rejects learning anything related to the military and armed forces, which also created anti-SDF sentiments among the Japanese (Fujioka 1993). He is also critical of the feeling that fosters a general atmosphere of Japanese saying "no wars anymore," without knowing why the state went to war or how to prevent it. The sentiment is a passionate refusal to engage in war or become involved in a war. However, it neither gives students a "sense of ownership" of the war nor fosters any consciousness of war responsibility.

To conclude, only discourses about "antinuclear atmosphere" and "fear of suffering casualties" are inherited by the postwar generations, because narratives of A-bombing and air raids are mainly used and told at school for peace education. On the other hand, elements such as "fear of entrapment" and "antimilitarism," which were shared by the direct war generations, are rarely inherited by the next generations. Therefore, it is a serious concern that fear of entrapment and antimilitarism will disappear when the war generations totally fade out of Japanese society.

How to Measure the Peace Sentiment?

The peace sentiment is the institutional side of the pacifist culture that constrains political actors in Japan. Opinion polls offer a measurement and can be used to assess the sentiment, although with some limitations. Hagström and Williamsson point out that modernist constructivists have used this method to measure the extent to which antimilitarist norms or a pacifist culture prevailed in postwar Japan (Hagström and Williamsson 2009). However, opinion polls are problematic for a number of reasons—for example, a decreasing percentage of replies to questionnaires in recent years due to growing concerns about privacy (Tanabe 2010). Results also tend to reflect the way questions are framed and worded, and many polls are not panel surveys, which provide longitudinal data on the same respondents.

All these criticisms aside, there is no other equally viable method to gauge normative change in society. Thus, let's draw on multiple opinion polls to quantify and evaluate public fears of the military in Japan, using data from the National Identity Modules of the International Social Survey Programme (ISSP) in 1995, 2003, and 2013. Public opinion surveys about SDF and defense issues conducted by the Japanese Cabinet Office to evaluate public sentiment and expectations about SDF are utilized as well. The opinion survey about peace conducted by NHK is also useful for analyzing the periodic transition of public consciousness on peace. In addition to quantifying these fears, it is necessary to evaluate the changes in Japanese society, mainly after the end of the 1955 system, and the impact of a shrinking population with direct war experiences on the pacifist culture. Following on this point, it is also necessary to evaluate the effectiveness of the patrimony of war experiences, and discourse among successive generations.

Function of Armed Forces in Japan and Normalization

In general, armed forces are recognized as the ultimate yardstick of national power (Tellis 2000), because they comprise the basis of power and only a legitimate recognized authority can utilize this mechanism of violence (Paret 1989). In many countries, the armed forces are a symbol of national pride, strongly connected to positive narratives, patriotism, and nationalism.

However, in Japan, the word *Guntai* (armed force) is synonymous with subjugation, destruction, and disaster, because the Japanese people endured these negative experiences not only in attacks by Americans, but also under the assertive rule of Japan's military regime, even though many Japanese at the time strongly supported the war. *Guntai* also evokes negative images of the Imperial Army and Navy, which people feel should be under civilian control with several *hadome* (instrumental breaks), self-imposed measures to prevent the remilitarization of Japan. Therefore, to follow the transition of perceptions of "armed force"—called the Self Defense Forces in Japan—it is necessary to measure the pacifist culture. Assessing national pride in armed force is critical in measuring public fears of the military, because armed force is a core item in the heritage of Japan's dismal twentieth-century past.

Ha and Jang describe national identity and national pride as being mutually related but conceptually different from each other, because national identity highlights normative aspects of membership, while national pride is rooted in affective, emotional responses (Ha and Jang 2014). Thus, evaluating shared public fears of the military is required to measure the emotional aspect of public consciousness as it relates to national pride. De Figueiredo and Elkins point out that national pride can be based on positive feelings about a nation's accomplishments, and is sometimes called "patriotism." They also explain that national pride can represent beliefs about the superiority of one's own country, based on positive feelings about its cultural or historical characteristics, which are supposedly linked with nationalism. In this context, it is possible to say that national pride offers an index of how a nation recognizes and diagnoses not only itself, but other countries as well (De Figueiredo and Elkins 2003).

Empirical Evaluation of the Sentiment

The transition of public affinity for armed forces in Japan can be measured using data from the National Identity Modules, *International Social Survey Programme* (ISSP) in 1995, 2003, and 2013. Comparing changes across these three sample years, it is clear that national pride in Japan's armed forces increased dramatically in 2013 (Table 5.3). This increase is especially notable in comparing the ISIP 2003 figures (reply of "very proud" and "somewhat proud": 44.4%) and ISSP 2013 (78.8%).

	Very proud	Somewhat proud	Not very proud	Not proud at all
ISSP 1995	10	37.9	40.2	11.9
ISSP 2003	10	34.4	40.7	14.9
ISSP 2013	28.1	50.7	17.8	3.4

Table 5.3: How proud are you of your country's armed forces? (%). Source: International Social Survey Program in 1995, 2003, and 2013, ISSP

It is easy to imagine this change coming from the dedicated contribution of SDF to search and rescue efforts after the disaster at the Fukushima Daiichi nuclear power station and the Great Northeast Earthquake in March 2011. This shows how successful SDF has been at improving its public image through nontraditional means such as disaster relief.

It is also useful to look at opinion polls conducted by NHK in 2013 and 2014 to assess the public sense of peace (see Table 5.4). Because of the Senkaku Islands (Diaoyu Dao/Diaoyu) issue, especially after nationalization of the islands was announced by the Node administration (DPJ) in September 2012, tension between Japan and the PRC heightened at the time the 2013 and 2014 polls were taken. It is clear evidence of the peace sentiment among the Japanese that major respondents still preferred to deal with the situation through diplomatic or peaceful measures, such as improving cooperation with Asian countries, even though Chinese authorities allowed (and in some cases even encouraged) anti-Japanese demonstrations in China and increased deployments of Chinese Coast Guard vessels around the Islands.

	Improving bilateral relations between Japan and PRC	Responding with American military deterrence	Responding with improved SDF	Improving cooperations with other Asian countries	others	don't know
7/2014	23.1	5.2	9.5	50.0	3.5	8.6
8/2013	21.3	6.6	13.8	47.2	2.9	8.3

Table 5.4: How should Japan react to China's increasing military activities? (%). Source: *Opinion polls about peace*, NHK, 2013, 2014

Opinion surveys about SDF and defense issues conducted by the Japanese Cabinet Office provide additional evidence of the growing public support for SDF. Table 5.5 shows the changes in people's opinion of SDF from 1969 to 2018. It is clear that the long-term tendency is toward an improving impression of SDF in Japanese society. The latest figure shows an 89.8% positive impression of SDF, compared with just 58.9% in 1972. It is an interesting fact that the favorable impression (total of "positive" and "relatively positive") of SDF has been steadily increasing, even during the Cold War and after the end of the Cold War era, with two exceptional years, 1972 and 1991. The influence of *Ampo Toso* (the campus disturbances and demonstrations by university students who opposed extension of the 1960 Japan-U.S. security treaty) around 1970 can be identified as a major factor in the temporary worsening of 1972. And division of opinion on the deployment of MSDF's minesweepers in the Persian Gulf after the Gulf War can be mentioned as a significant reason why the impression of SDF in 1991 worsened. The deployment was actually the first overseas mission by SDF after the end of WWII, and a crucial moment for SDF to start contributing to international security along with its original mission of national defense.

	Sep. 1969	Nov. 1972	Oct. 1975	Dec. 1978	Dec. 1981	Nov. 1984	Jan. 1988	Feb. 1991	Jan. 1994
Positive (Total)	68.8	58.9	69.2	75.4	71.3	74.3	76.7	67.5	76.8
Negative (Total)	14.1	24.3	17.6	13.4	17.5	16.7	15.6	19.4	13.4
don't know	17.1	16.9	13.1	11.1	11.2	9	7.8	13.1	9.9
	Feb. 1997	Jan. 2000	Jan. 2003	Feb. 2006	Jan. 2009	Jan. 2012	Jan. 2015	Jan. 2018	
Positive (Total)	80.5	82.2	80.3	84.9	80.9	91.7	92.2	89.8	
Negative (Total)	11.7	10.5	12.9	10	14.1	5.3	4.8	5.6	
don't know	7.8	7.3	6.8	5.1	5	3	3	4.7	

Table 5.5: Impression of the Self Defense Force (%). Source: Opinion survey on SDF and national defense, Cabinet Office of Japan, 2018

This long-term increase in support for SDF suggests that the Japanese have distinguished between SDF and "land, sea, and air forces, as well as other war potential," which are defined as unconstitutional under Article 9 of the Constitution, and have gradually come to accept SDF. The sincere efforts of SDF in non-combatant missions, such as participation in the PKO mission and disaster relief, have fostered public support and contributed to the overall improvement of SDF's image since the end of the Cold War as well.

The next table shows the expectations of the Japanese public regarding SDF missions (see Table 5.6). According to figures for 2018, the most respected mission of SDF is disaster relief, with national defense coming in second. In fact, expectations for SDF in regard to national defense dropped almost 13% between 2015 and 2018. It is reasonable to assume that this reduction reflects public fears of being dragged into an actual conflict with DPRK due to the nuclear and missile brinkmanship of Kim Jong-un. These fears are also reflected in the inversely increasing expectation of "missile defense," from 26.9% in 2015 to 40.2% in 2018. Another factor was fear of potential casualties among SDF members, due to the military legislation that was passed in 2015 and came into effect in November 2016.

	1991	1994	1997	2000	2003	2006	2009	2012	2015	2018
Disaster relief	23.8	66.0	66.9	67.1	71.8	75.3	78.4	82.9	81.9	79.2
National defense	48.9	57.2	56.6	59.0	68.6	69.4	70.0	78.6	74.3	60.9
Maintaining public order	15.1	33.8	25.7	24.3	36.0	42.8	41.8	47.9	52.8	49.8
Intercepting spy ships and armed agents	–	–	–	–	24.9	22.6	25.7	33.4	–	–
Missile defense	–	–	–	–	–	16.2	19.6	26.4	26.9	40.2
Participating in PKO	5.7	17.3	25.0	25.1	35.3	41.8	43.6	48.8	42.1	34.8
Contribution to the public (construction assistance, bomb disposal, and so on)	1.6	8.9	9.3	7.6	20.1	22.1	24.7	26.8	26.2	26.0

Table 5.6: Expected mission of the Self Defense Force (%). Source: Opinion survey on SDF and national defense, Cabinet Office of Japan, 2018

The legislation paved the way for Japan to exercise a limited right of collective self-defense for the first time, both for itself and its allies, enhancing the likelihood of Japan becoming engaged in armed conflict. Abe's "proactive contribution to world peace" in 2015 also increased public fear of SDF casualties. This is clear in the response to the question "Why you do not recommend your relatives to join SDF?" Between 2015 and 2018, the answer "Because the mission of SDF is unsafe work" increased from 75.1% to 81.3%. Overall, expectations for SDF to participate in PKO missions have also decreased since 2015.

As these polls indicate, the image of SDF has improved in Japan. However, this improvement is not simply a result of the reduction or erosion of Japan's pacifist culture; SDF has also consciously kept a distance from the former Imperial Army and Navy (Frühstück and Ben-Ari 2002). This separation reinforces the legitimacy of its existence as "not an armed force but a constitutional self-defense force" in postwar Japan. That gives SDF another opportunity to improve its image in Japanese society, so people can feel proud of what SDF has done while maintaining their distrust of the armed forces and keeping their conviction that military forces should remain under strict civilian control.

Through many interviews with civil servants, officers, and soldiers, Frühstück and Ben-Ari conclude that Japan's SDF wants to be a "normal" military force. But normality does not mean a nostalgic return to the Imperial Army and Navy. SDF wants to be regarded like the military forces of other industrialized democratic countries, such as Germany and the U.S., which are respected in their societies (Frühstück and Ben-Ari 2002). They also point out that SDFs are not passive recipients. Rather, they actively attempt to improve their image.

Verifying Function of the Sentiment

The National Defense Program Guidelines for FY 2019 and beyond (*2019 NDPG*), a basic policy guideline for national defense setting out the country's defense capability targets for the next ten years, was officially approved on December 18, 2018. The formulating process for these guidelines allows us to identify the main actors shaping the basic defense policy of Japan and assess the influence of the pacifist culture on the political actors. In verifying the process through a positivist approach, I focus on what actors attempted but could not achieve, rather than what they were able to shape or change, as a measure of how well the pacifist culture functioned as a barrier to prevent serious changes to Japan's pacifism by political actors.

Three Focal Points through the Formulating Process

During the process of developing the guidelines, the media and opposition parties pointed out a number of controversial elements, including: (1) the conversion of Izumo-class DDH (a destroyer for anti-submarine warfare equipped with helicopters) to a kind of aircraft carrier, which would exceed the limitations on offensive weapons announced by Defense Secretary Kawara in 1988, which defined an aircraft carrier with offensive capabilities such as the U.S. Navy has, along with ICBM missiles and strategic bombers, as offensive weapons not allowed under the Japanese Constitution; (2) possession of preemptive attack capabilities, which would deviate from an exclusively defense-oriented policy (each administration has maintained the policy that Japan should not possess preemptive attack capabilities, even though they recognized that Japan has a right to conduct preemptive attacks within the policy); and (3) lifting "1% of the GDP" as a self-imposed limitation on the defense budget, which was formally abolished in 1986. In January 1987, the Nakasone administration introduced a "total defense budget ceiling" (*Sōgaku Meiji Hōshiki*), which set five-year plans for the defense budget. This change created the precedent of keeping the defense budget below 1% of GNP on average during the five-year period. Since then, successive Cabinets have kept the limitation as a self-imposed rule. To verify the process, evaluating the transition of these three focal points (discourses) is essential.

Evaluation of the Formulating Process of the National Defense Program Guidelines

The 2019 NDPG is the first set of program guidelines formulated by the National Security Council (NSC), which was established in 2014. The regular conference members are the prime minister, chief cabinet secretary, and foreign and defense ministers. The National Security Secretariat (NSS), which is the secretariat body of the NSC with approximately 70 officials from the Ministry of Defense (MOD) and the Ministry of Foreign Affairs (MOFA), did the practical preparation of the NDPG.

After a Cabinet reshuffling in August 2017, Prime Minister Shinzo Abe asked newly appointed Defense Minister Itsunori Onodera to formulate a new NDPG for FY 2019. Onodera worked with technocrats such as Satoshi Maeda, a Director General of the Bureau of Defense Policy of MOD. In the same month, discussion about the basic direction and contents of the new NDPG started at the Research Commission on National Security (RCNS), which is a special commission of lawmakers from the ruling LDP that studies and makes policy recommendations related to national security. Since then, the NSC, with the support of the RCNS and the National Defense Division (NDD) of LDP, has played a crucial role in shaping the draft of the NDPG. During this process, RCNS made three controversial proposals—acquisition of "counterattack capability against enemy bases," conversion of the Izumo-class DDH to a "multipurpose aircraft carrier for defense" that could operate F-35B fighter jets, and the abolishment of the "1% ceiling" for an adequate defense budget, both in reference to NATO's 2% alliance target and due to North Korea's nuclear tests and missile launches. These were reflected in the NDPG draft prepared by NSC.

On November 16, the first joint working team (WT) of LDP and its coalition partner, the Komeito party, was held. At the second negotiation of the WT on November 20, the two ruling parties agreed to drop "counterattack capability against enemy bases" from the language of the guidelines. The final version of the 2019 NDPG, which was officially approved at an NSC and Cabinet meeting, mentions converting the Izumo-class DDH to a "multi-purpose destroyer" (neither aircraft carrier nor depot ship) and possible purchase of 42 F-35Bs. After the approval, Prime Minister Abe praised the new guidelines as "more ambitious than the previous ones." However, there was no mention of "2% of the GDP" as a reference figure for the defense budget, nor any recommendation for possessing "counterattack capability" in the NDPG at all.

Here, there are clear indications that the Abe Cabinet (particularly Prime Minister Abe) pushed hard for unshackling Japan's straitjacketed defense policy, but fell short. Gen Nakatani, a former defense minister, testified that he and members of the commission interviewed several personnel from the SDF, none of whom asked them to convert Izumo-class DDH to STOVL aircraft carriers. Current Defense Minister Takeshi Iwaya also explained that there was no request or demand from SDF members to make Izumo-class DDH a STOVL aircraft carrier (*Tokyo Shimbun*, January 4, 2019). This is clear evidence that MSDF generals and officers did not want to convert Izumo-class DDHs to STOVL aircraft carriers. Some of them were worried about the negative impact on budget allocations for vessels that are actually required, while others noted that the conversion could impose limits on the original Anti-Submarine Warfare operation.

Civilian control of the military in a democracy means that elected officials make the final decisions in areas of public policy, including foreign affairs and national security. Roehrig defines three broad requirements for keeping civilian control: (1) the military must be subordinate to elected decision-makers; (2) appropriate governmental institutions must be in place and working to maintain civilian control; and (3) the military must stay out of political affairs, and civilian sectors must not attempt to draw the military into politics (Roehrig 2002). These three requirements were met throughout the formulating process of the NDPG—in particular, SDF was kept at a distance from politics. In this context, an amendment to the Self-Defense Forces Law in 2015, which allows the Chiefs of Staff of GSDF, MSDF, and ASDF to advise the Minister of Defense in a capacity equal to high-ranking civilian officials, also adheres to the principles of civilian control.

The defense technocrats are not military personnel, but career civilian bureaucrats with special knowledge about defense matters. In the early years of postwar Japan, the police technocrats, who prepared the establishment of "armed forces" rather than purged military technocrats and officers, made efforts to prevent the former Imperial Army and Navy from having any influence in the newly established National Police Reserve in 1950, the National Safety Forces in 1952, and the Self Defense Forces in 1954. Since then, they have kept the rules of civilian control over SDF in place (Sado 2015), even after defense technocrats and later the defense ministry started to exert control over the agency. In this context, "civilian" control in Japan means defense technocrats rather than lawmakers, who are recognized as "civilian" in the context of general civilian control. The influence of *Kantei* (the Cabinet Office) should also be noted as part of the process. This means that the major actors in formulating defense policy for Japan were several LDP lawmakers working in conjunction with technocrats from MOD.

A security expert who acted as an adviser to RCNS of LDP, interviewed in late November 2018, explained that some LDP lawmakers were worried about possible negative public reaction if a "2%" defense budget target and "counterattack capability" were written into the NDPG. In addition, another LDP lawmaker explained that the designation "multipurpose aircraft carrier for defense" was changed to "multipurpose depot ship" because some lawmakers worried about using the term "aircraft carrier," which has a connotation of "attack" (blog of Satoshi Nakanishi, an LDP Upper House member, May 25, 2018). Natsuo Yamaguchi, a party leader of Komeito, mentioned that the WT played an important role in explaining the requirements of the Constitution and the Exclusively defense-oriented policy to the nation and neighboring countries (website of the Komeito, December 19, 2018). Komeito requested eradicating the image of "aircraft carrier" because it might trigger criticism from voters. This is also evidence that political actors are influenced by structural pressure.

Transformation of Pacifist Culture?

We have verified the existence of a peace sentiment and some of its functions. However, the peace sentiment in Japanese society has been facing serious obstacles, such as the difficulty of inheriting direct wartime experiences; dwindling generations with direct wartime experiences; and a drastic change in the security environment surrounding Japan. These have the potential to change the nature of Japan's pacifist culture.

Difficulties in the Inheritance and Metamorphoses of Collective Memory

Antimilitarist politicians in LDP with wartime military experience such as Masaharu Gotoda (1914–2005), Kiichi Miyazawa (1919–2007), and Hiromu Nonaka (1925–2018) have already passed away. Toranosuke Katayama, the oldest parliament member, was born in 1935 (and therefore has no military experience), and Prime Minister Abe is the first P.M. born after the war. Beyond the political sphere, the general degeneration of collective memory is also serious. If direct war experience is an inseparable element of Japanese pacifist culture, helping people understand and inherit narratives of the misery of war and fostering a "sense of ownership," then it is clear that this culture is facing a growing crisis. War memories have been fading away steadily since the end of WWII. For example, many war veterans associations (*Senyu kai*), estimated to have a membership in the tens of thousands at their peak in the 1970s (Takahashi 2005a), have been dismantled due to the declining number of members. War bereavement associations also face an existential crisis.

Overall, Japanese society is facing a decline in the population with direct war experiences. According to 2016 statistics, the number of people born in

Japan before 1946 is 23.2 million. They represent about 18.56% of the total population. (As a matter of convenience, these figures include everyone born before 1946, even though it is hard to imagine infants who were born in 1945 remembering and sharing war experiences.) This means that over the next twenty-five years, the generation with direct war experiences will disappear entirely. The impact of this reduction has already been observed, especially at peace education sites. In 1999, volunteer guides, instead of actual survivors of the attack, started to explain the experience of A-bombing at the Hiroshima Peace Memorial Museum. Another example: Lectures about the ground battle of Okinawa by former girls' junior high school students who witnessed the battle stopped at the Himeyuri Peace Memorial Museum at the end of March 2015, due to their old age. On a more individual level, sharing collective memories within families, an important element in fostering a "sense of ownership," is becoming rare as the generation dies off that could pass their experiences along to their grandchildren.

Basically, there is a gap in the "sense of ownership" between the war generations and postwar generations. The postwar generations tend to wonder why they should take war responsibility, since they did not engage in the war. In addition, inheriting memory is also a difficult process, with some features that metamorphose during the process. For example, Fukuma points out the difficulty of passing along accurate war experiences with a case study of Chiran, a small town in the Kagoshima prefecture on the island of Kyushu, which became a kind of commemorative site for kamikaze attacks in the postwar period (Fukuma 2017). Through his study of the process that reproduces war memories in popular culture, Fukuma concludes that both the media and public passed down "pure sentiments" and "a beautiful spirit of self-sacrifice" from mementos of the young *Tokkō* pilots to the next generation, while tending to be indifferent to the essence of the war and the issues of war responsibility which forced the young pilots' self-sacrifice. We can observe this sensibility in a film like *The Eternal Zero* (2013). The author describes the main themes of the film as the revitalization of Japan's wartime experience and the importance of survival through the war. He also describes the current reproduction or inheritance of war memories in Japan as a "memorial service," good for consoling the souls of soldiers but with no place for inquiries into war responsibility.

Now there is a chance to view the war more objectively and amend education efforts to foster a "sense of ownership" of the war (Murakami 2018). This is due to the liberation from ideological confrontation brought about by the end of the 1955 system; a drop in the ratio of teachers from the Japan Teachers Union, from 86.3% in 1958 to 22.6% in 2018; and the declining population of direct war generations, who find it difficult to accept war responsibility. In this context, the decline is a trade-off between the increasing difficulties of passing along direct war experiences and reducing the emotional obstacles to accepting war responsibility.

In any case, sufficient knowledge about modern Japanese history is a basic premise to utilize this chance. However, postwar education has avoided an objective history of the modern era, in order to prevent a possible ideological clash of opinions about war responsibility and Japanese aggression. It is a clear fact that there is little chance of learning modern Japanese history in public school education, though historical textbook issues were known well in the world. Educating little about modern history makes neighbors of Japan worry about the country's potential remilitarization, even though the Japanese have no intention of becoming a military power again.

Increasing Legitimacy of "jiei [self-defense]"

According to the *Opinion survey on SDF and national defense in 2018*, expectations for SDF to contribute to national defense have been increasing, from 48.9% in 1991 to 74.3% in 2017 (see Table 5.7). In 2018 expectations dropped to 60.9%, but the specific expectation for missile defense by SDF almost doubled, from 26.5% in 2017 to 40.2% in 2018, amid North Korean missile brinkmanship that year. These figures show that Japanese recognize their country faces military threats from North Korea and China. The rising tension of the security environment surrounding Japan is reflected in the growing consciousness of the Japanese about self-defense.

The Social Democratic Party of Japan (SDPJ) insisted on "unarmed neutrality" for Japan and denied all manner of war until 1994, when it established a coalition government with LDP and declared SDF constitutional. During the 1950s, 1960s, and 1970s, there was a strong peace sentiment among the Japanese, who recognized that "peace means a situation without any weapons" and believed in the explanations of SDPJ lawmakers such as Masashi Ishibashi, a former party leader. He insisted that "Japan is safe because Japan is an island state surrounded by the ocean as a natural barrier, which protects Japan from any invasion" (Ishibashi 1980). SDPJ declared SDF unconstitutional again in 2006. However, the impact of the policy shift that began in 1994 damaged the party's base of support and its image of idealistic pacifism. Realists derided this as utopianism, and the number of Japanese who accept the legitimacy of self-defense has been increasing ever since. Currently, only SDPJ officially claims that SDF is unconstitutional, but the support of the party hovers at a very low level.

Ordinary Japanese have been persuaded by LDP administrations, especially the Abe administration, which emphasizes the threats of PRC and DPRK. For example, in the 2019 NDPG, the government describes not only China's intention to build "world-class forces" by the mid-twenty-first century with a high level of defense spending that lacks transparency and represents unilateral, coercive attempts to alter the status quo, but also North Korea's nuclear and ballistic missile brinkmanship. Nobody objects to this perception; instead, the Japanese people have accepted the necessity for defense preparation without any level-headed analysis of the threats. The increasing legitimacy of self-defense has been one of the factors slowly filling the gap between pacifism and public sentiment, which converges in claims by the government that Japan is an individual state with a right to its own self-defense, and Japan needs to maintain the Japan-U.S. security alliance to secure the country's defense.

Table 5.7 shows the long-term trend of filling the gap between governmental security policy and public consciousness. The figures show the growing

	Defend Japan with Japang–U.S. security arrangements and SDF	Abolish the arrangements and defend only with SDF	Abolish the arrangements and SDF	other	Don't know
Sep. 1969	40.9	12.9	9.6	1.3	35.3
Nov. 1972	40.7	10.8	15.5	1.1	31.9
Oct. 1975	54.3	8.6	9.5	0.6	27.0
Dec. 1978	61.1	8.2	5.0	0.8	24.9
Dec. 1981	64.6	6.1	7.6	0.9	20.8
Nov. 1984	69.2	5.0	6.8	1.1	17.9
Jan. 1988	67.4	5.9	7.2	1.3	18.3
Feb. 1991	62.4	7.3	10.5	1.0	18.7
Jan.1994	68.8	4.3	7.0	0.7	19.2
Feb. 1997	68.1	7.1	7.9	0.6	16.3
Jan. 2000	71.2	8.0	5.8	1.2	13.8
Jan. 2003	72.1	8.3	4.7	1.1	13.8
Feb. 2006	76.2	8.6	5.6	1.3	8.3
Jan. 2009	77.3	9.9	4.2	1.4	7.2
Jan. 2012	82.3	7.8	2.2	0.8	7.0
Jan. 2015	84.6	6.6	2.6	0.8	5.4
Jan. 2018	81.9	7.1	2.9	0.7	7.4

Table 5.7: Consciousness of appropriate measures to defend Japan (%). Source: Opinion survey on SDF and national defense, Cabinet Office of Japan, 2018

support for active measures to defend Japan, with the number of respondents who support defense "with the Japan-U.S. security arrangements and SDF" increasing from 40.9% in 1969 to 81.9% in 2018. On the other hand, the number of respondents who prefer to "abolish both the arrangement and SDF"—in other words, a position of unarmed neutrality—has been decreasing, from approximately 10% to about 3%. It is worth noting that the number of "Don't know" responses dropped by nearly 80% between 1969 and 2018.

Many Japanese have come to prefer realistic measures to secure national defense. The idealism once shared by the nation is seen as lame when the country faces an actual military threat. However, even though consciousness of self-defense has increased, ordinary Japanese still recognize "war except for self-defense is wrong." This recognition is crucial for the pacifist culture, which is expected to maintain a critical role in constraining and controlling political actors in order to prevent the remilitarization of Japan.

Conclusion

First, according to many evaluations using a pragmatic approach with structural constructivism and positivism, it is clear that a kind of vague pacifist sentiment such as "war is evil and I am against war" still exists in Japanese society, functioning as an institution to constrain political actors and prevent Japan's derogation from the postwar pacifist instruments. The instruments, which could also be called "results of the compromise between LDP and progressive opposition parties under the 1955 system," could be defined as: (1) renouncing any type of war (except self-defense) to settle international disputes; (2) prohibiting the possession of any kind of offensive weapons, such as nuclear weapons, aircraft carriers with offensive capabilities, ICBMs, and strategic bombers, and instead maintaining moderate defense capabilities with an exclusively defense-oriented policy; and (3) keeping "civilian (technocrats') control" to prevent SDF members from achieving strong political influence. In this context, explanation of postwar Japan's security policies only with elements and influences of the Japan-U.S. alliance would be one-sided.

Second, direct wartime experiences and a postwar peace education focused on sharing wartime experiences strongly influenced the creation of collective memory, which is the core of the peace sentiment. That sentiment, built on wartime experiences such as the atomic bombings, kamikaze attacks, air raids, and the Battle of Okinawa, has multilayered features, including antinuclear sentiment; fear of incurring casualties; fear of entrapment; and anti-militarism. This explains the contrasting character of the pacifist culture, which harbors a strong antinuclear sentiment and fear of entrapment while paying little attention to Japan's war responsibility, because there is gap between war generations with "sense of ownership" of the war and postwar generations without it. The postwar education also groomed students to feel repulsion toward war with narratives of A-bombing and air raids as symbol of war misery, even though it did neither tell students other narratives, modern history, why Japan went to war, nor why ordinary Japanese supported the war due to avoidance of responsibility and ideological confrontation between teachers and authority. Therefore, the peace education could foster neither a "sense of ownership" of the war nor war responsibility.

Third, national pride in SDF has increased in Japanese society for several reasons. While this has not resulted in remilitarization, SDF has gained broad support in Japanese society not only because of the increasing legitimate need for self-defense, but also because of improvement efforts like SDF's dedication to helping with disaster relief. Declining populations with direct war experience also contribute to improve the affinity. Moreover, the increasing affinity for SDF seems to foster "*Kawaisō* (those poor soldiers)," a hypersensitivity to possible SDF casualties in the minds of the Japanese. This is expected to function as a new dimension in Japanese pacifism, making political actors pay much more attention to avoiding actual SDF casualties. The sentiment was already utilized for certain political purposes by SDPJ without any theoretical consolidation during arguments over the 2015 Legislation for Peace and Security in 2014. It shows that each actor used narratives and discourses for his/her own political purpose. In any case, the fear would become a hindrance to Abe's "proactive contribution to the world" policy.

Therefore, the peace sentiment, a collective consciousness and shared norms among ordinary Japanese shaped by narratives of past war experiences, can be called the postwar national identity of Japan. Article 9 of the Constitution is a symbol of that sentiment, and in discourse Japanese have expressed their belief that Article 9 defends Japan's peace. However, Japanese have little consciousness of the inextricable relations between the Three Non-Nuclear Principles and the U.S. "nuclear umbrella," or between the Exclusively Defense-Oriented Policy and the U.S. military presence. In this context, renouncing Article-9 or amending it would have a serious impact on the future of this vague peace sentiment.

References

Akazawa, S. (2000). *Sengo nihon no senso sekinin ron no doukou* [The trend of argument on war responsibility in post war Japan]. *Ritsumeikan Law Review*, Ritsumeikan University, *6* (274), 2607–2633.

Akazawa, S. (2003). *Sengo nihon ni okeru senbotsusha no 'irei' to tsuito* [Consoling and mourning the soul of the war dead in post war Japan]. *Memoirs of Institute of Humanities*, Kyoto: Ritsumeikan University, *82*, 117–133.

Adachi, Y. (1987). *Kataritsugu senso taiken kara toikakeru heiwa gakushu he* [From inheriting war experience to peace education with debating on peace]. *Heiwa Kyouiku* [Peace Education]. Tokyo: Meiji Tosho Shuppan, 6, 16–23.

Bar-Tal, D. (2002). The elusive nature of peace education. In G. Salomon & B. Nevo (Eds.), *Peace education: The concept, principles, and practices around the world* (pp. 27–36). Mahwah.

Berger, T. (1998). *Cultures of antimilitarism: National security in Germany and Japan.* London: John Hopkins University Press.

Boswell, C., & Hampshire, J. (2016). Ideas and agency in immigration policy: A discursive institutionalist approach. *European Journal of Political Research*, *56*(1), 133–150.

De Figueiredo, R., & Elkins, Z. (2003). Are patriots bigots? An inquiry into the vices of in-group pride. *American Journal of Political Science*, *47*(1), 171–188.

Frühstück, S., & Ben-Ari, E. (2002). Now we show it all! Normalization and the management of violence in Japan's armed forces. *The Journal of Japanese Studies*, *28*(1), 1–39.

Fukuura, A. (2017). *Jieitai kenkyu no shoso: Mingun kankei to konkatsu* [Various aspects of studies on the Japan self-defense forces: Civil-military relations and marriage hunting]. *Kansai Sociological Review*, *16*, 117–130.

Fukuma, Y. (2009). *'Senso taiken' no sengo-shi* [Postwar history of 'wartime experience']. Tokyo: Chukoshinsho.

Fukuma, Y. (2017). *Popular culture ni okeru 'keisho' no kajo to datsu-rekishi-ka* [Reproduction of 'memories on war' and the Indifference of History in Postwar Japan's popular culture: The Invention of Tokko memorial Sites in Chiran and its politics]. *Kansai Sociological Review*, *16*, 104–116.

Fujioka, N. (1993). *Heiwa kyoiku saihen no toki* [Time to reorganize post-war peace education], *Yomiuri Shimbun*, April 30.

Ha, S., & Jang, S. (2014). National identity, national pride, and happiness: The case of South Korea. *Social Indicators Research*, *121*(2), 471–482.

Hagström, L., & Williamsson, J. (2009). Remilitarization really? Assessing change in Japanese foreign security policy. *Asian Security*, *5*(3), 242–272.

Hosaka, M. (2005). *Showa sengo-shi no shikaku* [A blind spot of post war history in Showa era]. Tokyo: Asahi Bunko.

Hosaka, M. (2015). *Senjo taikensha. chinmoku no kiroku* [People who experienced battlefield. Record in silence]. Tokyo: Chikuma Bunko.

Ienaga, S. (1985). *Senso sekinin* [The war responsibility]. Tokyo: Iwanami shoten.

Ishibashi, M. (1980). *Unarmed neutrality.* Social Democratic Party of Japan.

Izumikawa, Y. (2004). *The sources of Japanese antimilitarism: The fear of entrapment and Japanese pacifist discourse.* International Studies Association presentation, Honolulu, March 5. Retrieved from http:// www.allacademic.com/meta/p70941_index.html.

Katzenstein, P. (1996). *Cultural norms and national security: Police and military in postwar Japan.* New York: Cornell University Press.

Kauppi, N. (2002). Elements for a structural constructivist theory of politics and of European integration. *Center for European Studies Working Paper*, 104. Retrieved from http://aei.pitt.edu/9048/1/Kauppi101.pdf.

Kolmaš, M. (2019). *National identity and Japanese revisionism.* London: Routledge

Kin, E. (2012). *Shugouteki kioku gainen no saiko* [Reconsideration of the concept of collective memory: A reevaluation of Maurice Halbwachs]. *Kansai Sociological Review*, *11*, 3–14.

Lind, J. (2004). Pacifism or passing the buck? Testing theories of Japanese security policy. *International Security*, *29*(1), 92–121.

Maruki, M. (1965). *Senso wo oshieta kiroku* [Record of teaching about war]. *Seikatsu Kyoiku*, Tokyo: Japan Association for Life Education, pp. 8–19.

Miyashita, A. (2006). Where do norms come from? Foundations of Japan's postwar pacifism. *International Relations of the Asia-Pacific*, *7*(1), 99–120.

Murakami, T. (2009). *Sengo nihon no heiwakyouiku no shakaigakuteki kenkyu* [Sociological research on peace education in postwar Japan]. Tokyo: Gakujutsu Shuppankai.

Murakami, T. (2018). *Senso taiken keisho ni taisuru Tojisha-ishiki wo sodateru kyouiku no kousatsu* [A study of education to nurture parties' consciousness for passing on of war experiences]. *Journal of Educational Research*, *18*, 173–182.

Ogawa, T. (2001). *Tokko no jissho* [Empirical research of Tokko attack]. Nagano: Choeisha.

Paret, P. (1989). Military power. *The Journal of Military History*, *53*(3), 239–256.

Roehrig, T. (2002). *The prosecution of former military leaders in newly democratic nations: The cases of Argentina, Greece, and South Korea*, New York: McFarland Press.

Rothstein, B. (2000). Trust, social dilemmas and collective memories. *Journal of Theoretical Politics*, *12*(4), 477–501.

Sado, A. (2015). *Jieitai-shi* [History of the self-defense forces]. Tokyo: Chikuma Shinsho.

Schmidt, V. (2008). Discursive Institutionalism: The explanatory power of ideas and discourse, *Annual Review of Political Science*, *11*, 303–326.

Takahashi, Saburo, & Mizobe, A. (2005a). *Kyodokenkyu Senyu-kai* [Joint research on Senyu-kai]. Tokyo: Impact-shuppankai.

Takahashi, S. (2005b). *Senshuboeika no tekikichi kougeki nouryoku wo megutte* [Should Japan have a strike capability under its exclusively defense-oriented policy?]. *NIDS security studies*, *8*(1), 105–121.

Takahashi, M. (2017). *'Senso no kioku' keisyo no genriteki kousatsu* [Aiming to build a practical theory of inheriting 'memory of war' in the curriculum]. *Departmental Bulletin Paper*, *61*, 65–77.

Tanabe, S. (2010). *National identity no kokusai hikaku* [International comparison of the national identity]: Tokyo: Keio University Press.

Tellis, A., et al. (Eds.). (2000). *Measuring national power in the postindustrial age analyst's handbook.* Rand Army Research Division.

Went, A. (1999). *Social theory of international politics.* New York: Cambridge University Press.

6. *Collective (Historical) Memory and National Identity in Contemporary Japan: Contested War Narrative and Myth-Making in* Japan's Longest Day

Jan Sýkora
Charles University

Myth-making and their deliberate use or misuse for political and ideological interests is not only the matter of the distant past but constitutes an important attribute of modern and contemporary history of Japanese society. Modern myths played an important role in building and consolidating national identity at the dawn of Meiji period, strengthened the fighting spirit during the war years and after the losing war at the time of the occupation, when the Japanese nation lost most of its ideological support, including the myth of the divine emperor; they contributed to the formation of new goals and to the mobilization of the forces, indispensable for their achievement.

Collective (historical) memory plays an important role in the shaping and maintaining of national identity. Both history and collective memory are based on publicly available social facts, but unlike history which represents the remembered past to which we have no longer an organic relation, collective memory represents the active past that forms our identity. Thus, the construction and the reconstruction of national identity is closely related to the tricky problem of what kind of historical facts are selectively "remembered" or "forgotten," and through which means these facts are incorporated into or deleted from the collective memory.

The unconditional surrender of the country in 1945 has been one the most traumatic historical events which has significantly influenced the national narrative and had an appreciable impact on the national identity in postwar Japan. The decision to surrender has been emotionally interpreted as a result of the clash between realistic politicians who preferred the end of war in favor of peaceful survival of nation and the reactionary military circles that were resolved to fight to the bitter end. The event has been dramatized by several movies both in Japan and abroad, which significantly contributed to the stereotypic myth in which the historical figures were labeled as heroes or villains.

The chapter analyzes the different images of the two controversial historical figures involved in the tragic endgame of the war in Japan, namely Emperor Showa and the Minister of Army General Korechika Anami, as portrayed in two film adaptations (1967 and 2015) of the Kazutoshi Hando's book *Japan's Longest Day*. I will illustrate that the interpretations of historical events differ greatly with each respective film adaptation. This, in turn, reflects the changing content of war narrative, which has large-scale connotation for national identity through myth-making in contemporary Japanese society.

Theoretical Framework to the Concept of War Memory

It is now conventional wisdom to observe that history, memory, and identity are intertwined concepts (see, e.g., Heisler 2008; Kratochwil 2006; McGrattan 2013; Trefalt 2003). The memory is—to some extent—a specific way of interpreting the historical facts and constructing the historical narrative, while the identity is formed by a mixture of real and imagined histories. Although these three concepts are closely related, nobody can confidently say how they are related. All the three are contingent on context; on agents (institutions) such as state, church, or local communities; and on the purposes to which they are put together. The power to explore, interpret, and use the history, memory, and identity is exercised at each level of these agents—from the state, at one hand, to the individual, on the other (Kansteiner 2002: 188–189), and it depends on the social context, namely on the autonomy of the institutions and individuals, to produce and reproduce the historical narrative, and on the readiness of the state to promote or restrict such (re)production. Thus, dealing with history, memory and identity may be regarded as a strong political matter, and as Friedrich Kratochwil (2006: 6) argues, "The understanding of 'politics' requires a historical awareness that is *sui generis*. Politics is inherently *practical* since it deals with doing the right thing at the right time in view of the particular historical circumstances." In such view, one of the most sensitive topics in the political discourse is the war memory.

In the recent decades, the scholarship devoted to the study of war memory has developed dramatically. Special attention has been paid to the key term of "politics of memory" denoting the power relations in producing and representing the past in the present (see, e.g., de Brito 2001; Hodgkin and Radstone 2003; Lebow et al. 2006; Ricci 2017; Szczepanska 2014). In a sophisticated theoretical study on contemporary war memory, Timothy Ashplant, Graham Dowson, and Michael Roper have introduced the concept of politics of war memory which they define as "a struggle of different groups to give public articulation to, and hence gain recognition for, certain memories and the narratives within which they are structured" (2000: 16). The process of such articulation may be analyzed from three main perspectives, that is, agencies, narratives, and arenas. Agencies are viewed as "institutions through which social actors seek to promote and secure recognition for their war memories" (ibid: 17) and vary from the state at one end of the scale to individuals at the other. Narratives are understood as descriptions of historical events which are shared by social actors and deeply embedded in their memories. And finally, arenas are "socio-political spaces within which social actors advance claims for the recognition of their specific war memories" (ibid.).

Viewed in this light, Asplant et al. proposed to distinguish between three principal theoretical approaches toward war memories. The first one is the state-centered (or "orthodox") approach which represents the wide range of the official narratives disseminated from the top to the bottom of the society through various instruments and institutions such as government statements, official commemoration events, education system, etc. The second one is the social agency approach which is based on the psychological concept developed by Jay Winter and Emmanuel Sivan. In their understanding, the social agency is "a product of individuals and groups who come together, not at the behest of state or any of its subsidiary organizations, but because they have to speak out" (1999: 9). The third approach is the popular memory approach which focuses on private memories, mostly—but not exclusively—those who experienced war, and on the way of how these memories are influenced by the various narratives within a society. The three approaches have their own strong and weak points and as Philip A. Seaton argues, "the challenge is how to synthesize the strengths of the three approaches into an 'integrated theory' of war memory applicable to the Japanese case" (2007: 12).

In a general sense, historical memory represents the way through which we look back on the past events and judge them from the present perspective. As Philip A. Seaton points out, "looking back on the event of past may say as much about the present priorities and politics of the individual or society as it does about the past" (ibid.). In the case of war memory, the narrative of past is contingent on the fact whether the agent has or has not personal experience of war. While people with the direct war experience rely more or less on their own memories, the postwar generation looks back on the historical events through the narratives which are created as a mixture of the "second-hand" knowledge learnt from the war generation, and the interpretation of the war based on formal education, novels, short stories, manga, movies, television dramas, etc. However, since the memories and narratives exist on both individual and collective levels, there are two intertwined tricky problems of how the individual memories are transformed to collective memory and how the memories of the war generation are transmitted to the collective memory of the postwar generations. If the society is able to solve these problems in a non-conflict way and to agree on the generally accepted official (war) narrative, a dominant cultural memory emerges, but—on the other hand—if the official narrative is contested among various groups of the ruling elite and politicians, the cultural memory provokes the controversy within the whole society. Thus, the "cultivation" of the cultural memory, in other words the degree of the identification with the public narrative, is a *sine qua non* for getting an identity on various levels, and as Seaton concludes, "conversely, identities acts as a filter for public narratives" (ibid.: 18).

Japanese War Memories and Their Reflection in Japanese Cinema

Unconditional surrender of Japan undoubtedly represents the deepest and the most dramatic breaking point in the entire history of the country, with which perhaps the Meiji Restoration only can be compared. Although the overthrow of the shogunate and the restoration of the power of emperor in 1868 meant—in the historical context—the unprecedented and radical change of the regime, it could hardly reach the political, economic, social, and human drama of the crushing defeat. The general feeling of the irreversible breakup with the past prevailed even after the Meiji Restoration, but the number of war victims and millions of broken personal lives put the Asia-Pacific War on a sad first place on the list of national historical traumata. Thus, there is no surprise that the feeling of deep discontinuity, manifested in the effort to make a clean break with the past, dominated in the perception of the war for several decades after its end.

The ambivalent relationship with the past can be probably best illustrated by the term *sengo* and by the conceptual changes in its content. The term *sengo* means "postwar period" as an antonym to *senzen* ("prewar period"). It is quite obvious that any society creates comfortable and simplistic terms for its historical self-identification, but the term *sengo* does carry a special meaning. Unlike the modern way of the traditional periodization system in which the era name corresponds to the reign of one emperor (*issei ichigen*, or "one reign, one era name" principle), one can hardly find any historical precedent in the modern times for dividing one historical era into two periods. From the very beginning, the term *sengo* has been burdened by ideological associations. It was dominated by the aspect of inversion, where the "new," postwar Japan was supposed to be the opposite of the "bad," prewar one. Postwar Japanese tended to portray themselves as victim of (pre)war militarism (see Bukh 2007; Jeans 2005), and this victim mentality has been pervasive in the popular presentation of war in literature, television, and film for several postwar decades. Although the view of the past was later diversified and particularized, some kind of inversion kept a certain inertia in some simplistic approach, and—paradoxically—it created the potential for continuity with the past (see Gluck 1993; Gordon 1993).

Japan has one of the oldest and largest film industries in the world. According to Motion Picture Producers Association of Japan, the number of the Japanese films released in 2018 reached 613 and generated box office earnings of over 122 billion *yen* (2019). The war films represent the integral part of the Japanese film history and have played an important role in the process of (re)forming the national identity in postwar Japan. Philip A. Seaton compiled a list of publicly screened films which depicted the war and/or are set in the war years of 1937–1945, and identified 235 war films, that is, about 4 percent of the total number of films made in the period of 1946–2001 (Seaton 2007: 153). The heyday of Japanese war film production was in the 1950s and 1960s followed by a slight decline in the 1980s and 1990s; but since the turn of the century the revival of popularity of war films, particularly with a nationalistic tone, has been quite obvious. Several major phases could be found in the development of the Japanese war cinema (see, e.g., Sato 1995; Sharp 2011; Richie 2012; Yomota 2019).

During the period of the occupation (1945–1952) the film industry—as well as the whole society—was under strict censorship of the General Headquarters (GHQ). All film scripts had to be submitted to the Civilian Information and Education Division (CIE) of GHQ, for receiving the permission before shooting, and completed films underwent the second censorship at the Civil Censorship Detachment (CCD). Although the CIE was composed of the American civilians, the CCD was controlled by the military figures, which means that it was in principle military censorship. In November 1945, the CIE compiled a list of thirteen topics which were banned from Japanese films. The list forbade any demonstration of nationalism, patriotism, and loyalty, but also the more "innocent" things such as using a sword, praising suicide, an act of revenge, violence or cruelty, etc. (Yomota 2019: 100). Moreover, the censorship was also applied to (pre)war films, and any scenes considered incongruous with the antimilitaristic policy of the occupation administration were adamantly cut. Under such conditions, it was absolutely impossible to produce any film which could remind war experience or cast a critical view on the war history.

The end of the occupation system brought about the elimination of the censorship and caused the substantial shift in the perception of war. The negative approach based on refusing of militarism was replaced by the feeling of nostalgia for the war and the moderate glorification of the military heroes who act morally in their fight against the United States and other colonial power enemies. Indeed, many of the Japanese postwar filmmakers belonged to the progressive leftist camp, but underneath "they were anti-American patriots and ethnic nationalists" (ibid: 112). The new war films showed the war experience sentimentally and put stress on the sad fate of Japanese soldiers dying needlessly in distant corners of the Japanese empire or the suffering of children, women, or A-bomb victims in Japan. Although the war films made in the 1950s and 1960s were primarily antiwar, they completely marginalized the discussion on Japanese war responsibility and confirmed the consciousness of the Japanese people of themselves as war victims.

The growing competition from television in the 1970s caused a substantial decline in the Japanese film industry and the war film production suffered a same fate. Japanese society faced new problems and challenges starting from social and environment issues up to the widening generation gap and the self-identity crisis. The films utterly lost the melodramatic pathos and nostalgia for the traditional world, and shifted to the portrayal of the everyday reality. The few war films which were made during the 1970s mainly dealt with the Japanese military impact on the Asian countries—lacking the cardinal question of responsibility again—and provoked hot debates among Japanese historians.

The 1980s were marked by the onset of neo-conservatism in the Japanese politics and the revival of nationalism which provoked noticeable frictions particularly between Japan and its Asian neighbors, namely China and Korea. And yet, the 1980s were overall probably the golden age of Japanese war film with more domestically and internationally respected works than any other decade in the postwar period. The crisis of the studio system pushed the major studios into producing films that could mobilize mass audiences to buy tickets, and the war theme was a safe bet. On the other hand, financial distress and later the collapse of the studio system allowed unprecedented opportunity for new generation of directors who took a new approach toward the depiction of war. It varied from a jingoistic defense of Japanese imperialism (ibid: 166) to the sentimental portrays of soldiers on both sides of the battlefront as men who simply wanted to stop fighting and return home. Although some films featured the mild criticism of the Japan's colonial ambitions and conveyed the antiwar message, overall the war films of the 1980s "left the cinema audience little wiser about war responsibility issues," (Seaton 2007: 157) and they did not express any direct political stance.

The 1990s threw Japanese society into unprecedented continuous political, economic, and social crisis. The burst of bubble economy, the end of political system of 1955, the sarin attack in Tokyo done by the Aum Shinrikyo religious group, unprecedented earthquake in Kobe, growing number of non-Japanese staying illegally in Japan, all these events were the obvious signs that the way of living that the Japanese share for a long time could no longer function. Such unprecedented changes had a tangible influence on the Japanese cinema including the war film production. Since Japan was exposed to the international competition and had to tackle the problems of self-reflection, Japanese films turns their focus on the international, mainly Asian, context. New wave of directors commenced to produce "action documentaries" on untouched problems of war history such as suffering of Asian people under Japanese occupation. However, not only the war genre *per se* but also the composition of the audience changed. Since the key target audience became young people who were not interested so much in hearing the sentimental narrative from war generation, filmmakers used the various methods of how to make the war more attractive and comprehensible to postwar generation. Elements of comedy, mystery, and adventure began to appear in war films, not to mention the anime films with war theme that achieved high popularity both in Japan and abroad. On the other hand, such representations of war in the format of entertainment provoked the reaction in the camp of right-wing conservatives and caused the revival of nationalism on the turn of century (Kushner 2007: 799). Thus, the clash of view to (war) history and different approaches to the war films as a key tool for reconstruction of national identity is still obvious in Japanese society and can be perfectly demonstrated on the comparison of the two film adaptations of Kazutoshi Hando's book *Nihon no ichiban nagai hi*.

The Politics of War Memory and the Japan's Longest Day

On August 12, 1967, just a few days before the 22nd commemoration of the surrender of Japan and the end of the Asia-Pacific War (*shusen kinenbi*), the Toho Studios released its massively advertised film *Nihon no ichiban nagai hi* (*Japan's Longest Day*) directed by Kihachi Okamoto (1925–2005). The all-star film which attracted a huge crowd of spectators became the blockbuster and encouraged the studio management to continue the production of films with war themes. Between 1967 and 1971 the Toho Studios made five big-budget war films, generally known as "8.15 series" (see Shimazu 2003; Salomon 2014). The spearhead of the series was followed by a hugely popular movie *Yamamoto Isoroku* in 1968, directed by Seiji Maruyama, *Nihonkai daitaisen* (*The Battle of the Sea of Japan*) in 1969, Hiromichi Horikawa's *Gunkaku* (*The Military Clique*) in 1970, and Okamoto's *Okinawa kessen* (*The Decisive Battle of Okinawa*) in 1971. Although the individual films did not have high artistic ambitions, nor they fundamentally changed the pacifistic stance toward the war, the series as a whole provoked a hot discussion, particularly in Japanese media, on the very traumatic moment in modern Japanese history. In doing so, they opened the gate to the process of the recreation of the national identity.

Toho project was implemented during the period which former Prime Minister Takeo Fukuda (1905–1995, in office 1978–1978) euphemistically called in June 1964 Showa Genroku, invoking the popular image of the Genroku Period (1688–1704) as the Golden Age of Tokugawa period for political stability, economic growth, and general well-being. Indeed, the governments of two LDP Prime ministers—Hayato Ikeda (1899–1965, in office 1960–1964) and Eisaku Sato (1901–1975, in office 1964–1972)—are still regarded as a period of peace and prosperity. The national economy demonstrated double-figure growth, Japanese products (particularly cars and electronics) conquered the foreign markets one by one, and the standard of living unprecedentedly improved. Moreover, Japan won the adequate place in the international community and got the high credit internationally for carrying out several ambitious projects: In 1964 Tokyo hosted the Summer Olympic Games, in 1970 the International World Exposition (Expo '70) was held in Osaka, and in 1972 Winter Olympics in Sapporo drew attention of the sport fans from all over the world.

However, the late 1960s and the beginning of 1970s were not the idyllic times at all; on the contrary, it was a period of sharp social and cultural conflicts. The revision of US-Japan Security Treaty in 1960 elicited all-national unrests. Although not directly involved in the Vietnam war (1955–1975), Japanese government allowed the stationing of American troops on Japanese territory, which provoked the strong opposition and protests coming not only from left-wing intellectuals and students but also from general public who held deeply rooted anti-war sentiments. Radical student movement which demanded reforms in education and politics swept the universities, and the ever-widening generation gap between those who experienced the war and young generation who was born during the peace times became obvious. The apt example of the effort to rebel against the elder generations who denounced younger people for weak-mindedness and lack of self-discipline and patriotism was the highly popular song *Senso wo shiranai kodomotachi* (*Children who do not know war*) written and composed in 1970 by the young duo Jiros (Osamu Kitayama and Jiro Sugita). Although the duo had no affiliation to the pacifistic movement, the song was composed to express the mild anti-war message and became an iconic expression frequently used in discussion on contemporary war memory (Salomon 2014).

In response to the concern over the common loss of Japanese identity, the Sato cabinet implemented several measures for enhancing the positive identification with the nation. The government actively used the Olympic Games in 1964 and 1972, as well as Expo Osaka in 1970 for presenting the new image of postwar Japan that took pride in its recent achievements (Wilson 2011). In 1972 the Japan Foundation (*Kokusai koryu kikin*) was established as a semi-governmental organization to promote the dissemination of Japanese culture, arts, and Japanese language education all over the world.

Moreover, the ethics curriculum was reintroduced to elementary and junior schools in 1958. It was the last step in the process of the revival of more conservative forces within Japanese society which started in the early 1950s and steered education away from liberal experiments (McCullough 2008: 24). In 1950 Teiyu Amano (1884–1980), philosopher and the Minister of Education in the 3rd Yoshida government (in the office 1950–1952), emphasized the necessity of moral education and proposed to replace the former Imperial Rescript on Education (*Kyoiku ni kansuru chokugo*, 1890) which considered the cultivation of virtues, particularly loyalty and filial piety, as the fundamental purpose of education, and was officially abolished in 1948, by the similar code of ethics. In 1952 the Prime minister Shigeru Yoshida delivered his renowned speech in which he emphasized the necessity of the fundamental change in social sciences—particularly in geography and history—and moral education, and finally, the policy of the revision of all textbooks used at the compulsory education system was implemented in 1958 (Kobayashi 1976: 60).

The last but not the least attempt to promote the spirit of patriotism was the National Foundation Day (*Kenkoku kinen no hi*), celebrated on February 11, which was reestablished and included in the official calendar in 1966. The day, originally named *Kigensetsu* (Empire Holiday), and designated by Meiji government in 1873 as a national holiday in order to promote the imperial cult that underlined the concept of *kokutai* (national identity, essence, and character), was abolished after the surrender of Japan for its reliance on the State Shinto (*kokka shinto*), Japanese nationalism and militarism.

Thus, all these events, together with the celebration of the centennial of the Meiji Restoration in 1968, provoked strong pressure on the reevaluation of the national history including war one, in order to recreate the Japanese national identity. And there is no doubt the Toho 8.15 project, which started with the film *Nihon no ichiban nagai hi* directed by Kihachi Okamoto, perfectly fit to the spirit of time.

The film distributed also under the English title *The Emperor and the General* was the adaptation of the book written by a historian and non-fiction writer Kazutoshi Hando (b. 1930) but originally published in 1965 under the name of Soichi Oya (1900–1970), famous journalist noted for his research and commentaries on popular culture (Hando 1965). The book was a combination of documentary footage, historical records, and fictional scenes. The story covered the period between noon August 14, 1945, when the Emperor expressed his decision to surrender and noon August 15 when the Emperor's message was broadcasted all over the country, and showed the different responses of the country's top leaders, namely the Prime Minister Kantaro Suzuki, the Minister of War Korechika Anami and the Minister of Navy Mitsumasa Yonai, to the simple fact of the inevitable defeat of Japan. The plot also included the *Kyujo incident* (*Kyujo jiken*)—the military coup d'état by young officers of the Ministry of War and Imperial Guard to stop the move to surrender.

The coup began on August 15, 2019, between 1 a.m. and 2 a.m. when junior officers led by Major Kenji Tanaka seized the Imperial Guards Division after killing Lieutenant General Takeshi Mori, commander of the Division. The rebels then issued a set of false orders in Mori's name and attempted a series of assassinations, including that of Prime Minister Suzuki. They also detained the president of NHK after the public broadcaster recorded the Emperor's speech at the Imperial Palace, but he had left the recording in the palace, fearing the rebels might catch him. A frantic search for the recording ensued until the early morning, when General Shizuichi Tanaka of the Eastern District Army showed up at the palace and quelled the coup. The Emperor and his household were safe, and the speech was aired from a broadcasting center right next to the Imperial Palace in Uchisaiwaicho in Chiyoda Ward.

The film became a great commercial success. The media in Japan called it as a "film for the nation" (*kokumin eiga*) using the wartime propaganda label (High 2003: 224–225). As Harald Salomon proved in his study on Toho's 8.15 series (Salomon 2014), the investigation of the audience done by Studios managers provided the surprising feedback on the emotional impact of the film. Not only middle and older age audience but also families and female students were represented in high numbers. However, there was a remarkable generation gap in the reception of the film. The younger generation under 25 years tended to emphasize the "horror of war" (48 %) while older spectators focused on the "courage of the people who saved the country" (43 %). Some answers stressed that "Toho attempt to tell 'the history that schoolbooks omitted' and even younger audience member were struck by the passionate patriotism of the young officers who opposed the ending of the war" (ibid.: 125). There are no doubts the Toho film project felt into the fertile ground and perfectly corresponded to the urgent need of the recreation of national identity during the late 1960s and early 1970s.

The second adaptation of Hando's book was released in 2015, almost a week before the 70th anniversary of the end of the war, and distributed abroad under the English title *The Emperor in August*. The director Masato Harada basically worked on the same story but in a slightly different way. The comparison of the two adaptations can provide a vivid picture of how the changing content of war narrative reflects the different approach to the national identity in the postwar Japanese society.

It may be beneficial to start the analysis with the personalities of both directors. Kihachi Okamoto, born in 1924, had to suspend his university studies during the war times and in 1943 was drafted into the elite Air Force. The personal war experience had a profound effect on his later film works; one-third of almost forty films of various genres he directed during six decades relates directly to the war. Masato Harada, to the contrary, has been a classic representative of the generation of the "children who never knew war." Born in 1949 he left Japan in 1972 and studied in Great Britain and USA where he spent number of years training as a filmmaker and working as an English-Japanese subtitle translator. His foreign experience has allowed him to take more complex and detached approach to the war narrative.

Main difference between the two adaptations lies in the way of how the historical narrative is built and how the key historical figures are portrayed. Okamoto relies to some extend on the "conspiracy theory" based on the idea supported by the occupation administration that it was the military circles who de facto usurped the state and led the Japanese nation astray.

However, the unexpected hero of the Okamoto's film is General Korechika Anami (1887–1945), the Minister of War in the surrender cabinet, played by Toshiro Mifune, one of Japan's most internationally recognized actor. Although Anami was one of the toughest opponents of the acceptance of the Allied surrender terms, once the imperial decision was made, he became its strong and determined supporter in the few but critical hours before his death. His dramatic ceremonial suicide appears to be an almost rationally conceived solution to the intolerable internal conflict between the values of his professional career and his loyalty to his Emperor, whose decision meant their destruction. Thus, although the militarists in general are labeled as villains, the true soldier imbued with the feelings of devotion to the country and loyalty to the Emperor is regarded as hero. His ritual suicide is not just an act of taking responsibility but also as a step toward the catharsis and purification (*harae*) in the name of new Japan. Such an interpretation is evident from the scene just before his suicide. When one of his subordinates expresses his firm determination to follow his commander in death, Anami forbids him to do so in a very emotional speech in which he stresses the necessity to live on and rebuild the new Japan. Such a strong ideological message of Okamoto's film to the young generation is completely absent in Harada's adaptation.

Both films present the Emperor Showa (Hirohito) in a completely different light. Okamoto follows the generally accepted view on the lack of the Emperor's responsibility. Although the Emperor is physically presented at any important moment, he is not a key person on the stage and does not participate in serious discussions in the Imperial Council about the important issues that involved both the Emperor and the Big Six, a group of six supreme civilian and military leaders of the country in 1945. His presence is more or less implied, and he himself is highly impersonalized; his voice can be heard but his face is taken in long shots or from behind, and the camera focuses on the symbolic details—a back collar of his ceremonial uniform, his hand in a white glove put on an armrest of his chair, etc. On the other hand, Harada goes in his adaptation more deeply into the characters. He pays more attention to the individuality and personal motivations of three key persons, that is, Prime Minister Suzuki, Minister of War Anami, and the Emperor. The three historical persons are described as ordinary people—including the Emperor (sic!)—with their visions, doubts, and personal sufferings. Moreover, his Emperor plays a key role in bringing the war to the end, despite the fact that young military hotheads mount a coup d'état to thwart his surrender announcement and fight the enemy on home soil.

Unlike in Okamoto's adaptation, in Harada's film the Emperor's decision to accept the surrender conditions laid down by the Potsdam Declaration of July 26, 1945, is not immediately approved. The Big Six is deeply divided over the surrender question, with Prime Minister Suzuki firmly in the peace camp and Imperial loyalist General Anami among the bitter-enders. But when Anami sees the Emperor's strong desire for peace, he changes his mind. With the backing of Suzuki and Anami, the Emperor feels emboldened to announce his decision for peace to the Imperial Council. Such interpretation did not appear in Hando's book *Nihon no ichiban nagai hi*, but has been based on the new researches which had been published since the end of 1960s, including Hando's *Seidan* (Hando 1985).

Both adaptations are anti-war films and can be regarded as a coherent tool for exploring the collective historical memory. But while both represent periodical attempts to interpret the dark side of the national history, they have failed to overcome a narrow national perspective. They reduce war to a confrontation between Japan and the USA while they exclude the effects of the Japanese aggression on the soldiers and civilians in China, Korea, and other Asian countries. Thus, both films are imprisoned in the narratives of war experience within national boards and do not provide a necessary instrument for coping with the past and for potential reconciliation.

Conclusion

The film as a fiction seems to be the perfect tool for molding the collective memory and national identity. Unlike the non-fiction which based on the historical facts and may be seen as inconvenient because of the intentional selection of historical events in (re)producing the historical narrative, the fiction offers a large scale of possibilities of how to distill the key factors for forming national identity into the collective memory. Indeed, all the historical "errors and inaccuracies can be simply defended as a 'creative licence'" (Seaton 2007: 151). Moreover, there is also an emotional aspect. For many people such "creative licence" may play greater significant role in the process of formation of their historical consciousness than true and objective historical evidence.

Japanese war films have gained a great success for more than seventy years since the end of war. The secrets of such success have been numerous starting from the technical and economic aspects (i.e. best timing, national-wide publicity and distribution) via famous directors and actors up to the ability of story that reached the audience. Thus, although the war films have displayed ideologically very different perceptions of war, the audience has been willing to accept nationalistic films with military heroes as well as progressive and critical ones which revealed the suffering of Japanese victims, on one hand, and the horror of atrocity, on the other. However, the core question in the search of the relation between historical narrative, collective memory and identity consists of how the war stories can be told in such a way that the postwar generations can positively identify with the experiences of the war generation. There is no simple answer to such a tricky problem, but it is obvious that the Japanese filmmakers have elaborated several conceptual frameworks within which nationalistic, conservative and progressive interpretations of war narratives are acceptable. No matter how different these concepts are, there is a common denominator underneath which consists of a simple moral—mainly antiwar—message that the Japanese identify with since the end of war.

References

Ashplant, T.G., Dawson, G., & Roper, M. (2000). *The politics of war memory and commemoration.* London: Routledge.

Bukh, A. (2007). Japan's history textbooks debate: National identity in narratives of victimhood and victimization. *Asian Survey, 47*(5), 683–704.

De Brito, A.B., Gonzalez-Enriquez, C., & Aguilar, P. (2001). *The politics of memory: Transitional justice in democratizing societies.* Oxford: Oxford University Press.

Gluck, C. (1993). The past in the present. In A. Gordon (Ed.), *Postwar Japan as history* (pp. 64–95). Berkeley and Los Angeles: University of California Press.

Gordon, A. (1993). Conclusion. In *Postwar Japan as history* (pp. 449–464). Berkeley and Los Angeles: University of California Press.

Handō, K. (1965). *Nihon ichiban nagai hi* [The Japan's longest day]. Tokyo: Bungei shunju.

Hando, K. (1985). *Seidan: Tenno to Suzuki Kentaro* [Imperial decision: The Emperor and Kentaro Suzuki]. Tokyo: Bungei shunju.

Heisler, M.O. (2008). Challenged histories and collective self-concepts: Politics in history, memory, and time. *The Annals of the American Academy of Political and Social Science*, 617(1), 199–211.

High, P.B. (2003). *Imperial screen: Japanese film culture in the fifteen years' war, 1931–1945.* Madison: Wisconsin Press.

Hodgkin, K., & Radstone, S. (Eds.). (2003). *Contested pasts: The politics of memory.* London and New York: Routledge.

Jeans, R.B. (2005). Victims or victimizers? Museums, textbooks, and the war debate in contemporary Japan. *The Journal of Military History, 69*(1), 149–195.

Kansteiner, W. (2002). Finding meaning in memory: A methodological critique of collective memory studies. *History and Theory*, 41(2), 179–197.

Kobayashi, T. (1976). *Society, school and progress in Japan.* Oxford: Pergamon Press.

Kratochwil, F. (2006). History, action and identity: Revisiting the "second" great debate and assessing its importance for social theory. *European Journal of International Relations, 12*(1), 5–29.

Kushner, B. (2007). Nationality and nostalgia: The manipulation of memory in Japan, Taiwan, and China since 1990. *The International History Review, 29*(4), 793–820.

Lebow, R.N., Kansteiner, W., & Fogu, C. (Eds.). (2006). *The politics of memory in postwar Europe*. Durham, NC: Duke University Press.

McCullough, D. (2008). Moral and social education in Japanese schools: Conflicting conceptions of citizenship. *Citizenship Teaching and Learning*, *4*(1), 21–36.

McGrattan, C. (2013). *Memory, politics and identity: Haunted by history*. New York: Palgrave MacMillan.

Motion Picture Producers Association of Japan. (2019). *Statistics of film industry in Japan*. Retrieved from http://www.eiren.org/statistics_e/.

Ricci, G.R. (Ed.). (2017). *Justice and the politics of memory*. Abingdon and New York: Routledge.

Richie, D. (2012). *A hundred years of Japanese film: A concise history, with a selective guide to DVDs and videos*. Tokyo: Kodansha international.

Salomon, H. (2014). Japan's longest days: Toho and the politics of war memory, 1967–1972. In K. Tam, T.Y. Tsu, & Wilson, S. (Eds.), *Chinese and Japanese films on the second world war* (pp. 121–136). London, Routledge.

Satō, T. (1995). *Nihon eigashi* [History of Japanese film], Vol. 1–3. Tokyo: Iwanami shoten.

Seaton, P.A. (2007). *Japan's contested war memories: The 'memory rifts' in historical consciousness of World War II*. London: Routledge.

Sharp, J. (2011). *Historical dictionary of Japanese cinema*. Plymouth: The Scarecrow Press.

Shimazu, N. (2003). Popular representations of the past: The case of postwar Japan. *Journal of Contemporary History*, *38*(1), 101–116.

Szczepanska, K. (2014). *The politics of war memory in Japan: Progressive civil society groups and contestation of memory of the Asia-Pacific war*. London: Routledge.

Trefalt, B. (2003). War, commemoration and national identity in modern Japan, 1868–1975. In S. Wilson (Ed.), *Nation and nationalism in Japan* (pp. 115–134). London: Routledge.

Wilson, S. (2011). Exhibiting a new Japan: The Tokyo Olympics of 1964 and Expo '70 in Osaka. *Historical Research*, 85(227), 159–178.

Wilson, S. (2013). Film and soldier: Japanese war movies in the 1950s. *Journal of Contemporary History*, *48*(3), 537–555.

Winter, J., & Sivan, E. (1999). *War and remembrance in the 20th century*. Cambridge: Cambridge University Press.

Yomota, I. (2019). *What is Japanese cinema: A history*. New York: Columbia University Press.

7. *Through the Eyes of Others: Postwar Reconciliation Narrative in Contemporary Japan*

Emilia S. Heo
Ritsumeikan Asia Pacific University

Introduction

"Does peace studies contribute to peace?" was the very first essay question I gave to my students in international peace studies class. While grading 200 papers, one captured my eyes. The title was "Your question is wrong!" I paused for a moment and, with a mild irritation, started reading it. The essay bluntly states that I should not have asked whether peace studies contributes to peace. I should have asked *how* peace studies contributes to peace. I realized I did make the question wrong.

This research is about postwar reconciliation in contemporary Japan, and this, through the eyes of the younger generation. Why youth? Just like any canonical international relations (IR) scholars, I love concept and theory—I wrote my doctoral dissertation on creating a conceptual framework of reconciliation in IR. To analyze state behaviors, I look into foreign policy, power relations, and structural constraint. My paper often argues that joint political leadership or a regional institutional framework plays a pivotal role in rebuilding a broken relation between historical enemies. Nonetheless, university teaching gradually made me discover that it is important to listen to students if we want peace studies to contribute to peace, in other words, to connect research with reality: To what extent does Japanese youth's understanding about the country's past affect the way they perceive their home country's relations with neighboring states today? How do they perceive their own role in promoting peace and reconciliation?

World War II and its aftermath remain a vital reference point for how countries perceive themselves and are perceived by others in the Asia-Pacific region. The constant interactive process between the past and present poses challenges since the current generation did not experience the traumatic historical event themselves. Japanese youth are not *remembering* what happened. They are *learning* from what they see in the media, what they hear from their grandparents, and what they learn at school. It now becomes even more challenging since governmental efforts in globalizing Japanese higher education bring students into a situation where competing national narratives coexist in and outside the classroom.

Working with data through an online survey and multiple class observations in Japan, I elucidate that Japanese university students, especially those exposed to a global educational environment, display critical engagement with World War II teaching and conflict knowledge acquired at school. The research findings also show how they connect themselves with the country's past influences their perspective on what role youth can play in promoting peace with former enemy states. I therefore argue that if we want the younger generation to become an active agent of reconciliation, it is crucial not only to create a locus where youth can learn world history and current affairs through the eyes of others, but also to offer them an opportunity to think and share their reflections with their compatriots as well as with students from other countries.

The purpose of this study is not to question *which* historical knowledge is taught or should be taught in Japan. Rather, it is an attempt to discover how conflict knowledge affects youth perception toward themselves and others and what challenges they face today.

Conflict Knowledge and Identity

Although World War II came to an end more than seventy years ago, it still continues to haunt the Japanese relations with former enemy states, China and Korea in particular. Nanjing massacre, sex slavery, territorial dispute, Yasukuni shrine visits, and apology issue are to name but a few. The question of how to remember has long become official business. States choose various ways of remembering the conflicting past in an attempt to shape a national collective memory that could be transmitted from generations to generations. Takayama (2009) problematizes how Japanese and American elites construct postwar hegemonic narratives and create official knowledge in the Japanese history textbook. Since high school students today are born after 2000, so distant from past violent events, history education easily becomes the major source of conflicts between corresponding governments (see, for instance, Wang 2014; Yang 2003). Callahan (2006) shows how China produces and consumes patriotic nationalism by focusing on the external other, Japan, through rituals on public holidays such as national humiliation day and how it deeply affects the public memory and collective identity. War memorials, museums, and statue constructions are also a powerful means to build up collective memory. By illustrating how conflicting past is narrated in the war memorial museums in Korea and Japan, Kal (2007) convincingly demonstrates the danger of ethnic nationalism construction: "The unchallenged concept of nation and citizenship based on an ethnic collectivism poses a critical obstacle to the task of reconciling historical injustice between the nations as well as within them" (p. 151).

Whether it is through education, practiced national rituals, public holidays, or memorials and museums, how people understand or learn about their past reflects not only how they perceive themselves but also others. From social constructivist and poststructuralist perspectives, identity formation whether it is personal or collective is relational and interdependent (Diez 2004; Hagström 2015; Hansen 2006; Neumann 1996). When it comes to conflicting past, the otherness becomes inseparable from the notion of enmity. By definition, otherness or being different is neutral and does not automatically contain any judgment of perceiving the other as hostile, violent, or fearful (Harle 2000). The otherness becomes the source of enmity only when it is associated with an asymmetric relationship: the victim and the victimizer, the weak versus the strong, the superior versus the inferior, and the winner versus the loser.

What counts as conflict knowledge therefore strongly affects the shaping of national identity. Neil Macgregor, the former director of the British Museum, highlighted the danger of selective history while exhibiting "Memories of a Nation," German history from the British view: "In Britain we use our history in order to comfort us to make us feel stronger, to remind ourselves that we were always, always deep down, good people [...] Maybe we mention a little bit of slave trade here and there, a few wars here and there, but the chapters we instate on are the sunny ones" (cited in Connolly 2016).

Glorifying the wartime past while keeping silent on the dark side of one's history is not an uncommon practice when it comes to the collective identity formation. It, however, has an alarming consequence to the youth today living in the era of globalization. The memorialization of the past is now beyond national boundaries: "How a nation deals with its past is never entirely within its own control, least of all with the growing globalization of intellectual life and popular culture in the twentieth and twenty-first centuries" (Evans

2003: 9). Youth today are easily exposed to a situation when they discover a different version of what happened while discussing history and politics with youth from the former enemy states. Capturing how they narrate about their past thus provides us a better understanding of how conflict knowledge shapes the self versus the others.

On Reconciliation Narrative

Exploring narratives to understand or to make sense of our life is not new. But it made a recent turn in IR both as concept and research methodology (Bouza García 2017; Suganami 2008; Roberts 2006; Czarniawska 2004). Scholarly works in peace and reconciliation studies have also joined this "recent turn." Auerbach (2009) develops an analytical framework of what she calls "Reconciliation Pyramid" indicating the relationship between metanarratives, national metanarratives, and national narratives—mainly based on the Israeli-Palestinian and Turkish-Armenian reconciliation cases. Wigura (2012) explores alternative historical narrative to review the meaning of forgiveness in the Polish-German reconciliation process. By applying Mishler's (2015) model of narrative analysis, Manners and Murray (2016) propose six European integration narratives to make new sense of what European Union (EU) means after the awarding of the Nobel Peace Prize in 2012. Rosoux (2017: 333) goes to the opposite direction arguing that the common narrative defining EU as a peace builder is not accepted any more: "This symbol both of reconciliation between French and Germans, and of EU integration, does not seem to resonate with the same intensity among the younger generations." She concludes that there is no need to create a new interpretation of *Pax Europeana* but rather to make efforts at connecting all existing narratives about past and present realities.

Narrative, as a unit of analysis, has found its place in peace and reconciliation studies. But which narrative or whose narrative? Bouza García (2017: 286–287) notes that the "narrative turn" in European studies raises important questions around the agency, the narrator: "Are all stories on European integration to be analyzed? [. . .] Does a narrative require a certain degree of spread among the public – and methodologically, what is this extension? Who are the key producers of narratives?" Rouhana (2004), for instance, shows how power relations create an unbalanced treatment in dealing with the narratives of the perpetrator and the victim in identity conflicts. To better understand why EU lacks democratic foundations today, Tonra (2011) criticizes the élite-focused narrative poorly disseminated within the society. He claims that collective identity can become a reality through shared narratives, not only by political and diplomatic élites but also by writers, educators, artists, intellectuals, and engaged citizens. So, to answer Bouza García's question, yes, not all individual agencies are equally assessed.

Holmes (2018) chooses diplomats and political leaders to explain how face-to-face encounters shape key events in global politics. Bode (2015) talks to international civil servants to assess the role of individual agency in policy change at the United Nations. Little (2011) interviews representatives of the main political parties to rethink reconciliation and conflict transformation in Northern Ireland. Barkan (2009) zooms into the challenges and contributions of historians in dealing with Turkish-Armenian reconciliation. Radnitz (2018) listens to adults to assess the attitudes of people in a post-conflict society towards their former enemies in Azerbaijan. Many scholars (Clarke-Habibi 2018; Halai and Durrani 2018; Zembylas, Charalambous, and Charalambous 2011) have explored teacher agency in promoting peace and reconciliation. There is every reason for its justification. When it comes to international reconciliation, political elites shape foreign policy; regional institutions offer incentive to sustain bilateral peace condition; scholars provide theory and suggest future implications (hopefully to be taken seriously by practitioners); mass media holds power to easily create collective hatred; and professors influence students by how and why they teach. They all do matter but youth does, too. "Students count in a variety of ways, but perhaps their main significance is that they constitute future generations. [. . .] The motivations they develop are bound to affect what a society will become with the passage of time," states Rosenau (2008: 122) in his recent monograph *People Count!* How students perceive the education they receive will in return provide indicators for those who make and revise the education policy. Exploring youth narratives on postwar reconciliation in Japan therefore offers insights into how conflict knowledge shapes the way they perceive their home country's relations with former enemy states and what role they think they can play in promoting reconciliation.

Data Collection

The empirical findings in this chapter are based on data gathered through an online survey and classroom observations. The survey included 19 content-based questions subdivided into four thematic sections: sources of World War II knowledge, conflict narrative, history education, and reconciliation. It followed a mixed-structure approach, including both multiple choice and open-ended questions, the latter being particularly relevant to explore youth narratives and perspectives on postwar reconciliation. The average completion time for the survey was 15 minutes. I shared this survey among my professional networks across different universities. For a larger sampling, I also shared the survey link on Facebook, Twitter, and official websites of research institutes. However, the major survey respondents are students from Sophia University, then Nagoya University, Osaka University, Hokkaido University, and others in the Tokyo area. To diversify the sample, I tried to increase the number of departments and faculties within my institution. The majority of respondents study subjects in the areas of social sciences and humanities and were between 18 and 24 years of age enrolled in a BA program. Students were given the choice between English and Japanese to complete the survey. All student answers were translated into English while translations were done with sensitivity to connotations in the national discourses. A parallel data collection for German students was done by my former UN University colleague, Ingvild Bode (for a full description of survey content, question list, and research method, see Bode and Heo 2017). A prior research outcome was published focusing on a subset of five questions contained in World War II knowledge sources and conflict narrative parts. In addition to the 155 Japanese responses used for the coauthored article, 55 responses are added here, summing up to 210 respondents in total. The 55 responses were not used at that time in order to keep the quantity of Japanese samples comparable to the German ones.

The current research focuses on four questions included in the history education and reconciliation parts and analyzes 210 responses completed by Japanese university students. Class observations are limited to peace-related undergraduate courses I taught at Sophia University (2013–2016) and Ritsumeikan Asia Pacific University (2016–current). All names mentioned are pseudonyms. The purpose of narrative analysis here is to put into light unheard stories (Chase 2011: 427–428) through thematic representations of provided answers. By doing so, the study attempts at engaging youth as "key producers of narratives" (Bouza García 2017: 287), often neglected in IR. Narrative research is "still a field in the making" but is worth pursuing as it "encourage[s] creative explorations of self, identity, community, and reality" (Chase 2011: 429–430). The data result as well as its interpretation does not aim at generalizing and only provides an indication of youth narrative in Japan.

Data Analysis

To the question whether World War II knowledge affects their view on the home country's relations with neighboring states, 65% (123 out of 189 answered, 21 skipped) of Japanese students surveyed answered yes. What they learn or do not learn at school matters. Do they know what they know? Do they know what they do not know? In other words, do Japanese students take conflict knowledge and history teaching seriously? Why or why not?

Finding 1: Conflict Knowledge Helps Us Become More Sensitive to Others

About 98.8% respondents (176 out of 178 answered, 32 skipped) said it is relevant to learn about World War II today. Only 0.2% (2) clearly stated that "we have nothing to do with the generation and the time" and that "there is no hurt in knowing, but I have never personally encountered a situation in which I was troubled by not having enough knowledge." The main reason provided with the why of history learning is based on the conventional interpretation of the connection between the past and present: "There is no future for those who forgot history," "We should learn from the past not to repeat the same mistake," "History makes what it is today." These types of reflection do not tell us whether students will actually make more efforts to study. World history is not a hot subject to many of them. I often ask my Japanese students whether they enjoyed learning world history in high school. Ryosuke told us that he chose not to learn since the subject was optional. Midori said it was all about memorizing dates and places and names. They looked puzzled when Claire shared her passion on learning about the world. Still, their narratives reveal a high awareness of what history learning means and what consequence it brings to them: "To learn World War II is effective in making sense of the now of world affairs." And since past gives sense to the present, "I cannot understand the current problem among nations because I do not have knowledge about them at all." What counts as historical knowledge is crucial in shaping their worldview perception today. But why is it so? Students go on to argue:

> If we do not learn about the Second World War, we might hurt Koreans or Chinese. Since we learned what Japan did to Koreans and Chinese a little, we understand that the Second World War is a sensitive issue to talk about.
>
> There will be a larger number of immigrants and exchange students from China and Korea in the future. In order to minimize a clash created by ignorance, it is important to have the correct understanding of history.
>
> Learning it [World War II] can make people more considerate of each other. If we do not learn it, we are easily controlled to hate one another.

These narratives are particularly significant as they imply an interactive process of history learning. Conflict knowledge affects not only how we perceive them. It also affects how they perceive us. And it matters since "the way how next generations interpret Japan's position during the war can change the relationship between other countries in both good and bad ways." To the generation that did not experience the war, historical enmity is not given. It is socially created and respondents here are aware of it.

Finding 2: I Want to Know How Koreans and Chinese Learn About World War II

When I ask students where they acquired their conflict knowledge, they do not have difficulty in naming the sources. It ranges from history classes, mass media, internet (mainly referring to Wikipedia or Google) to oral stories from their grandparents, visits to museum (often as a compulsory school trip), movies, and animes. But when I twist the question and ask "what makes you believe what you believe true?" it is not the same. Several justifications could be made. The best, I would argue, is that the question requires a certain degree of self-assessment and reflective criticism, not always obvious to Japanese students. It therefore came out with surprise when 76.9% (130 out of 169 answered, 41 skipped) of the respondents explained why and in which way World War II history should be taught *differently*. This question presupposes that students are well aware of what history education they received and how it is viewed by neighboring states. It also requires them to be ready to question it. Some misunderstood, others simply skipped the question. But there was a certain pattern observed around repeated keywords such as "multiple perspectives," "diversified views," and "various aspects." What they mean by multiple, diversified, or various differs but they largely fall into three categories: victim and aggressor sides, Japanese and non-Japanese views, and official and hidden narratives.

First, 21 respondents highlighted the importance of learning conflict knowledge not only from the victim side but also from the aggressor side. Examples are as follows:

> I think we should teach the facts from the aggressor side.
>
> As I remember, history classes did not discuss current problems such as comfort women. I do not agree with the Japanese way of thinking 'do not touch what is dangerous [*abunai kotoniwa hurenai*]'.
>
> Japan should teach the real story of what Japan did to people in Okinawa and other Asian countries.
>
> People in Japan have too much sense of victimization because of atomic bombs. We should learn more specifically what we did.
>
> Japan is too victimizing themselves. It is true that many people were killed but Japan killed millions of people, too, which are not clearly cited. We should learn more about what Japan did wrong, and learn from our mistakes.

> I feel that in Japan, students are taught about the Second World War as if Japan was only a victim. It's such a one sided perspective, so we should see it from other countries' perspectives as well.
>
> Japanese education emphasizes on Hiroshima/Nagasaki atomic bomb, the event which Japan got damaged when they teach about WW2. I strongly feel that we need to learn what we have done to other countries even if they are too painful and shameful for us.
>
> Stories always have two or more sides. Yes we have a lot of victims in our country but we need to recognize that we also caused sorrow to other countries.
>
> I think that we need to face the fact that we were also causing damage to countries such as the other Asian countries more deeply, because some history classes still teach the war from a perspective where Japan is the victim.

These self-reflective narratives display critical engagement with history teaching and knowledge acquired in high school. Respondents know that what they learned at school is a not a complete version of World War II history. Some students specifically pointed out the victimhood education on atomic bombings. Prior research demonstrated that the most frequently mentioned terms when asked to write down key expressions about World War II were Nagasaki, Hiroshima, and atomic bomb (Bode and Heo 2017: 12–14). However, it is also to note that some provided a counter narrative by emphasizing that "it is never enough to learn and remember the pain of the loser's side (like atomic bombs)." To explain the rationale behind why to learn the dark side of national history, two students referred to international community. While one explains that it is politically correct to teach both sides of aggressor and victim as we live in a globalizing world, the other raises concern about the danger of ignorance:

> We have always emphasized that war should never be an option. On the other hand, we do not teach how cruel we were when we invaded other countries. I think it is important to include it in history education as a consideration to international community [*kokusaitekina hairyou*].
>
> I think that in Japan, the history of Japan as the aggressor is downplayed so much that I find wrong and needs immediate correction. I hear that in high school, some schools finish Japanese history before WW2, which leaves out everything from 1940s and later, which is a crime considering how we fail to educate Japanese youth to be able to discuss these issues with others from other countries. We are viewed internationally as having little knowledge of our own past and our own role in the war.

Second, 32 respondents showed eagerness to learn history through the eyes of others, meaning other countries:

> At an international school I used to attend, where the student body was predominantly white American, we had a German classmate teaching us how she

was taught about WW2 back in her German elementary school. It provoked a lot of reflection and constructive discussion and I think it left us with quite a different impression of history than what we would have if we were only told one point of view.

Since we learn about the Second World War from Japanese perspective, I wish to learn from other perspectives. I am interested in learning about what Koreans and Chinese learn about the Second World War.

When I was in the U.S., the teacher taught us that dropping the atomic bombs was necessary in order to end the war and the US contributed the end of the war. However, Japanese people think themselves as the victims and it was not necessary because there were not enough military power left in Japan. There is such different perspective and people tend to tell differently about this war so I would like to be taught in different country's perspective.

Professors coming from other countries, especially from Southeast Asia or from United States, hold courses over 2WW.

Classes should be taught more from multiple perspectives. In addition, I believe that why it happened is more important than who is or is not at fault.

These narratives clearly demonstrate that students are more and more aware of the fact that what they learn as official history in school is not always the same as what their classmates from other countries learn in their own nation. One student mentioned history textbook suggesting that a comparative analysis might be beneficial to them: "There is a need for change. Regardless of what is true, there needs to be a chance to compare the history textbooks from different countries." More than who is right or wrong, students surveyed here are more interested in studying how a single historical event, World War II in particular, is taught differently in other countries. It is to highlight that some respondents narrate their experience of studying abroad while others mention the international composition of faculty body. With the government's efforts in globalizing higher educational system in Japan, the clash of national narratives will drastically increase and poses further challenges to university teaching in IR and peace studies. At my current institution, it is not rare to have students from more than 25 nationalities in one classroom: we have Pakistani students sitting next to Indian students, Chinese next to Japanese, French next to German, and Tamils next to Singhalese. Compared to my courses at the previous institution where more than 95% of students were Japanese, this multinational composition of student body will lead Japanese students to be more and more confronted with a new reality of discovering official knowledge different from what they learned.

Third, students used words such as "true," "hidden," or "distorted" to explain how history teaching in Japan should be changed:

Some facts are rejected and only the most important facts are taught.

I believe that much of the information about the war is still hidden. I think that people must face the reality of what actually happened during the war.

I heard that the facts of comfort women or group suicide in Okinawa are distorted in education.

We know little what happened in the past, neither what Japan did to other countries. So we have to take more time to learn it and should learn how Korea, China or other countries were thinking of Japan.

It should be covered thoroughly especially Japanese textbooks exclude things like the comfort women, or where exactly did they invade. Aside from that, it should extend its vision towards other countries view points.

In particular, Japan tries to conceal the fact Japan illegally attach other countries. Therefore, all countries should not conceal any facts and should accept their own mistakes, then they should teach them.

Japanese government does not provide the truth to let Japanese people know about it.

There are a lot of events the government chose to look over or not put too much emphasis on.

It should be changed if it is taught with the Japanese government's point of view.

I've heard that some adults are hesitant to teach about the war these days because they are afraid of hurting children's feelings. But I think it's even more scarier that future generation might start a war again because of lack of history knowledge.

When I was in the US and learned about the war in the US history class, even though I was supposed to be learning the same thing about the war as I learned it in Japan, it seemed very different. It might be because each country tries to make their own country look innocent and just. In my opinion, people who did not experience WW2 need to learn what truly happened in the war, and keep on telling that to next generations.

Because it is self-centred in many countries and taught in the way that is beneficial for their own countries.

These answers show that students question the process of selecting which conflict knowledge is to be taught. While some place responsibility on "government" or "adults" for the consequences of selective history, others provide deeper reflection of why certain countries glorify their past and what it means to open up the dark side of one's own history.

Finding 3: Let's Promote Friendship and Anime to Bring Peace!

We have seen that Japanese students surveyed have a clear understanding that what and how they were taught affect their perception on Japanese relations with neighboring states. Now with what they know or do not know, how do they perceive their own role in promoting peace and reconciliation between

Japan, China, and Korea? A total of 165 respondents (45 skipped) shared their thought on the potential role of individual agency to build peace relations among nations. Various ideas—all meaningful—were developed but I will focus on three main representative patterns: *let's make friends*, *let's appreciate culture*, and *let's promote Japan*.

Creating interpersonal relations or simply becoming friends with youth from the former enemy states contribute to peace: "I personally interact with Chinese or Korean exchange students. I believe that by establishing good relationship with them, I contribute to improvement of relations with neighbouring countries in the future." Becoming friends for what? The ultimate purpose is to avoid stereotype, bias, prejudice, to eliminate discrimination, or not to judge them. This reflection ironically implies that there is rather a negative collective perception portrayed toward "them" and respondents consider it as a major obstacle to creating peace conditions in East Asia:

> To establish personal network with people from neighbouring countries. To make sure Koreans and Chinese are not discriminated against in Japan.
>
> By knowing the people from the country and getting along with them, we can prove that the stereotypes that we Japanese tend to have to other Asians are not true in all cases, and we are all alike and different in good ways.
>
> Actually talking or having relations with the people in neighbouring countries to know their personality, not just having a solid image.
>
> Never use or judge those people by stereotypes.
>
> Not to have faulty thinking [*ayamatta kangae kata*] or stereotypes towards neighbouring countries.
>
> Elderly people have stereotypes. We do not have that kind of stereotypes and many of us know we cannot judge by which country you are from.
>
> Play a role to reduce the adult's stereotypes towards China and Korea. If we have more connections to the younger people of those countries, our views towards each other's countries would change as well.
>
> Through direct interaction, to reduce antagonism [*tekitai ishiki*] on a personal level.
>
> What I can do is to interact with people of other countries without bias [*henken*].
>
> To interact with them to change the bad image of Japan.

What they mean by bad image or stereotype is not always described but some narratives talk about anti-Japanese feeling, often created by media:

> When meeting people from neighbouring countries, treat them as individuals and do not create unnecessary boundaries by viewing them all as an anti-Japanese.
>
> To deepen understanding of each other through interacting with people of neighbouring countries. Negative views [*warui mikata*] are often spread because people understand those countries through opinions on the Internet

> and politics, rather than meeting them in person. I believe that reconciliation is brought closer if we understand their ways of thinking.
>
> Getting along with Korean and Chinese students is the best. Korean and Chinese I am acquainted with are nice persons. Japanese media and neighbouring countries media tend to broadcast bad aspects of each other. The young have to judge by themselves. We must not be susceptible to the media.
>
> Actively seeking for correct knowledge rather than being influenced by distorted media.

Apart from the potential danger of distortion through media, one student mentioned that not knowing causes problem: "To share my personal experience to others and try to reduce misunderstandings caused by ignorance." For this, "to know, prior to all" [*mazuwa shiru koto*] was another recurring pattern observed in assessing their role as peace agent:

> We can think of the history of war not emotionally but critically so that we understand the other countries.
>
> To know the neighbouring countries deeply, not only TV media and newspaper but form another aspects.
>
> To understand the history from both sides and have own ideas to construct better relation.
>
> Getting not only the information of Japan but also that of other countries.

Students surveyed demonstrate an active engagement by raising the necessity not only to understand how Chinese or Korean students learn about the past conflict but also to discuss and exchange ideas: "Study more, from various sources not only in Japanese, and discuss with friends, although I find this very difficult because I don't want to ruin friendship. But certainly discussion on internet is not the way forward. The anonymity is good but it can lead to over statement which can lead to unsolvable discussion." Direct communication is the best way to learn:

> It is needed that young people of each country have an honest interchange of thought or opinion in an unofficial place.
>
> To communicate and discuss with friends or colleagues in neighbouring countries, and tell that it's not only one viewpoint that tells the whole story.
>
> Now I cannot contribute to promote Japanese relations directly, but I want to know a lot about same generation of Chinese and Korean people. And I would like to know their opinions about the relations with Japan and I also want them to know our opinions. I want to get more first-hand education.
>
> We should listen to people who have opposing opinions and talk with them friendly.
>
> To talk about what should be changed and how it should be changed.
>
> To know how they think about Japan and to understand that we are all the same humans.

Grass-root communication, talking to many Asian friends and feel the differences and similarities, it affects me a lot.

Acquiring knowledge and interacting with them is a shortcut to reconciliation, but about what? Interestingly, although some narratives touch upon historical issues, most of the respondents direct their interest to culture and art:

As a Japanese youth I think I have to show an attitude that I am willing to understand the cultures and the way people of our neighbouring countries think.

We can promote amity relationship in exchanging studies and culture. It can help people-to-people reconciliation.

Cultural exchange is the best way to promote Japanese relations with them.

I would like to be involved in education that promotes cultural exchange.

Culture has a very general connotation that could mean anything and nothing. But some go further and specify what they mean by culture:

I want to use Japanese anime culture as a tool for reconciliation.

Try to understand the countries from culture such as cuisine, arts, pop cultures etc.

Personally, I like music produced by China and Korea. I tell people that music should be appreciated and the historical background should not hurt the quality of the art.

We can more get to know each other sharing about our favourite person, food or music rather than political issues and we have to be friends as Asian people.

To learn their language.

If cuisine, pop music, art, or language can be used as a two-way communication element, the following narratives provide examples of how promoting Japan to the outside world may contribute to peace:

We don't have to stick on the past, we can be a good friend with neighbouring country's young people. I want to promote Japan's tourist industry. Foreign country's tourist will realize the wonderfulness of today's Japan first hand to come to Japan.

Since I am in the Spanish department, I can take action to convey Japanese culture to the Philippines.

To let neighbouring countries people know Japanese subculture.

Encouraging foreign people to come to Japan to see what the country is really like.

Introducing Japanese culture such as manga and advanced games, we can make foreigners have a great understanding of Japanese culture.

Visit those countries and show how good Japanese people are or make many friends then they might change their images of Japanese.

Teach Japanese culture.

> Promote that Japan has accurate and developed technologies.
> I can take action to convey Japanese cultures to other countries.
> We can use social media to promote Japanese relations with neighbouring countries.

Respondents consider reconciliation as a one-way and outbound process: Promoting (the wonderfulness of) Japanese culture to others helps transform enmity into amity relations. The causal link between the depth of conflict knowledge they possess and the way they perceive their own role as peace agent is not tested here. Nonetheless the postwar reconciliation narratives provided demonstrate a strong disconnection from politics and history.

Discussion and Implications

This research provides evidence that conflict knowledge influences Japanese youth perception on their home country's relations with former enemy states. By examining their postwar reconciliation narratives, the study reveals two key points to discuss.

On the one hand, there are a growing number of Japanese students displaying critical engagement with conflict knowledge acquired at school and the way it is taught. The survey results show that respondents believe that what they learned is often one-sided and does not always provide the whole picture of conflict history. The globalizing educational setting—strongly promoted by the Japanese government—undertakes a major role in this change. Students with experience studying abroad or those commuting universities with multinational classrooms are more and more exposed to conflict knowledge other than what they have learned at school. While some worry that they will be perceived internationally as ignorant, others are surprised with how history is taught in the United States is different from Japan. Many of them discover untold stories inside the classroom while discussing history and contemporary affairs.

Miki, for example, wrote in her final paper how she was astonished but then ashamed to learn about the Japanese colonization in Indonesia during a group discussion. Her main embarrassment was not about whether what was told is true. It was more about the fact that she had to face an official narrative unknown to her and was expected to respond in public. Shintaro who will start working for a governmental institution after his graduation showed a very violent reaction when faced with alternative narratives. He came to my office to convince me that Nanjing massacre is a lie and Koreans are exaggerating with the number of comfort women. As long as cultivating *guro-baru jinzai* (global human resource) remains one of the primary goals of the Japanese higher educational reform, students are more likely to face with the clash of national narratives. Feeling ashamed, wanting to learn more on what was not taught, or strongly rejecting all other narratives are few reactions observed, but there will be more.

On the other hand, the study illustrates that how Japanese students relate themselves to the country's past influences their perspective on what role youth can play in bringing peace. Most postwar reconciliation narratives suggest making friends, using anime or music, or promoting the greatness of Japan as a tool for reconciliation. There is an overwhelming trend of detaching politics when thinking of how to break the stalemate of unresolved issues in East Asia. The more one disconnects oneself from the country's past, in other words, knows little about it, the more it is likely to express a future-oriented view that concentrates on friendship, culture, and arts. (Previous data findings show that 75% of German students rate their knowledge about World War II as either deep or very deep, while 90% of Japanese students do not think they have developed sufficient knowledge. The deep/very deep ratings were insignificant in the Japanese survey group [4.2%]; See Bode and Heo [2017].) Is *a*-political means insufficient to rebuild a broken relationship in IR? Who knows, in a few decades, k-pop or *hallyu* (Korean wave) may lead to South Korean-Japanese reconciliation. In a century, manga or anime may ease Japanese-Chinese relations. Any prediction goes beyond the scope of this study. What counts here is that whether students consider themselves as an active agent of peace largely depends on how they relate themselves to the country's past.

Coming back to my student's essay on "Your question is wrong!" the chapter concludes that in order to connect peace studies with peace, youth should deepen their own reflection not only on what they can do but also on how they can take concrete actions in their daily life. Without using any sophisticated academic jargon such as individual agency or micro-level narrative, the chapter touches upon one of the most salient issues in IR: the importance of individualizing IR (see, for instance, Wheeler 2018). From these observations, I argue that if we want research to be connected with reality (reconciliation studies with reconciliation in this study), and if we want our students to become an active agent of peace, it is essential to offer them an opportunity to learn history and current affairs with and through "others." Being exposed to multiple narratives does not automatically lead to a better understanding of the past, nor does it make students become an active agent of peace. Learning *through the eyes of others* requires practice through a thoughtful pedagogy that encourages "student consciousness-raising rather than the absorption of materials and facts" (Lea and Sun

2014: 249). This pedagogical initiative emphasizes the commitment of social change by helping students become aware of their own role in the psychological transformation from enmity to amity and engaging them in action-generating learning (Pherali 2016; UNICEF 2011). I conclude this chapter with Stella's reflection, which leaves space for further reflection on the role of peace education:

> Conflict resolution classes merely focus on what states are capable of doing, not much encouraging how youth are potential to be involved in the process. Unfortunately, perhaps the majority of International Relations lecturers come to a realization of embracing the realist thought. Yet this does not bring youth to act further and actually provide any possible efforts for peace and reconciliation. I experienced a period of passiveness until I encountered topics regarding reconciliation that involves not only political theories but also the theories that makes an individual regarded as a human being. I believe most of other students would feel the same way as well, that the level of wanting to engage to a community to a degree increases when youth are constantly exposed to possibilities of how they can contribute to reconciliation.

References

Auerbach, Y. (2009). The reconciliation pyramid—A narrative-based framework for analyzing identity conflicts, *Political Psychology*, *30*(2), 291–318.

Barkan, E. (2009). Truth and reconciliation in history. *American Historical Review*, *114*(4), 899–913.

Bode, I. (2015). *Individual agency and policy change at the United Nations.* London: Routledge.

Bode, I., & Heo, S.E. (2017). World War II narratives in contemporary Germany and Japan: How university students understand their past. *International Studies Perspectives*, 18(2), 131–154.

Bouza García, L. (2017). Introduction: A narrative turn in European studies. *Journal of Contemporary European Studies*, 25(3), 285–290.

Callahan, W.A. (2006). History, identity, and security: Producing and consuming nationalism in China. *Critical Asian Studies*, *38*(2), 179–208.

Chase, S.E. (2011). Narrative inquiry: Still a field in the making. In N.E. Denzin & Y.S. Lincoln (Eds.), *The SAGE handbook of qualitative research* (pp. 421–434). Thousand Oaks, CA: Sage.

Clarke-Habibi, S. (2018). Teachers' perspectives on educating for peace in Bosnia and Herzegovina. *Journal of Peace Education*, *15*(2), 144–168.

Connolly, K. (2016). Britain's view of its history 'dangerous', says former museum director. *The Guardian*, October 7.

Czarniawska, B. (2004). *Narratives in social science research. Narratives in social science research.* Thousand Oaks, CA: Sage.

Diez, T. (2004). Europe's others and the return of geopolitics. *Cambridge Review of International Affairs*, *17*(2), 319–335.

Evans, R.J. (2003). Introduction—redesigning the past: History in political transitions, *Journal of Contemporary History*, 38(1), 5–12.

Hagström, L. (2015). The 'abnormal' state: Identity, norm/exception and Japan. *European Journal of International Relations*, 21(1), 122–145.

Hansen, L. (2006). *Security as practice: Discourse analysis and the Bosnian War*. New York: Routledge.

Halai, A., & Durrani, N. (2018). Teachers as agents of peace? Exploring teacher agency in social cohesion in Pakistan. *Compare*, *48*(4), 535–552.

Harle, V. (2000). *The enemy with a thousand faces: The tradition of the Other in West political thought and history*. Westport, CT: Praeger.

Holmes, M. (2018). *Face-to-face diplomacy: Social neuroscience and international relations*. New York: Cambridge University Press.

Kal, H. (2007). The aesthetic construction of ethnic nationalism: War memorial museums in Korea and Japan. In G.W. Shin, S.W. Park, & D. Yang (Eds.), *Rethinking historical injustice and reconciliation in northeast Asia* (pp. 133–153). New York: Routledge.

Lea, S.G., & Sun, T. (2014). Diversity and controversy in the facilitated classroom. In M. Baildon, L.K. Seng, I.M. Lim, G. Inanc, & J. Jaffar (Eds.), *Controversial history education in Asian contexts* (pp. 248–264). New York: Routledge.

Little, A. (2011). Disjunctured narratives: Rethinking reconciliation and conflict transformation. *International Political Science Review*, *33*(1), 82–98.

Manners, I., & Murray, P. (2016). The end of a noble narrative? European integration narratives after the Nobel Peace Prize. *Journal of Common Market Studies*, *54*(1), 185–202.

Mishler, E.G. (2015). Models of narrative analysis: A typology. *Journal of Narrative and Life History*, *5*(2), 87–123.

Neumann, I.B. (1996). Self and other in international relations. *European Journal of International Relations*, *2*(2), 139–174.

Pherali, T. (2016). Education: Cultural reproduction, revolution and peacebuilding in conflict-affected societies. In O. Richmond, S. Pogodda, & J. Ramovic (Eds.), *The Palgrave handbook of disciplinary and regional approaches to peace* (pp. 193–205). New York and London: Palgrave Macmillan.

Radnitz, S. (2018). Historical narratives and post-conflict reconciliation: An experiment in Azerbaijan. *Conflict Management and Peace Science*, *35*(2), 154–174.

Roberts, G. (2006). History, theory and the narrative turn in IR. *Review of International Studies* 32 (4): 703–714.

Rosenau, J.N. (2008). *People count: Networked individuals in global politics*. London and New York: Routledge.

Rosoux, V. (2017). Reconciliation narrative: Scope and limits of the Pax Europeana. *Journal of Contemporary European Studies*, *25*(3), 325–339.

Rouhana, N.N. (2004). Group identity and power asymmetry in reconciliation processes: The Israeli-Palestinian case. *Peace and Conflict, 10*(1), 33–52.

Suganami, H. (2008). Narrative explanation and International Relations: Back to basics, *Millennium: Journal of International Studies, 37*(2), 327–356.

Takayama, K. (2009). Globalizing critical studies of 'official' knowledge: Lessons from the Japanese history textbook controversy over 'Comfort Women'. *British Journal of Sociology of Education, 30*(5), 577–589.

Tonra, B. (2011). Democratic foundations of EU foreign policy: Narratives and the myth of EU exceptionalism, *Journal of European Public Policy* 18 (8): 1190–1207.

United Nations Children's Fund [UNICEF]. (2011). *The role of education in peacebuilding: Literature review*. New York: United Nations Children's Fund.

Wang, Z. (2014). History education: The source of conflict between China and Japan. *The Diplomat*, April 23.

Wheeler, N.J. (2018). *Trusting enemies: Interpersonal relationships in international conflict*. New York: Oxford University Press.

Wigura, K. (2012). Alternative historical narrative: 'Polish bishops' appeal to their German colleagues' of 18 November 1965. *East European Politics and Societies, 27*(3), 400–412.

Yang, D. (2003). Reconciliation between Japan and China. In Y. Funabashi (Ed.), *Reconciliation in the Asia-Pacific* (pp. 61–90). Washington, DC: United States Institute of Peace.

Zembylas, M., Charalambous, P., & Charalambous, C. (2011). Teachers' emerging stances and repertoires towards reconciliation: Potential and challenges in Greek-Cypriot education. *Journal of Peace Education, 8*(1), 19–36.

8. *China as an* Other *in Japanese Media: Construction of National Identity*

David Kozisek
Ritsumeikan University

Introduction

This chapter presents an analysis of the contemporary Japanese media discourse on the People's Republic of China as depicted by Japan's largest national daily newspapers *Yomiuri Shimbun* and *Asahi Shimbun*. Adopting a post-structuralist understanding of language, power, and society, we explain how the media portray China as one of Japan's several discursively constructed Others, and how they construct a certain image of Japan as Self. This relational dichotomy helps understand how images and notions of national identity are articulated and presented to the public through a specific media discourse. Given the rather peculiar links between the Japanese government and the media regarding their handling of information, this raises questions about the possible future normalization/remilitarization of Japan as envisioned by the conservative Liberal Democratic Party (LDP) government. Critical discourse analysis (CDA) further serves as a convenient and powerful tool for analysis concerned not only with the actual contents on a micro-textual level, but also the circumstances of production and consumption, as well as the encompassing wider social practices of the contemporary Japanese society.

In a postmodern globalized world, national identity matters perhaps more than ever before. Through a discursively constructed image of similarities we acquire a national identity which is at the same time juxtaposed against a contrasting Other delineating its boundaries and defining what we are not, helping organize social actions. National identity as a narrative constructed by a state is something so essential and omnipresent that we rarely think of it, as it comes as guaranteed. Within an international environment it needs a recognition from Others to achieve stability and ontological security (Ringmar 2007). However, the concept is elusive, and analytically difficult to grasp, and some have argued that national identity is simply too vague and unspecific to have much analytical value (Brubaker and Cooper 2000). Furthermore, very different perspectives have been brought by research in sociology, social psychology, social anthropology, or political science showing contrasting approaches and assumptions.

The possibility of constitutional change provides critical context during which identity may experience a more significant change. But such change is at the same time also constrained by the already existing national identity. Identities are constituted within representations, and individuals get their sense of identity from public institutions such as education systems or the media by forging the link between identity and culture by negotiating national identity, which may differ from the official government discourse putting constraints on carrying out education reforms.

Designating China as one of the Others utilized in the contemporary Japanese discourse, the background of the Senkaku Island territorial dispute serves as an event study providing analytical context. The analyzed data was gathered from Japan's two largest national daily newspapers: the typically conservative *Yomiuri*, which also happens to be the largest newspaper in the world, and *Asahi*, commonly viewed as more left-leaning. The genre can be predominantly classified as hard news but also includes editorials and comments.

This research is concerned with the question by what means is China portrayed as one of Japan's Others, focusing on the media's emphasis of potential security threats posed by the country, and by extension Japan's own image vis-à-vis a similar discursively constructed enemy. Furthermore, the emotions and implied meanings associated with the depiction of the Other are also of particular interest. This research design is different from previously published analyses of Japan's national identity, as it is not concerned with foreign policy directly but rather chooses to explore the mutually constitutive link between texts and social practices existing in the contemporary Japanese society by limiting its focus on the media and their discourse related to the images of Japan vis-à-vis an Other they attempt to construct. Nevertheless, a similar concept comes with certain limitations. It does not directly answer the question of what the contemporary Japanese identity is but rather how its construction might be facilitated by the media discourse due to its ties to the government.

One might argue that the newspapers simply relay what is occurring in the remote region of the East China Sea. However, as the theory of CDA suggests, each text is ultimately produced by choice and heavily reflects its author, as well as the social context in which it was created. In contrast to more common foreign policy analyses (see, e.g., Cooney 2015; Langdon 2011), this approach attempts to provide a different point of view by understanding the media as one of identity agents. Given the peculiar link between Japanese media and politics, it is a topic worth examining. To what extent do Japanese newspapers duplicate the official governmental discourse personified by Shinzo Abe, and where do they deviate from it? Ultimately, media contents in various forms are deliberately and often unconsciously and uncritically consumed by the majority of the population through different outlets perhaps for several hours every day. It is the media discourse rather than distant foreign policy that has the potential of shaping one's concept of national identity and policy preferences much more directly while reflecting on the possible course of Japan's identity sedimentation.

Theoretical Conceptualization, Discourse, and Identity

Setting the concept of national identity as our main focus, the approach suggested by this chapter relies on the study of discourse as an effective analytical tool. The post-structuralist understanding insists that identities are inherently rational, and they function as basis for actions and are deeply linked with language and discursive practices existing in the society. There is a wide body of literature dealing with identity construction through foreign policy on the level of national elites (see Campbell 1992; Hadfield-Amkhan 2010; Luther 2001; Prizel 1998), as well as several foreign policy-based analyses of Japan's possibly changing national identity (see, e.g., Bukh 2010; Hagström 2005; Tamaki 2010). In contrast to those, this chapter focuses solely on the media and their own discourse of Self and Other, attempting to present a different point of view and contribute to the debate of relevance of media in national identity construction. Critical understanding of the discourse and its various strands on this level may help understand the situation and societal mood pertaining to the possibility of Japan's military normalization, successive reinterpretations of the Constitution, and the future possibility of its change, which is an endeavor very clearly undertaken by former PM Shinzo Abe. The media discourse with all its features peculiar to Japan (e.g., the tight link between the media and politics) does not only reflect the official discourse of the government, but also adds other alternative strands, further giving properties and ascribing adjectives to both the Japanese Self and its many Others.

The post-structuralist view utilized in this chapter understands truth as a system of ideas, beliefs, and practices constructed within a particular discourse, while discursive and narrative power constructs and cultivates identity, stressing language as a constitutive element of society. Language maintains and reproduces existing social identities and relations while also acting as a transformative element. Such change is slow but perpetual. Most importantly, the relationship between discourse and society is of a circular character. Texts produced within particular social practices shape the context of their own production and in the end impact and shape the viewpoints of their consumers who operate within the discourse. By combining this discursive epistemology with an emphasis on ontological properties of language, we can identify and analyze how discursive images related to identity are produced on various levels of society.

We adopt understanding of identity as made up of variously sedimented layers (Kolmaš 2019). This concept presented by Ole Waever (2003) proposes a three-layer model based on relational understanding of identity and discourse. Identity is simultaneously constructed on these three interacting levels.

The base sedimented layer represents the fundamental understanding of a state and its nation, and their mutual relationship. This connection between state and nation exists in various constellations around the world, making a general typology rather difficult to produce. It is the narrative of shared origins, history, and culture. In the Japanese understanding of national identity the ideas of state and nation are fused together producing concepts such as *kokka*, which quite ambiguously carries the notions of and translates into English as nation, state, country, or government; as well as the idea of *kokutai*, national polity, and the emperor as a symbol of the nation's mythical origins and its ethnic continuity. Thus, this layer of identity stresses harmony, clear geographic boundary, as well as boundaries of identity by specifying who insiders and outsiders are (see also the Japanese concepts of *uchi* and *soto*). The national mythos produced in a historical process (see Oguma 2002) on this layer also defines Japan as a monoethnic homogenous state, largely disregarding existence of minorities. It is this layer of identity that is the most sedimented and thus represents the backbone of national identity, the most resilient to change and as such presenting the biggest constrains for the possibility of change.

The second, middle layer is based on a relational position based on distinguishing Self from Others and incorporates recent identity changes or specific identities created vis-à-vis other states. Multiple identities and concrete self-descriptions coexist on this level (Hagström and Gustafsson 2015: 7). The multiple Others are not only spatial but can be also temporal (a country's reflection of its own history). Change on this level is not impossible, yet can be only achieved through a significant structural change. The middle identity layer portrays Japan as democratic, rational, law-obeying, peaceful, and moral. The change occurring on this level represents a shift from Japan as an "economic giant" to a mature, moral, and law-abiding country threatened and even victimized by morally inferior neighbors who abuse Japan's perceived weakness (ibid.: 17).

The third layer of identity is the least sedimented, dynamic, and negotiated on the discursive level by endeavors of agents (called identity entrepreneurs by Waever) pursuing a specific concept of identity. These agents are most prominently political actors, but also include media and interest groups. The change on this level occurs by reflecting on the previous two sedimented levels and challenging the narratives they encompass. Individual agents pursuing a specific agenda may thus create their own narratives. Should a change on this level occur, it may eventually sediment deeper into the other two layers. The agents' discourse is often focused on bilateral problems and brings attention (often through securitization) to their individual properties to reconstruct them as a problem in order to promote a desired image of national identity, for example, by discursively constructing Japan's postwar peaceful identity as abnormal and weak. In the 2000s, the Japanese discourse on China and North Korea was largely transformed from victims to bullies and aggressors, reinforcing Japan's own perception of the Self as a victim and leading to the reactivation of several from the multitude of bilateral issues. The increasing portrayal of Asia as a threat may in the future contribute to Japan's normalization.

Despite the fact that the discursive space is very broad and difficult to cover, Japanese media share a certain level of uniformity and homogeneity (see Cooper-Chen 1991), perhaps owing to the journalistic process, described more as a collective effort.

The issues of importance of history and historical memory have been repeatedly examined in the past (see Halbwachs 1992; Neal 1998; Wang 2014). Historical animosity is often described as one of the underlining factors determining relations between state actors due to its long-term sedimentation in national identities. However, Fairclough suggests that a group's identity is constructed through a shared narrative providing a sense of community which is necessary in order to maintain a level of unity and cohesion within a group. Individual memory is constructed within wider social structures, and it can be understood only within the context of a group, regardless of its size (Fairclough 1993: 37–60). Some suggest that historical narratives are formed as a response to the present status quo through selective historiographic means in the service of interests and emotive charging (Burger 1994: 168 in Wodak et al. 2009: 20). National identities are thus discursive products building upon narratives of national culture and are hugely affected by the demands of the present, as states as imagined communities require constant maintenance (Clifford 1997: 9). Despite undeniable and well-documented historical facts, deliberately selected memories can serve as a basis for construction of a social narrative rendering history merely a continuously reinvented and reimagined chain of representations of causally linked events and occurrences within a specific discourse.

As Gillis suggests, memories and identity are not things we think about, but rather things we think with (1996: 5). Furthermore, Martin explains that the national identity narrative conveys political emotions providing a new interpretation of the world order in order to modify perceptions of the past and the present (1995: 13). Thus, there is no historically determining context, only the discursive practice and identity reflecting on the past through allusions to specific symbols. Fairclough further conceptualizes discourse as consisting of three interrelated layers: the object of analysis (text), social conditions of both production and interpretation, and sociohistorical conditions governing these processes (2014: 57–58). He also suggests that media texts function ideologically in social control and social reproduction, operating as cultural commodities and representing ideology in discourse easily transformed into common sense (1995: 47). Power in media can be conceived not only as power over but also as hidden power behind the discourse. Fairclough's theory of discourse proposes that the effect of media is very much cumulative and capable of exercising pervasive and powerful influence in social reproduction due to the scale of modern mass media, as well as extremely high level of exposure to a relatively homogenous output (Fairclough 2014: 82). Typically, different media outlets may have certain notions of prestige attached to them. For reasons explained later in this chapter, this is particularly the case with Japanese national newspapers.

Self and Other Relational Dichotomy

According to Campbell (1992), a state's national identity is deemed to be inherently relational and its existence is possible through a simultaneous delineation between itself and something which is different. The meaning is constructed by a discursive juxtaposition of two related but oppositional terms, the Self and Other, researched extensively by many (see Gries 2005; Mercer 1995; Neumann 1998; Rumelili 2004; Wodak 2009). A stable national identity requires establishing of an external 'enemy,' and a sense of Self is formed only through social interaction (Olick 1999: 343). Identity is a discursive construct maintained in relational categories of Self and Other, bound to the relationship of sameness and difference mediated by an identity narrative within the state. Narratives on Others are constructed as the main building blocks in the discursive identity construction of the national Self (Bukh 2015: 48). Additionally, Hansen further calls for an analytical perspective that views the dichotomy rather as a series of related but slightly different juxtapositions through the crucial processes of linking and differentiation (2013: 37). CDA works with linguistic features that imply construction of the Other through employment of attributes with negative denotations and connotations. As an extension, the Self is ascribed the opposite positive characteristics. The discursive construction of Self and Other is thus often very black and white (e.g., democratic-undemocratic, rational-irrational). Here Hansen also argues that the process goes beyond designating particular signs for the Self or the Other, but rather through the location of a particular sign within a larger system as a series of interlinked signs which constitute a relation of sameness, as well as a differentiation to another series of juxtaposed signs situated within the discourse (ibid.: 42). Only through this juxtaposition the discourse achieves stability. The theory assumes that there are multiple dynamic Others though which the difference of Self is expressed.

Ever since its surrender in 1945, Japan has been portrayed as an abnormal state due to the changes in foreign and security policy constricted by the explicit renunciation of war by Article 9 in the Constitution drafted by American lawyers. The core of postwar identity culminates in the critical question of remilitarization (Hashimoto 2015: 16), and the elites also commonly construct their narratives on the premise that World War 2 (WW2) and its end was the starting point of contemporary Japan; they commonly presuppose that all social contradictions in contemporary Japan are a result of the war (Hidaka 2016: 33). Japanese identity is unfixed; it has been created and recreated over the past century and a half by Japanese elites with different objectives at different times. The discursive representation of issues of external security can be fundamentally identified as built upon the same rubric as national identity, that is, from the standpoint of the difference between Self and Other. Security within any state is conventionally conceived primarily as national security, and as such it is given importance in the state's political discourse due to the state being traditionally conceptualized as a security guarantor, providing an environment devoid of violence.

Japanese Media and Relevance of Newspapers

Media create a narrative serving as an organizing principle that allows us to make sense of the world, helping form our social values. Most media texts are carefully selected and highly constructed representations of the world. Due to the often enormous distance between the consumer and the events portrayed by the media, it has been argued that the media no longer try to represent the real world; they have in fact replaced it (Rayner et al. 2001: 89). News media in particular are assumed to reproduce 'national' culture as they help to frame what it means to be 'national' by reporting and portraying events in a particular way and using key descriptors (Bechhofer and McCrone 2009: 14).

Located in the East China Sea, relatively far away from the Japanese main island of Honshu, the Senkaku Island dispute is a good example. Japanese media consumers rely on representations construed as a problem of national security and sovereignty with connotations of danger and insecurity. The question of the effect of media, that is, to what degree are these messages internalized and what impact they have on consumers, is a difficult one and has been one of the central themes of media studies for decades. Kadobayashi argues that social engineering via informational management has started to control the privacy and security of the individual (2017: 90). Nevertheless, research shows that the effect of media on its consumers is larger than what individuals perceive. Despite audiences declaring they do not trust the media, in practice media messages are still accepted at least in some aspects of their thinking (Kitzinger 2009: 413). Inarguably in order to understand the contemporary society anywhere in the world, one cannot ultimately ignore the media and their impact.

Media are typically classified as occupying one of the following three positions (see, e.g., Le 2006): (1) The one of a spectator, where they function as passive transmitters and are perceived as generally neutral. (2) A 'watchdog' essentially serving as the fourth branch of the government, and possessing the power to shape politics and set agenda. This position also gives the media the ability to reflect on and ultimately limit the government's decisions, creating a control mechanism. The final role (3) is the one of a servant of the state, forging consensus on social and political values, generating support for the regime. Japanese media are often seen as collaborators in state managing of the society. Nevertheless, empirical evidence suggests that they in fact occupy different positions on this spectrum. Pharr (1996) presents a synthetic and cumulative view describing the Japanese media as a trickster that fulfills different functions simultaneously. Nevertheless, there is a noticeable difference in the media's behavior depending on the topic. In case of foreign bilateral issues the media do not have an objective reason to drastically differ from the official narrative of the government, thus enforcing and perpetuating stereotypes is much easier. Media texts as cultural products are ideological, and ideology is ultimately linked to social identity and discourse which constructs topics and is present across texts. Narratives in the media have thus ideological implications.

Being established during the period of Japan's quick modernization and Westernization in the second half of the nineteenth century, Japanese media have a fairly long tradition experiencing periods of relative freedom, as well as periods of control by the state during the Taisho period, and censorship by the occupation forces (SCAP) directly after WW2. Owing the existence of the constitutional guarantee of freedom, contemporary Japanese media operate in an environment free from all overt forms of control. However, norms and conventions constrain what the public is allowed to know.

As this research is concerned mainly with national newspapers and their portrayal of Japan and its Others, the issue of relevance of newspapers in the twenty-first century needs to be addressed. Despite having the largest readership in the world resulting into Japan being a newspaper culture, similarly as elsewhere in the world, the readership of newspapers in Japan has been steadily declining in the recent years. Particularly among the younger generation newspapers have been largely replaced by the Internet owing to the ubiquity of mobile devices and fast data connection speeds. Furthermore, across the generations, newspapers seem to have been replaced by television. Given these empirical facts, one might question the relevance of newspapers and their role and value in shaping the discourse. Regardless of the declining readership, Japanese newspapers manage to maintain a high degree of trustworthiness. Polls suggest that 68.6% trust newspapers. Japanese television is deemed trustworthy by 62.7%, yet 20- and 30-year-olds seem to find TV somewhat less reliable than the other generations. The Internet is viewed as a reliable source of information by less than 30%, and only 16.7% trust the information in magazines (Nippon Shimbun Kyokai 2016). Moreover, based on topic, Japanese newspapers are perceived as particularly trustworthy when reporting domestic political and economic news, domestic social issues and foreign news, placing them as the most reliable media outlet in Japan (ibid.).

The Japanese media system has a peculiar feature that is not found in the media culture elsewhere in the world: the way official information is gathered and subsequent news reporting is facilitated through the existence of *kisha kurabu* (reporters' clubs), resulting in cartelization of information. These professional organizations have serious impact on the content and flow of information. They are managed by highly educated professional elites and hold proprietary access to information. This leads to homogenization of opinion and results in a certain level of predictability, as news articles in the newspapers are written by groups rather than individuals (Hirose 1994; Seward 2005). The Japanese press will usually decide what is or is not news by reference to 'the national interest' rather than to the public's right to know (Hadfield 1991: 15).

The *kisha kurabu* have exclusive access to information sources, that is, government offices and officials. Reportedly 90% of news in Japan comes from these official sources. Despite the aforementioned constitutionally guaranteed freedom of speech, the reporters engage in self-censorship. Breaking the rules can result in sanctions within the club, resulting in denial of access to information. The system is thus self-regulating and based on personal relationships between the source and the journalists. Japanese newspapers are thus an integral part and defenders of the established order as the journalists' current affluence and professionalism, and their dependence on official sources through the reporters' club system, create the basis for the 'servant' role (Krauss 1996: 366). The link between the government and the media is a strong one. Criticisms of the above described media culture in Japan include the fact that rather than critical reporting based on the information gathered from the source, journalists internalize the opinion of the source and simply present it as it is.

Furthermore, the newspapers are connected through Nihon Shinbun Kyokai (NSK), the Japan Newspaper Publishers & Editors Association. The NSK is an entirely independent and autonomous professional organization operated by daily newspapers, news agencies, and broadcasters. The organization aims to set ethical standards in news reporting and has been criticized for monopolizing representation with government officials, especially in regard to censorship. Japanese newspapers further serve as a source of information for other media outlets, most importantly television. Typically, a particular TV station uses a certain major newspaper as its source. Japan's most powerful and prestigious newspapers such as *Yomiuri* and *Asahi* form the apex of extended groups (*keiretsu*) that typically include television and radio networks, a family of weekly magazines (*shukanshi*), and a variety of non-media firms. The clubs are not the actual root of the problem, but cartels set up by rigidly hierarchical media groups that do not regard the critical quest for information as a fundamental institutional goal (McCargo 2003: 54). The existence of *keiretsu* represents another step in information control and possible censorship due to their interest in profits from advertising. Nevertheless, in the end Japanese newspapers, especially the national dailies, remain by far the most important media outlet in the news-making process (Freeman 2012: 16).

China as Japan's Other—from a Weak State to a Military Threat

China and Japan share a long history, the notion of which can never be completely removed from the bilateral relationship. Sometimes the relationship is described as two thousand years of friendship and fifty years of war. To a degree, the discourse stemming from past historical experience shapes identities but is also utilized for pressure during alternating times of relatively positive perception of one another, and those less favorable, depending on the political situation at the time. Historically, the ancient Chinese civilization served as a source of inspiration and cultural import for the Japanese archipelago, yet, perhaps due to a bit of luck, Japan was never successfully conquered by its much older, larger, and stronger neighbor, as a typhoon repeatedly crushed the invading Yuan (Mongol) dynasty on the sea. Without officially acknowledging it, Japan existed within and complied with China's tributary state system; and the Middle Kingdom never really posed a threat, as the majority of ruling Chinese dynasties did not desire expansion outside the mainland. Even during Japan's period of relative isolation (*sakoku*) during the Edo period, cultural and trade relations were never completely severed.

However, the relationship between China and Japan changed drastically after Japan was forced to open by Western powers and began the race for modernization and Westernization, a change initiated by the Meiji government. At the same time, Japan witnessed China's failure to react to Western presence in Asia, resulting in China's exploitation and colonization by Europeans. During that time, China in Japan was perceived as a victim of Western imperialism, provoking fear that Japan might become the next target. Thus, indirectly China's weakness and failure to modernize and react accordingly were understood as a threat to Japan's own identity. Ironically, as much as Meiji Japan was preoccupied with China being a weak state, the situation in the twenty-first century is exactly the opposite, as it is China's rise through economic modernization and strengthening of its military that are perceived as threats to Japan's security and identity and make China an important Other for Japan.

In order to protect its strategic interests, Japan clashed with China over the Korean Peninsula in 1984, resulting in Japan's victory over its neighbor. This victory served as the first milestone for Japanese identity, as the country was under China's cultural influence more or less since the beginning of its recorded history. Notwithstanding its crushing defeat, China then for a brief moment looked up to Japan, sending Chinese students to learn about successful Japanese modernization. The image of China's perception as a weak state did not change, and the country became the main victim of Japan's expansion at the beginning of the twentieth century, resulting in the loss of Taiwan and the loss of influence over Korea. Incidents orchestrated by the Japanese, the establishment of the puppet state of Manchukuo, and later the Marco Polo bridge incident in 1937 brought an all-out war between China and Japan. This damaged mainly China's perception of Japan and the atrocities committed by the Japanese during WW2 often serve as a basis for contemporary China's discourse on Japan. As a result, this presents the Chinese Other as unreasonable, driven by emotion and unaccepting of Japan's many apologies, ignoring past development assistance, and essentially denying Japan's postwar peaceful identity.

Following Japan's defeat and surrender in 1945, Japan was pressured by the United States to recognize Chiang Kai-shek's Kuomintang regime in Taiwan (Radtke and Liao 1990: 88); and as a result, until the normalization of diplomatic relations in 1972, the relationship toward the communist People's Republic of China remained in line with American policies. Despite the strained political situation during the Cold War, Japan managed to revive its economic relations with Mainland China, mainly through expansion of trade volume which essentially created an important pillar for future positive cooperation. After the normalization, Japan, China, and the United States all shared a concern with Soviet military intentions. Japan was, however, hesitant to side with China, as the government saw it as a possible obstacle in the future possibility of the resolution of the Northern Territories dispute. Yet, during the Cold War both the Japanese left- and right-wing politicians utilized Soviet Russia as an Other to emphasize Japan's peaceful and democratic characteristics (Suzuki 2015: 109). In order to hasten Japan's signing of the mutual Treaty of Peace and Friendship in 1972, China skillfully provoked a conflict over the Senkaku Islands (see Kawashima 2013). After this, the issue was put aside, yet Chinese intrusions into the territorial waters remained a convenient tool to pressure the Japanese government (Koo 2009).

The 1980s saw a number of official visits from China to Japan and the relationship thrived, and again China looked up to Japan praising it for its miraculous economic performance. Yet at the same time, Beijing became more aware and cautious of the possibility of Japan's transition from an economic power to a political one. The trend became apparent particularly in Japan approaching relations with developing countries. The economic weakness of the USSR was long apparent toward the end of the 1980s, and as soon as the idea of the Soviet threat dissipated China reverted into a more independent state, increasingly voicing concerns about Japan's future direction. Before 1982 China had not shown any interest in the long-running disputes over the presentation of Japan's past aggressions and colonial expansion before 1945. PM Nakasone Yasuhiro's visit to the controversial Yasukuni Shrine in 1985 spurred protests of the Chinese government (Drifte 2005: 27) and also student protests (Mochizuki 2010: 40) concerning a perceived Japan's economic invasion into China. A rather faint and soft reaction to the Tiananmen Massacre in 1989 demonstrated that, unlike the United States, Japan did not share the same hopes for China's democratization, possibly in an interest to maintain the prosperous economic ties. Moreover, the burden of Japan's own past perhaps did not allow for a stronger moral stance. Contrastingly, in the twenty-first century the discursive strand of morality is frequently present in Japan's own narrative of national identity. Despite being pressured into imposing sanctions on China by Western powers, Japan was rather resistant to do so, and later only suspended a loan package to China. Japan's government even tried to actively reduce foreign criticism of China, and the relation was again fully restored after only two years.

The post-Cold War unipolar environment brought a new era of economic and political development for China, as well as military assertiveness and thus also raised security concerns to Japan. Beijing largely focused on the importance of military modernization and defense of territorial sovereignty, gradually but noticeably increasing its military spending. The Japanese government was, and to this day is, mainly concerned with China's non-transparency and maritime presence in both the East China Sea and the South China Sea. With uncertain political conditions, China has been portrayed as an increasing threat. Neither country has a clear understanding of the nature of the Other's domestic politics, as well as foreign policy direction (Zhao 2001: 675). With resumption of China's nuclear tests, Japan became increasingly more worried about the development of ballistic missiles and their potential export to countries such as North Korea or Pakistan. The topic of nuclear weapons resonates very strongly with the Japanese public. The discourse on both sides of the bilateral relation thus developed into perceptions of mutual threat (see He 2008; Takamine 2005; Suzuki 2008).

With increasing military expenditures since the 1990s, China has argued territorial claims in both the East China and the South China Seas. This rising confidence helped construct an image of China as a brazen aggressor encroaching upon Japanese territorial waters around the disputed Senkaku Islands and competing for rich maritime resources. Needless to say, the issue of sovereignty and territorial security strongly echoes with national pride and is therefore one of the best opportunities to create a strong image of the Other. Securitization of the problem allows actors such as politicians and the media on the most superficial level of identity to construct particularly strong discursive images. China quickly emerging as an economic power and its link to Japan's economic woes reinforce the general perception of China as a multifaceted 'problem.' By the same token the lack of transparency and reliable information about China tend to further enhance these negative perceptions (Drifte 2005: 80).

The over-time worsening image of China can be easily observed in public opinion polls. According to surveys regularly conducted by YS, in 1998, 64% perceived Japan-China relations to be very good or somewhat good. In 1992, mentioning the Tiananmen massacre and possible selling of weapons of mass destruction, China's trustworthiness decreased by 15%. The perception of China further worsened during the 1990s and early 2000s. A survey from 2010 expressed that 89% Japanese were concerned by China's aggressive foreign policy, and 79% perceived China as a military threat, identifying Chinese fishing boats' incursions into the territorial waters around Okinawa and Senkaku as the source of deepening mutual mistrust. The related discourse often relies on words such as threat (***kyoui***) or caution (***keikaikan***). A survey from 2016 then announced that 91.6% perceived the China-Japan relations as "not good," again identifying the incursions into Japan's territorial waters and airspace as the main reason. The discourse of national identity does not necessarily cause negative feelings toward other countries or their citizens. However, when relations between two countries continue to deteriorate, national identity is more likely to generate negative feelings toward the Other (Zhai 2017: 104).

In the modern Japanese mind, China has been repeatedly perceived as a security threat, albeit for different reasons. In the nineteenth century, the Japanese discourse portrayed China as a weak state unable to modernize and defend itself against Western colonizers, thus increasing the risk of Japan being the next target. This perception was further solidified after clashing over the Korean Peninsula, famously described by Aritomo Yamagata as a "dagger pointed at the heart of Japan" (Murata 2004: 140) and culminated in Japan's own conquest for power and resources leading to the Pacific War. The Cold War image of China was long influenced by the U.S.-Japanese Security Treaty and Japanese politicians closely following American foreign policies. After transforming into a largely economic dimension in the 1970s, the Japanese image of China was briefly positive, but relations started to deteriorate quickly after China began pursuing a path of military modernization in the 1990s. China as Japan's Other has been thus portrayed increasingly as a threat, an irrational or arrogant neighbor who tries to intimidate the 'weak' Japanese state into making concessions (Suzuki 2015: 96) and therefore cannot be thrusted. Chinese behavior especially in the East and South China Seas since the 2000s has contributed to the perpetuation of this discourse and has permitted Japanese politicians and the media to use these images to solidify a certain notion of Japanese identity, portraying China as an undemocratic bully ignoring international law, the opposite to Japan's democratic, rational, and law-obeying peaceful and responsible Self.

Empirical Context of the Dispute

In order to analyze the portrayal of China as one of Japan's Others, the research chooses the Senkaku Islands territorial dispute, particularly a set of selected events from 2016, to provide empirical context, as well as a representative sample of the newspapers' discourse. Concerned with events surrounding the Senkaku Islands and the surrounding area of the East China Sea between August 6 and 13, 2016, the analyzed data corpus contains 25 articles of varying length and genre from *Yomiuri*, and 22 articles from *Asahi*.

The territorial dispute represents only one out of the three territorial problems Japan is currently involved in. However, it is the only disputed territory that the Japanese government maintains control of. Despite their rather large geographical distance, all the three disputed territories share one common feature and therefore need to be treated as a complex rather than three separate issues. It is their precedential value. A hypothetical concession or an attempt to compromise in one could have serious repercussions toward the other two, resulting in a weaker position of the Japanese government vis-à-vis China, South Korea, or Russia.

Both China and Japan have produced historical evidence claiming sovereignty over the Senkaku Islands. Interestingly, out of the two examined newspapers, only YS stresses Japan's historical claim over the disputed islands. The analysis of both Japanese and Chinese claims is beyond the scope and aim of this chapter and has been already provided by many before (see, e.g., Chansoria 2018; Suganuma 2000; Urano 2005). During the 1980s and most of the 1990s, the islands meant little or nothing to the average Japanese. In a *Yomiuri* opinion poll from 1988 the Senkaku were listed as the least important area of Sino-Japanese relations by its respondents. However, tensions have repeatedly spiked since the 1996 ratification of United Nations Convention on the Law of the Sea (UNCLOS). While the actual economic value of the uninhabited islands remains marginal compared to the value of the surrounding waters, the impact and interpretations of UNCLOS are crucial, as the islands create a 200 nautical mile exclusive economic zone (EEZ) that confers full sovereignty over the waters, providing access to maritime resources located in the zone. From the 2000s onward, the discourse on Senkaku has been transformed into a perceived invasion of Japan's sovereign maritime territory, and subsequently as such incorporated into government-approved textbooks. Finally, in 2012 the Japanese government nationalized the islands, causing diplomatic tensions with Beijing. Among rising tensions, Beijing established an air defense identification zone (ADIZ) over the East China Sea in 2013, requiring that all aircraft in the region report to Chinese ATC which further escalated the conflict with Japan and solidified the image of China as an aggressor attempting to one-sidedly change the status quo.

At approximately 1:30 p.m. on August 5, 2016, following Chinese fishing vessels, a Chinese government vessel (a ship belonging to the Chinese government) sailed into the territorial waters surrounding the Senkaku Islands. Then, between this time and August 26, a group of as many as 15 Chinese government vessels entered the contiguous zone, and a total of at least 36 Chinese government vessels were detected in Japan's territorial waters. There were approximately 200–300 fishing vessels operating in the contiguous zone of the Senkaku Islands, and a large number of Chinese government vessels, in this case as many as 15. They congregated in the same waters and then repeatedly entered Japan's territorial waters following Chinese fishing vessels. Activity of this scale was recorded for the first time. Furthermore, the increased activity in the East China Sea resulted into a collision of a Chinese fishing vessel with a Greek cargo ship on August 12. As a result, the former sank and Chinese fishermen had to be rescued by the Japan Coast Guard (JCG, *kaijohoancho*). The presence of Chinese vessels in the waters surrounding the islands is not uncommon; however, this time the sheer number of ships is repeatedly described as unprecedented, as both *Yomiuri* and *Asahi* reported the number of Chinese vessels to be around 400 at one point.

China as an Other in the Discourse of Japanese Newspapers

While the discourse on Senkaku indeed has a hard security aspect, in its very core we can identify the topic of sovereignty. The above-described events are portrayed as territorial incursions or invasions (*shinnyu*, *shingai*) by both examined newspapers. Both descriptions clearly have negative meanings and connotations attached to them, portraying the behavior of China in the East China Sea as encroaching upon Japan's sovereign territory. The discourse distinguishes between civilian fishing vessels (*gyosen*) and government vessels (*kousen*). The latter essentially consists of the Chinese Coast Guard, and

Marine Surveillance and Fisheries Enforcement Command. Both *Yomiuri* and *Asahi* report that some of the military vessels are equipped with what 'appears' to be machine guns or cannons. Despite the rather careful wording this can be viewed as an attempt at securitization, as an invader equipped with weapons is most definitely a more dangerous one than one without weapons. Moreover, the newspapers commonly list previous Chinese territorial incursions from recent history in order to maintain intertextuality between the events and stress that this is not a one-time occurrence. This intertextuality presents China as increasingly more determined and impudent.

The discourse is further constructed upon quotes from various government officials, stating that Chinese incursions and other actions in the territorial waters around Senkaku are a violation of Japan's sovereignty and as such cannot be accepted and are resolutely condemned. In this context Japan is referred to as *wagakuni* (our country), a term that has slight patriotic connotations and would be often utilized in a similar context of Japan vis-à-vis another state. While this expression appears in both newspapers, it is much more commonly used by *Yomiuri*.

Due to the news collecting process described above and overall vagueness of the Japanese language, sources are quite often not identified by name and simply appear as a generic description such as 'a source connected/related to the Ministry of Foreign Affairs,' etc. The degree of homogeneity between the two analyzed newspapers is also apparent. The same stance is reiterated by both *Asahi* and *Yomiuri* throughout the analyzed articles; and similarly strong claims are presented from the Chinese, thus constructing a direct opposition between the two countries.

Asahi Shimbun suggests that the JCG is actively preventing the Chinese from landing on the actual islands, reinforcing the image of further violation of Japan's sovereignty and territorial rights while conveying emotions best described as anxiety or fear of 'our country' being encroached upon by an aggressive invader. The newspaper also expresses concern that China is trying to establish its continuous presence in the East China Sea as a normal state of affairs and thus effectively weaken Japan's position in the remote region. China is clearly presented as unwilling to compromise and ignoring all of Japan's protests and complaints. *Asahi* also directly criticizes China by describing the background logic under which the Chinese government operates: The more Japan complains the more ships are going to appear in the disputed waters since China strives to avoid domestic criticism for appearing too weak in its stance toward Japan. It is concluded that no matter what Japan does, the situation will not change, thus conveying a sense of hopelessness to the reader. Furthermore, China's image in the newspaper discourse is constructed as clearly arrogant. *Asahi Shimbun* gives an example of the Chinese ambassador talking to a group of Japanese reporters. He reportedly states in Japanese that both countries should avoid complicating the issue and strive to resolve the issue. Yet it is pointed out that he consequently switches to Chinese to say that "Japan should not raise trivial complaints" (*nihon wa, tsubekobe wo iu beki dewanai*).

The image of China in YS is constructed as the one of a brazen and hostile expansive aggressor, actively escalating the situation in a one-sided attempt to change the status quo. In a direct opposition, Japan is then portrayed as cooperating and involved in the international society, while China is recognized as a clearly destabilizing element in the Asia-Pacific, threatening the region's security. Contrastingly Japan's approach and actions in these situations is conveyed as calm, composed, and acting in resolute manner (*kizen to reisei ni taiou suru*) and not giving way to China's expansion. While the possibility of deploying the JSDF (*jieitai*) is briefly mentioned, it is suggested that the government is not going to deploy them in order avoid further escalation. China is identified as the one who carelessly escalates the situation. The discourse portrays Japan as defending its sovereignty against China's arrogant expansion, with the latter being identified as a trespasser. It also relies on the intertextuality between the current events and China's behavior in the South China Sea, predicting the same course of action for the East China Sea which further conveys a sense of danger and urgency. *Asahi Shimbun* stresses Japan's active international involvement and cooperation, particularly with the United States, citing America's support on the issue which is guaranteed by Article 5 of the Security Treaty between the two countries. *Yomiuri* warns that China is increasingly more forceful and "[we] have to think about new strategies of responding" (*aratana taiousaku wo kangaenakute wa ikenai*).

In a direct contrast to China, the discourse on the Senkaku Island dispute portrays Japan as law-obeying and seeking a peaceful resolution. It is pointed out that China is the one who essentially expresses various grievances against Japan while being simultaneously presented as ignoring the international law. The newspapers largely present the events as China's expansionism fueled by grudge against Japan, as well as an attempt to divert attention to an external enemy in an attempt to maintain domestic stability, thus identifying anti-Japanism as a strategy utilized by the Chinese Communist Party. *Yomiuri* specifically points out the fact that Japan is viewed as unpopular in China and expects that there is a possibility that China will continue using various techniques to shake (destabilize) Japan (*samazamana shuhou de nihon wo yusaburi tsudzukeru kanousei ga aru*). The discourse points to a more recent grievance that is discovered in Japan siding with South East Asian states by publicly supporting the verdict of the international tribunal on the South China Sea, and the current situation around the Senkaku Islands is viewed to be an act of China's retribution or perhaps vindictiveness. The discourse hereby posits Japan as a victim of irrational and childish negative sentiments.

Conflicting Discourses of Japanese Identity

Between the two analyzed newspapers, the left-leaning *Asahi* is clearly more critical of China's behavior and presents a harsher image of the country. In an editorial, the newspaper claims that China threatens the stability of neighboring countries, wishing that China would follow actions appropriate to its self-proclaimed large country with responsibility. Here we can identify a strand of the discourse that is concerned with righteousness, ethics, and moral responsibility, and is present in the discourse on several different Others as well.

Asahi describes China's behavior as unacceptable and calls for the country to take responsibility and properly react to Japan's continuous diplomatic protests. Despite all criticism *Asahi* is quite optimistic and actually sees a possibility of dialog and improvement of the currently escalated situation. The newspaper calls for mutual understanding on many different levels—political, diplomatic, economic, and cultural—in order to avoid misunderstandings that could further deepen the crisis. Nevertheless, *Asahi* also heavily criticizes the lack of transparency of the Chinese military, as well as its motives and goals. China is reprimanded for ignoring all of its neighbors and using its power to change the status quo while obeying international law only when it is convenient. The image of China as a brazen expanding aggressor who cannot be trusted is articulated very clearly. *Asahi* uses imperative forms to criticize China's behavior—"China, do not increase tensions!" (*chuugoku wa kinchou wo takameru na*)—and modal constructions to convey necessity, for example, "[China] must immediately stop these actions" (*sokkoku kono ugoki wo yameru beki da*). The newspaper clearly points to China as the one who complicates the situation of the territorial dispute, also suggesting that China's behavior is difficult to predict, which poses a serious risk to its neighboring countries and is the main reason why Asia's security environment is unstable. The discourse suggests that China cannot be trusted and the trust cannot be gained if the country keeps behaving the same way. In an editorial, *Asahi* expresses the wish that China would act accordingly to its size and responsibility, stressing an idea of moral duty the understanding of which is absent in the thinking of China's government. Here it is implied that Japan occupies a morally higher position and understands responsibilities toward the international community and peace. Japan is ascribed adjectives such as peaceful, moral, and rational. This is further emphasized by pointing out the fundamental difference between Japan's democracy and China's ruling Communist Party which contributes to the othering discursive practice.

By analyzing the portrayal of China and the Senkaku Islands territorial dispute in *Yomiuri* and *Asahi*, we can see that the discourse is far from homogenous and contains more than a single narrative. Hashimoto (2015) identifies three conflicting strands of the contemporary Japanese discourse related to the postwar national identity. (1) The discursive strand of nationalism is concerned with advancing national strength and constructs a social identity derived from traditional heritage. The patriotism-cultivating discourse has a varying spectrum of intensity, and in contemporary Japan is the most clearly represented by the former PM Abe and the LDP. The goal of this discourse strand is overcoming the cultural trauma of defeat while facing a steady decline of national pride. (2) The discourse of pacifism is constructed upon an antimilitary ethos, humanist pride, recovering moral prestige and ultimately morality. Here the appropriation of Article 9 is used as a form of civic identity, condemning immoral acts of violence and desiring human security. This discourse is also linked to a certain notion of pride in the pacifist identity through an elevated moral status. (3) Reconciliationism represents the third and final strand that is concerned mainly with improving of relations and acknowledgment of the past guilt. Justice is identified as a universal value built upon mutual respect and trust.

In the postwar period, the Japanese political discourse on China consisted of several different strands. While the Left typically viewed China as a victim of Japanese aggression and the Self as a perpetrator, the Right understood Japan as a weakened state that had stood up against China's rise and aggressive behavior. Meanwhile the Left frequently utilizes the discourse of morality, highlighting Japan's higher moral ground as a pacifist and antimilitarist country and stresses the importance of maintaining this identity. China is portrayed as a state hugely lacking moral responsibility toward the international society. Suzuki points out that the two discourses have recently converged together: Regardless of one's political preference once thing is certain—China has become a bully that Japan has to act assertively toward and resist Beijing's amoral demands (2015: 98). China's 'history card' seen as an attempt to discursively keep Japan in a permanently weakened state (victimizer) often further fuels more antipathy toward Beijing. Particularly after 2010, the discourse of China as a rising threat has been adopted even by left-wing media, thus giving more prominence to the perception of Japan as a weak or inferior state. As seen later in this chapter, this trend can be observed particularly in *Asahi* editorials.

Despite an undeniable degree of cultural affinity, the Japanese discourse on China has inevitably reflected on the often strained historical relationship. In China's modern discourse on Japan, the postwar relationship is characterized by distrust, which is, however, often instrumentalized by Beijing as a diversion tactic from domestic political scandals, realization of various political goals, and overall support of the Communist regime (Reilly 2011: 142). The Chinese discourse is rooted in historical determinism and promotes the idea that Japan, having failed to accordingly recognize, acknowledge, and repent for its past as an imperialistic aggressor, is bound to repeat the same wrongdoings again in the future. The state-constructed discourse of Chinese national identity consists mainly of the following three strands: China as a victim (looking back at its past), as a developing and modernizing country (present oriented), and finally China as a great power (a future-focused narrative). Similarly to Reilly, Atanassova-Cornelis also suggests that the victimization narrative is focused, first and foremost, on preserving the legitimacy of the one-party regime (2012: 106), as China's identity as a victim, in its past aspect, has been forged primarily in relation to Japan as the victimizer. This has made balancing between domestic anti-Japanese sentiments and economic relations with Japan particularly difficult. However, negative sentiments toward Japan are much more deeply embedded in the Chinese society. If the broader spectrum of the population did not share some form of anti-Japanese feelings, nationalist sentiment is hardly going to arise from manipulating memories of Sino-Japanese war history (Suzuki 2007: 28).

Even though whitewashing of history in Japan, often conveniently presented as 'looking for truth,' is an issue, China is similarly guilty of distortion of historical facts in school textbooks (see He 2007). Even though China's identity vis-à-vis Japan as a victim remains stable, some suggest that the discourse of Chinese textbooks has changed. While the emphasis on Japan's invasion remains strong, history books began to praise Japan's modern reforms, as well as democratic reforms after WW2 and its fast economic recovery and development (Su 2011: 147). Yet Gustafsson objects that China's patriotic education is regarded as anti-Japanese because its historical narrative largely ends in 1945. Japan's development as a peaceful country is consequently denied, creating a one-sided image of Japan (2015: 126). This lack of recognition effectively contradicts Japan's peaceful Self that the postwar identity has been built upon.

Nevertheless, Japan as the victimizer has been much more inclined to stay away from the issue of history and focus on economic relations instead.

On the other hand, the Chinese narrative on Japan largely focuses on its past aggressions and ignores the postwar period. Japan's postwar development as a peaceful state and aid, as well as official apologies (more than 20 since 1972) remain largely ignored. Japan is not recognized as peaceful which essentially denies a part of its identity discursively constructed after WW2. As an example, after 2012 nationalization of Senkaku Chinese vice premier excluded Japan from the peace-loving international community (Gustafsson 2014). Japanese identity discourse is centered and built upon the postwar period and is consensual without creating much debate, unlike Japan's militaristic past.

However, the tarnished memory and ambivalent sentiments about heroes, victims, and perpetrators of the militarist totalitarian past have erupted to the surface in many proxy political disputes, such as the question of remilitarization/normalization in the new global geopolitics. The diversity of views in the defeat culture is shown time and time again in opinion polls and national surveys, and tends to hold a steady pattern across generations; they cannot be explained monocausally by generation, gender, or political party affiliation (Hashimoto 2015: 19). Deep mistrust between constitutional revisionists and preservationists has given shape to the patchwork of practices and compromises that have long sustained Japan's postwar military defense structure. The constitutional revisionists (*kaikenha*) claim that contradictions between the ideal of unarmed peace and the practice of armed peace—made possible by successive reinterpretations of Article 9—have now reached a limit in the post-Cold War global age. The constitutional preservationists (*gokenha*) counter that the original ideal must be protected to ensure and reassure the world that there will be no military escalation ever again in Japan.

Another contradictory feature of Japanese identity, as suggested by Bukh, is represented by the coexistence of conflicting discourses of Pan-Asianism and a Japanese version of Orientalism (2015: 60). While the former is built upon a notion of a certain horizontal affinity between Japan and the rest of Asia based on racial sameness, the latter anchors Japan as spatially located in Asia but temporally superior to its Asian neighbors. For Japan this layer of national identity entails an idea of perceived hierarchy that understands Japan as superior to other Asian states. Since the second half of the nineteenth century, Japanese identity narratives have positioned the country between Asia and the West, the former being inferior and the latter superior. Japan was constructed as a nation that emerged from the Orient while maintaining positive aspects of Asian culture, but developed a degree of cultural and historical autonomy comparable to the West (Bukh 2010: 17), providing legitimacy to Japan's claims for equality with the West and giving birth to the discourse on Japan's cultural uniqueness and constructing Japan as Asian yet modern (Tanaka 1995).

This discourse has developed during and after Japan's nineteenth-century modernization and became the drive for Japanese imperialism in the first half of the twentieth century as a reaction to the presence of Western powers in the Asian region, and a way to justify expansive colonial ambitions based on a reflection of the notion of hierarchy of states and a perceived sense of moral responsibility of liberating the Asian continent. Although the postwar discourse reconstructed Japan as a peaceful nation, and militarism was replaced by pacifism, the discourse of morality responsibility related to the ideas of the unique character of the Japanese nation and a resulting perception of hierarchy and superiority in its core remained largely unchanged. It was later transformed into economic dimension; however, the collapse of the bubble economy in the early 1990s again resulted in a certain crisis of identity and is followed by a new phase of reassessing, looking for, and constructing of the Self. Despite the discourse of morality or ethicality being largely implicit, it remains an integral part of the present discourse vis-à-vis other Asian powers.

The analysis of the Senkaku discourse on China in this chapter clearly identifies an implicitly included discourse of moral superiority and responsibility that corresponds or perhaps can be identified as a part of the above-mentioned pacifist strand. The newspaper discourse focuses on articulations of moral identity aiming at discursive construction of ethics, morality, and responsibility that is particularly accented by *Asahi* emphasizing the principles of international law and order and a certain sense of a moral duty toward their protection.

Conclusion

The analyzed contemporary discourse on China with the Senkaku Islands territorial dispute providing empirical context portrays the country as a brazen and hostile expansive aggressor actively destabilizing the region. While the hard security aspect of the discourse identified by securitization is more apparent in the case of *Yomiuri*, both analyzed newspapers rely on the discourse of Japan's sovereignty, identifying China's arrogant expansion encroaching upon Japan's remote territory and serving as a direct opposition to Japan's calm, composed, and resolute behavior that values cooperation, democracy, and the rule of law. The Japanese Self is formed upon a discourse of morality and related ethical responsibility, resulting in an image of continuing moral superiority of Japan vis-à-vis China, and by extension also vis-à-vis its additional Asian Others. This implicit discourse of morality, an elevated moral status, has direct links to Japan's discourse of pacifism adopted after WW2 as a mechanism of overcoming the country's defeat.

Contrastingly, if we look at the Japanese newspaper discourse on North Korea, the People's Republic of China is not portrayed in a similarly negative way. Instead the discourse stresses China's role as a permanent member of the UNSC and its potential stabilizing influence on North Korea's behavior. This contextual fluidity of the same Other being constructed in a different manner depending on the contextual background confirms the social constructivist quality of the examined Othering process. In many cases, individual Others appearing in the discourse of identity agents (e.g., politicians or the media) serve as a tool to challenge the sedimented aspect of Japanese identity. Even though Japan's Others are portrayed negatively, often as enemies, their existence and continuous discursive construction is essential to maintaining the stability of the Self; and it can be viewed both as a product of the currently existing discursive strands in the Japanese society, as well as the impetus behind social practices possibly leading to the arduous path toward Japan's ultimate moral recovery and the possibility of normalization, as the postwar reinterpretations of Article 9 have reached their limit against the concepts of proactive pacifism (*sekkyokuteki heiwashugi*) or collective self-defense (*shūdanteki jieiken*) advocated for by the successive LDP governments, carrying the legacy of former PM Shinzo Abe in the twenty-first century.

Despite abandoning its military past in 1945 and following a path of peaceful resolution of conflict and the rule of law, the discourse of Japan as an imperial aggressor is heavily maintained by China to this day, refusing to recognize Japan as a pacifist country. Some admit that it is possible that the political elites are using China's denial of Japan's identity to refashion the country's identity in a way that constructs it less in relation to its wartime past and to a greater extent in relation to an undemocratic China (Suzuki 2015: 133). This brings an opportunity for identity agents on the least institutionalized layer of identity to push the agenda for Japan as a weakened and abnormal state that needs to be normalized.

In the contemporary Japanese newspaper discourse, as well as the discourse of political elites, China is now universally understood as a security threat. While there is a degree of similarity between the discourse used by both examined newspapers, which can be attributed to the information-gathering process, it is particularly the left-leaning *Asahi* which also utilizes an implicit discourse of morality that is largely absent in *Yomiuri*. The image of China as an increasingly aggressive and unreasonable bully contributing to Japan's weakness might fuel nationalist tendencies and their politicization, leading to an even more strained political situation between the two countries and potentially perpetuating the security dilemma in the region.

References

Atanassova-Cornelis, E. (2012). Chinese nation building and foreign policy: Japan and the US as the significant 'others' in national identity construction. *East Asia: An International Quarterly*, *29*(1), 95–108.

Bechhofer, F., & McCrone, D. (2009). National identity, nationalism and constitutional change. In F. Bechhofer & D. McCrone (Eds.), *National Identity, Nationalism and Constitutional Change* (pp. 1–16). Springer.

Brubaker, R., & Cooper, F. (2000). Beyond 'identity', *Theory and Society*, *29*(1), 1–47.

Bukh, A. (2010). *Japan's national identity and foreign policy: Russia as Japan's other.* London: Routledge.

Bukh, A. (2015). Shimane Prefecture, Tokyo and the territorial dispute over Dokdo/ Takeshima: Regional and national identities in Japan. *The Pacific Review*, *28*(1), 47–70.

Burger, R. (1994). Patriotismus und Nation. Bemerkungen zu einem (nicht nur) österreichischen Problem. *Leviathan*, *2*, 161–170.

Campbell, D. (1992). *Writing security. United States foreign policy and the politics of identity.* Minneapolis: University of Minnesota Press.

Chansoria, M. (2018). *China, Japan, and Senkaku Islands: Conflict in the East China Sea amid an American shadow.* London: Routledge.

Clifford, J. (1997). *Routes: Travel and translation in the late twentieth century.* Harvard University Press.

Cooney, K.J. (2015). *Japan's foreign policy since 1945.* London: Routledge.

Cooper-Chen, A. (1991). *Mass* communication *in Japan.* Wiley.

Drifte, R. (2005). *Japan's security relations with China since 1989: From balancing to Bandwagoning?* London: Routledge.

Fairclough, N. (1993). *Discourse and social change.* Wiley.

Fairclough, N. (1995). *Media discourse.* Bloomsbury Academic.

Fairclough, N. (2014). *Language and power.* London: Routledge.

Freeman, L.A. (2012). *Closing the shop: Information Cartels and Japan's mass media.* Princeton University Press.

Gillis, J.R. (1996). *Commemorations: The politics of national identity.* Princeton University Press.

Gries, P.H. (2005). Social psychology and the identity-conflict debate: Is a 'China Threat' inevitable? *European Journal of International Relations*, *11*(2), 235–265.

Gustafsson, K. (2014). Is China's discursive power increasing? The 'power of the past' in Sino-Japanese relations. *Asian Perspective*, *38*(3), 411–433.

Gustafsson, K. (2015). Identity and recognition: Remembering and forgetting the post-war in Sino-Japanese relations. *The Pacific Review, 28*(1), 117–138.

Hadfield, P. (1991). Japan: Keeping in with the Club. *Index on Censorship, 20*(7), 15–17.

Hadfield-Amkhan, A. (2010). *British foreign policy, national identity, and neoclassical realism*. Rowman & Littlefield.

Hagström, L. (2005). *Japan's China policy: A relational power analysis*. Psychology Press.

Hagström, L., & Gustafsson, K. (2015). Japan and identity change: Why it matters in international relations. *The Pacific Review, 28*(1), 1–22.

Halbwachs, M. (1992). *On collective memory*. University of Chicago Press.

Hansen, L. (2013). *Security as practice. Discourse analysis and the Bosnian war*. London: Routledge.

Hashimoto, A. (2015). *The long defeat: Cultural trauma, memory, and identity in Japan*. Oxford University Press.

He, Y. (2007). History, Chinese nationalism and the emerging Sino–Japanese conflict. *Journal of Contemporary China, 16*(50), 1–24.

He, Y. (2008). Ripe for cooperation or rivalry? Commerce, realpolitik, and war memory in contemporary Sino-Japanese relations. *Asian Security, 4*(2), 162–197.

Hidaka, K. (2016). *Japanese media at the beginning of the 21st century: Consuming the past*. London: Routledge.

Hirose, H. (1994). The press club system in Japan. Its past, present and future. *Keio Communication Review, 16*, 63–75.

Kadobayashi, T. (2017). The media theory and media strategy of Azuma Hiroki, 1997–2003. In M. Steinberg & A. Zahlten (Eds.), *Media theory in Japan*. Duke University Press.

Kawashima, S. (2013). The origins of the Senkaku/Diaoyu islands issue. *Asia-Pacific Review, 20*(2), 122–145.

Kitzinger, J. (2009). A sociology of media power: key issues in audience perception research. In S. Thornham, C. Bassett, & P. Marris (Eds.), *Media Studies: A Reader* (pp. 405–417). Edinburgh University Press.

Kolmaš, M. (2019). *National identity and Japanese revisionism*. London: Routledge.

Koo, M.G. (2009). The Senkaku/Diaoyu dispute and Sino-Japanese political-economic relations: Cold politics and hot economics? *The Pacific Review, 22*(2), 205–232.

Krauss, E.S. (1996). The Mass Media and Japanese Politics: Effects and Consequences. In S. J. Pharr & E. S. Krauss (Eds.), *Media and Politics in Japan* (pp. 355–372). University of Hawaii Press.

Langdon, F. (2011). *Japan's foreign policy*. UBC Press.

Le, E. (2006). *The spiral of anti-other rhetoric: Discourses of identity and the international media echo*. John Benjamins.

Luther, C.A. (2001). *Press images, national identity, and foreign policy: A case study of U.S.-Japan relations from 1955–1995*. London: Routledge.

Martin, D.C. (1995). The choices of identity. *Social Identities, 1*(1), 5–20.

McCargo, D. (2003). *Media and politics in Pacific Asia*. Psychology Press.

Mercer, J. (1995). Anarchy and identity. *International Organizations, 49*(2), 229–252.

Mochizuki, M. (2010). The Yasukuni Shrine Conundrum: Japan's contested identity and memory. In M. Kim & B. Schwartz (Eds.), *Northeast Asia's difficult past: Essays in collective memory.* Springer.

Murata, K. (2004). Japanese domestic politics and the US-Japan-ROK security relationship. In T. Kim and B. Glosserman (Eds.), *The future of U.S.-Korea-Japan relations: Balancing values and interests*, edited by CSIS.

Neal, A.G. (1998). *National trauma and collective memory: Major events in the American century.* M.E. Sharpe.

Neumann, I.B. (1998). *Uses of the other: The east in European identity formation.* Vol. 9. Minneapolis: University of Minnesota Press.

Oguma, E. (2002). *A genealogy of 'Japanese' self-images.* Melbourne: Trans Pacific Press.

Olick, J.K. (1999). Collective memory: The two cultures. *Sociological Theory, 17*(3), 333–348.

Pharr, S.J. (1996). Media as trickster in Japan: A comparative perspective. In E. Krauss & S.J. Pharr (Eds.), *Media and politics in Japan* (pp. 19–43). University of Hawaii Press.

Prizel, I. (1998). *National identity and foreign policy: Nationalism and leadership in Poland, Russia and Ukraine.* Cambridge University Press.

Radtke, K.W., & Liao, C. (1990). *China's relations with Japan, 1945–83: The role of Liao Chengzhi.* Manchester University Press.

Rayner, P., Wall, P., & Kruger, S. (2001). *Media studies: The essential introduction.* London: Routledge.

Reilly, J. (2011). *Strong society, smart state: The rise of public opinion in China's Japan policy.* Columbia University Press.

Ringmar, E. (2007). *Identity, interest and action: A cultural explanation of Sweden's intervention in the thirty years war.* Cambridge University Press.

Rumelili, B. (2004). Constructing identity and relating to difference: Understanding the EU's mode of differentiation. *Review of International Studies, 30*(1), 27–47.

Seward, R. (2005). Fish nor fowl: Kisha clubs and Japanese journalism. *Asia Pacific Media Educator, 1*(16), 17–26.

Su, Z. (2011). The 'Others' in Chinese history textbooks. In G. Mueller (Ed.), *Designing history in East Asian textbooks: Identity politics and transnational aspirations.* Taylor & Francis.

Suganuma, U. (2000). *Sovereign rights and territorial space in Sino-Japanese relations: Irredentism and the Diaoyu/Senkaku islands.* University of Hawaii Press.

Suzuki, S. (2007). The importance of 'Othering' in China's national identity: Sino-Japanese relations as a stage of identity conflicts. *The Pacific Review, 20*(1), 23–47.

Suzuki, S. (2008). Can apology serve as a security policy? Responsible scholarship and breaking the chains of negative history in Sino-Japanese relations. *Korean Journal of Defense Analysis, 20*(4), 319–333.

Suzuki, S. (2015). The rise of the Chinese 'Other' in Japan's construction of identity: Is China a focal point of Japanese nationalism? *The Pacific Review, 28*(1), 95–116.

Takamine, T. (2005). A new dynamism in Sino-Japanese security relations: Japan's strategic use of foreign aid. *The Pacific Review*, *18*(4), 439–461.

Tamaki, T. (2010). *Deconstructing Japan's image of South Korea: Identity in foreign policy*, Basingstoke: Palgrave Macmillan.

Tanaka, S. (1995). *Japan's orient: Rendering pasts into history.* University of California Press.

Urano, T. (2005). *Senkaku shoto—Ryukyu—Chugoku, Nicchu kokusai kankeishi.* Tokyo: Sanwa Shoseki.

Wæver, O. (2003). Identity, communities and foreign policy: Discourse analysis as foreign policy theory. In L. Hansen & O. Waever (Eds.), *European integration and national identity: The challenge of the Nordic states* (pp. 20–49). London: Routledge.

Wang, Z. (2014). *Never forget national humiliation: Historical memory in Chinese politics and foreign relations.* Columbia University Press.

Wodak, R., De Cillia, R., Reisigl, M., & Liebhart, K. (2009). *The discursive construction of national identity.* Edinburgh: Edinburgh University Press

Zhai, Y. (2017). Identity, contact, and the reduction of mutual distrust: A survey of Chinese and Japanese youth. *The Pacific Review*, *30*(1), 93–113.

Zhao, Q. (2001). China and major power relations in East Asia. *Journal of Contemporary China*, *10*(29), 663–681.

Notes on Contributors

Emilia S. Heo is an associate professor of international relations and peace studies at Ritsumeikan Asia Pacific University and the author of *Reconciling Enemy States in Europe and Asia* (Palgrave Macmillan, 2012). She was an assistant professor of global studies at Sophia University, a JSPS research fellow at the United Nations University with joint affiliation to the University of Tokyo, a research associate at the Sigur Center for Asian Studies at the George Washington University, and a visiting scholar of Harry & Helen Gray AICGS reconciliation fellowship at the Johns Hopkins University. Her current research focuses on postwar reconciliation narratives, peace education, and the role of arts in processes of reconciliation beyond national borders. Heo holds an M.A. in European studies from Université Paris VIII and a Ph.D. in international relations from the Graduate Institute of International and Development Studies, Geneva, Switzerland.

Takashi Hosoda is a lecturer in Asian security at Faculty of Social Science, Charles University in Prague and a research fellow of Foreign Policy Center Tokyo in Japan. After he obtained a Ph.D., he worked at Japan Institute of International Affairs (JIIA) as a research assistant, and Japanese Embassy in the Czech Republic as a researcher. His academic interests include the influence of people's mutual perception, rivalry, and reconciliation to security policy; alliance theory including autonomy-security trade-off model; Asia-Europe security cooperation; and nuclear and maritime security.

Yoshinori Kaseda is a professor at Ritsumeikan Asia Pacific University in Japan. He received his B.A. in philosophy from Kumamoto University in Japan and his M.A. and Ph.D. in political science from Northern Illinois University in the U.S.A. His research interests include Japan's security policy,

Japan's relations with neighboring countries, Japan-U.S. relations, and international politics over North Korea's nuclear development. His recent works appeared in such books as *North Korea and Security Cooperation in Northeast Asia* (Ashgate, 2014), *The North Korea Crisis and Regional Responses* (East West Center, 2015), *United States Engagement in the Asia Pacific* (Cambria Press, 2015), *One Korea: Vision of Korean Unification* (Routledge, 2016), and *Regional Institutions, Geopolitics and Economics in the Asia-Pacific* (Routledge, 2017).

Michal Kolmaš is an assistant professor of international relations at Metropolitan University, Prague. He focuses on Japan's foreign policy, contemporary international relations theory, and environmental security. His recent publications include *National identity and Japanese revisionism* (Routledge, 2019) and various articles on Japan and security in Asia in journals such as *Cambridge Review of International Affairs, The Pacific Review, Japanese Journal of Political Science, Social Science Japan Journal,* and *China Report.*

David Kozisek is a doctoral candidate of international relations at Ritsumeikan University in Kyoto, Japan. His research focuses on critical discourse analysis and the role of media discourse in identity construction in contemporary Japanese society. He holds degrees in Asian Studies with a focus on East Asia, as well as the English language. David has published several peer-reviewed articles on state image construction and portrayal of the Other on the background of territorial disputes involving Japan and South Korea. His core research interests are post-structuralism and social constructivism in IR, and the media.

Yoichiro Sato is a professor at Ritsumeikan Asia Pacific University. He holds a B.A. (law) from Keio University, M.A. (international studies) from University of South Carolina, and Ph.D. (political science) from University of Hawaii. Previously, he also taught at multiple tertiary and governmental institutions including the U.S. Department of Defense's Asia-Pacific Center for Security Studies, Auckland University (New Zealand), and University of Hawaii. His major works include *The Rise of China and International Security* (coedited with Kevin Cooney, Routledge, 2008), *The U.S.-Japan Security Alliance* (coedited with Takashi Inoguchi and G. John Ikenberry, Palgrave, 2011), *U.S. Engagement in the Asia Pacific* (coedited with See Seng Tang, Cambria, 2015), and *Re-rising Japan: Its Strategic Power in International Relations* (coedited with Hidekazu Sakai, Peter Lang, 2017). He and his comments have appeared in various international media, including *Time*, *Newsweek*, *USA Today*, National Public Radio, Voice of America, Agence France-Presse, Al Jazeera, Radio Australia, Bloomberg, MSNBC, Nikkei Asian Review, *Japan Times*, and TVNZ.

Jan Sýkora is an associate professor of Japanese Studies at the Institute of Asian Studies, Charles University in Prague. Being educated both in Asian studies (Ph.D., Charles University) and economics (M.A., Saga University, Japan), he majored in Japanese economic history with a special focus on economic thought in early modern and modern Japan. He worked as a visiting associated professor at *Nichibunken* in Kyoto (1997–98) and a visiting research fellow at Seinan Gakuin University (2000–01), Kansai University (2012), and Osaka University (2005–06, 2017). His field of studies covers social-economic and intellectual history of early modern and modern Japan, and current issues of the contemporary Japanese society. He is currently focusing on the phenomenon of the consumer in modern and contemporary Japanese society.

Utpal Vyas is associate professor (international relations and political economy) at Ritsumeikan Asia Pacific University, Japan. He obtained his Ph.D. at the University of Sheffield, and he is the author of *Soft Power in Japan-China Relations: State, Sub-state and Non-state Relations* (Routledge, 2010); coeditor of *The North Korea Crisis and Regional Responses* (East-West Center, 2015); and coeditor of *Regional Institutions, Geopolitics and Economics in the Asia Pacific* (Routledge, 2017). His current main research interests are in Japan and China's international relations and political economy, and in regionalism and populism in Asia and Europe.

Hidetaka Yoshimatsu is professor of politics and international relations at Ritsumeikan Asia Pacific University, Japan. His recent publications include *Comparing Institution-Building in East Asia: Power Politics, Governance, and Critical Junctures* (Palgrave Macmillan 2014) and *The Political Economy of Regionalism in East Asia: Integrative Explanation for Dynamics and Challenges* (Palgrave Macmillan 2008).

Index

B

C

K

L

M

N

O

P

Q

R

www.ingramcontent.com/pod-product-compliance
Ingram Content Group UK Ltd.
Pitfield, Milton Keynes, MK11 3LW, UK
UKHW021838100926
8556IPUK00004B/417

9 781433 172021